Opposing Viewpoints®
American
GOVERNMENT

Other Books of Related Interest in the Opposing Viewpoints Series:

American Foreign Policy
American Values
Economics in America
The Political Spectrum
The Welfare State

Additional Books in the Opposing Viewpoints Series:

Abortion
AIDS
The American Military
America's Prisons
The Arms Race
Censorship
Central America
Chemical Dependency
Constructing a Life Philosophy
Crime & Criminals
Death and Dying
The Death Penalty
Drug Abuse
Latin America & US Foreign Policy
Male/Female Roles
The Mass Media
The Middle East
Nuclear War
Problems of Africa
Religion & Human Experience
Science & Religion
Sexual Values
Social Justice
The Soviet Union
Terrorism
The Vietnam War
War & Human Nature

Opposing Viewpoints®

American
GOVERNMENT

David L. Bender & Bruno Leone, *Series Editors*

David L. Bender, *Book Editor*

87-457

OPPOSING VIEWPOINTS SERIES ®

Greenhaven Press   577 Shoreview Park Road   St. Paul, Minnesota 55126

Library of Congress Cataloging-in-Publication Data

American government.

  Bibliography: p.
  Includes index.
  1. United States—Politics and government.
2. United States. Constitution. 3. Elite (Social sciences)—United States. 4. Democracy.
I. Bender, David L., 1936-
JK274.A54785 1987   320.973   87-19791
ISBN 0-89908-398-6 (lib bdg.)
ISBN 0-89908-373-0 (pbk.)

"Congress shall make no law... abridging the freedom of speech, or of the press."

First Amendment to the US Constitution

The basic foundation of our democracy is the first amendment guarantee of freedom of expression. The *Opposing Viewpoints Series* is dedicated to the concept of this basic freedom and the idea that it is more important to practice it than to enshrine it.

Contents

Why Consider Opposing Viewpoints?

"It is better to debate a question without settling it than to settle a question without debating it."

Joseph Joubert (1754-1824)

The Importance of Examining Opposing Viewpoints

The purpose of the Opposing Viewpoints books, and this book in particular, is to present balanced, and often difficult to find, opposing points of view on complex and sensitive issues.

Probably the best way to become informed is to analyze the positions of those who are regarded as experts and well studied on issues. It is important to consider every variety of opinion in an attempt to determine the truth. Opinions from the mainstream of society should be examined. But also important are opinions that are considered radical, reactionary, or minority as well as those stigmatized by some other uncomplimentary label. An important lesson of history is the eventual acceptance of many unpopular and even despised opinions. The ideas of Socrates, Jesus, and Galileo are good examples of this.

Readers will approach this book with their own opinions on the issues debated within it. However, to have a good grasp of one's own viewpoint, it is necessary to understand the arguments of those with whom one disagrees. It can be said that those who do not completely understand their adversary's point of view do not fully understand their own.

9

A persuasive case for considering opposing viewpoints has been presented by John Stuart Mill in his work *On Liberty*. When examining controversial issues it may be helpful to reflect on this suggestion:

> The only way in which a human being can make some approach to knowing the whole of a subject, is by hearing what can be said about it by persons of every variety of opinion, and studying all modes in which it can be looked at by every character of mind. No wise man ever acquired his wisdom in any mode but this.

Analyzing Sources of Information

The Opposing Viewpoints books include diverse materials taken from magazines, journals, books, and newspapers, as well as statements and position papers from a wide range of individuals, organizations and governments. This broad spectrum of sources helps to develop patterns of thinking which are open to the consideration of a variety of opinions.

Pitfalls To Avoid

A pitfall to avoid in considering opposing points of view is that of regarding one's own opinion as being common sense and the most rational stance and the point of view of others as being only opinion and naturally wrong. It may be that another's opinion is correct and one's own is in error.

Another pitfall to avoid is that of closing one's mind to the opinions of those with whom one disagrees. The best way to approach a dialogue is to make one's primary purpose that of understanding the mind and arguments of the other person and not that of enlightening him or her with one's own solutions. More can be learned by listening than speaking.

It is my hope that after reading this book the reader will have a deeper understanding of the issues debated and will appreciate the complexity of even seemingly simple issues on which good and honest people disagree. This awareness is particularly important in a democratic society such as ours where people enter into public debate to determine the common good. Those with whom one disagrees should not necessarily be regarded as enemies, but perhaps simply as people who suggest different paths to a common goal.

Developing Basic Reading and Thinking Skills

In this book carefully edited opposing viewpoints are purposely placed back to back to create a running debate; each viewpoint is preceded by a short quotation that best expresses the author's main argument. This format instantly plunges the reader into the midst of a controversial issue and greatly aids that reader in mastering the basic skill of recognizing an author's point of view.

A number of basic skills for critical thinking are practiced in the activities that appear throughout the books in the series. Some of the skills are:

Evaluating Sources of Information The ability to choose from among alternative sources the most reliable and accurate source in relation to a given subject.

Separating Fact from Opinion The ability to make the basic distinction between factual statements (those that can be demonstrated or verified empirically) and statements of opinion (those that are beliefs or attitudes that cannot be proved).

Identifying Stereotypes The ability to identify oversimplified, exaggerated descriptions (favorable or unfavorable) about people and insulting statements about racial, religious or national groups, based upon misinformation or lack of information.

Recognizing Ethnocentrism The ability to recognize attitudes or opinions that express the view that one's own race, culture, or group is inherently superior, or those attitudes that judge another culture or group in terms of one's own.

It is important to consider opposing viewpoints and equally important to be able to critically analyze those viewpoints. The activities in this book are designed to help the reader master these thinking skills. Statements are taken from the book's viewpoints and the reader is asked to analyze them. This technique aids the reader in developing skills that not only can be applied to the viewpoints in this book, but also to situations where opinionated spokespersons comment on controversial issues. Although the activities are helpful to the solitary reader, they are most useful when the reader can benefit from the interaction of group discussion.

Using this book and others in the series should help readers develop basic reading and thinking skills. These skills should improve the readers' ability to understand what they read. Readers should be better able to separate fact from opinion, substance from rhetoric and become better consumers of information in our media-centered culture.

This volume of the Opposing Viewpoints books does not advocate a particular point of view. Quite the contrary! The very nature of the book leaves it to the reader to formulate the opinions he or she finds most suitable. My purpose as publisher is to see that this is made possible by offering a wide range of viewpoints which are fairly presented.

David L. Bender
Publisher

Introduction

"In framing a government which is to be administered by men over men, the great difficulty lies in this: you must first enable the government to control the governed; and in the next place oblige it to control itself."

James Madison, *The Federalist*, #51

Most, if not all, American students are required to take courses in either American history or American government, or both. During these courses they are taught the mechanics of government and the interplay of the three branches. They learn how Congress makes the laws, how the executive branch executes them, and how the courts interpret them. The purpose of this book is to dig below this surface explanation of American government. The first two chapters focus on the basic philosophy that forms the foundation of American democracy. Later chapters examine more practical issues, such as the impact of special interest groups on the democratic process and the concrete steps to take to improve the functioning of government.

As this introduction is being written, congressional hearings are in process in Washington to investigate the misdeeds of government officials in the Iran-Contra affair. A decade ago the Watergate scandal shocked Americans into the realization that James Madison's observation, quoted above, is as applicable today as it was two hundred years ago. The founding fathers were well aware that government officials required constant surveillance. It is obvious that this need still exists. Men have not yet become angels.

Less sensational than large-scale political scandals, but perhaps more important in the overall scheme of events, is the daily impact of special interest groups on governmental affairs. In 1986, for example, Congress passed legislation that reduced the effectiveness of existing gun control laws. The House of Representatives voted 292 to 130 restricting the anti-gun law enacted in 1968 after the assassinations of Martin Luther King Jr. and Robert Kennedy. This lopsided vote took place in spite of the counter recommendations of six presidential commissions, fourteen key national law enforcement groups, and, based on opinion polls, an overwhelming majority of the American people. Why did the legislation pass? The answer is The National Rifle Association (NRA), a political action committee (PAC) with an annual budget of $60 million.

In 1984 members of Congress received over $100 million for their campaign funds from special interest groups. One member of Congress said he voted for the Firearms Owners Protection Act of 1986 because "the people forget but the NRA never forgets." Thus, these groups which represent only a small portion of the voting population, through financial support and private lobbying, can greatly influence politicians' lawmaking decisions. How severe is the problem of special interest group control and how should it be remedied? Chapter three debates this issue.

In the years ahead Americans will continue to be confronted with a varied list of problems. How can the budget deficit be eliminated, the arms race stopped, AIDS controlled? How should controversies like genetic engineering and other biomedical issues be dealt with? Is the Constitution and the present structure of government adequate to deal with these problems? Alexander Hamilton, in his last Federalist paper, argued for the ratification of the Constitution, claiming its defects could be corrected by later amendment. Thomas Jefferson recommended a new constitutional process every generation. Has the Constitution become obsolete? Should it be amended, or has the time come for a second constitutional convention? Chapter four debates the issue of the current relevance of the Constitution.

No book that raises difficult questions would be complete if it failed to propose solutions. This book's concluding chapter presents alternative views on how American democracy can be improved. Most observers of the American constitutional system agree that the system has worked well. At two hundred years old, it is the oldest government still functioning on the basis of its original written constitution. During that time it has had many detractors. Yet, most current critics advocate only minor changes in either the Constitution, other structures of government, or some other aspect of American political life.

In his closing address at the Philadelphia convention in 1787, Benjamin Franklin declared that it "astonishes me, Sir, to find this system approaching so near perfection as it does." Near perfect perhaps, but not quite perfect. Can American government be improved, or has it already reached the zenith of its perfection and is it now in decline? This volume of opposing viewpoints presents readers with a variety of opinions on which to base their answers.

What Is the Basis of American Democracy?

Chapter Preface

An American sociologist, Robert N. Bellah, suggests that America has a civil religion with values that parallel those of Christianity. He claims this civil religion was shaped by the words and acts of America's founding fathers and has been maintained since that time. Assuming this is true, does America also have a corresponding political belief system that was shaped by the founding fathers or by other forces? The purpose of this chapter is to explore this issue. It presents alternative views of political belief systems that may form the basis of American democracy.

The chapter begins with a viewpoint claiming that classical liberalism forms the basis of American democracy. Its authors identify six liberal assumptions they claim constitute the foundation of American democracy. Succeeding viewpoints offer different perspectives. A former president, Woodrow Wilson, claims Americans merely borrowed from their English forefathers. An earlier president, James Madison, who has been called the father of the Constitution, presents an argument originally used by the Constitution's drafters to convince their adversaries of the document's merits. Gordon Wood, an historian, argues that classical republicanism was the basic thinking of the founding fathers in 1787.

A different perspective was suggested by French representative Michel Chevalier on a diplomatic visit to America in the 1800s. He observed that "the United States constitutes a society which moves under the impulse and by the guidance of instinct rather than according to any premeditated plan." The last two viewpoints debate this possibility. Daniel Boorstin, the Librarian of Congress, claims that Americans so strongly agree on the tenets of democracy that there is little need to articulate an explicit philosophy. The book's editor, in the fifth viewpoint, suggests a slightly different explanation. He claims that the consensus Boorstin identifies has allowed Americans to develop a pragmatic method of dealing with issues that has replaced the need for a political philosophy.

"All major ideologies in the United States share liberal assumptions to some degree."

Classical Liberalism Is the Basis of American Democracy

William S. Maddox & Stuart A. Lilie

William S. Maddox is associate professor of political science at the University of Central Florida. Stuart A. Lilie is associate professor and chairman of the department of political science at the same school. The following viewpoint is excerpted from their book *Beyond Liberal and Conservative*, in which the authors claim classical liberalism forms the bedrock of American political thought. They identify six basic liberal assumptions that form an American consensus and provide the basis for most political thought and public opinion in the United States.

As you read, consider the following questions:

1. Unlike Europe, why did classical liberalism flourish in the United States, in the authors' opinion?
2. What role did the "social contract" concept play in the development of American political thought?
3. What six basic assumptions do the authors claim form the foundation of American political thought?

William S. Maddox and Stuart A. Lilie, *Beyond Liberal and Conservative*. Washington, DC: CATO Institute, 1984. Reprinted with permission.

Most of our ideological labels and ideas originate in European thought and history, even though the American and European political experiences are quite different. The two most obvious differences are the absence of a feudal tradition and the presence of the great frontier in the United States. Because we lack a feudal tradition, a European conservatism based on tradition and class privilege did not develop here. Furthermore the great frontier with its seemingly unlimited resources of land and wealth made the classical liberal concept of the independent and self-sufficient individual seem more realistic in the United States than was possible in relatively more developed Europe.

American Political Thought Is Marked by Consensus

In this setting what is called classical liberalism took root to such an extent that all major ideologies in the United States share liberal assumptions to some degree. As we shall soon discuss, only the libertarians retain these assumptions in their classical form. For the other ideologies classical liberal assumptions are the starting point though they are often modified and reinterpreted. Thus from a global perspective the most striking thing about American thought is the degree of consensus rather than conflict. This consensus is one of the reasons why Americans often think of themselves as nonideological. In the context of consensus, basic assumptions are rarely seriously challenged, so that these assumptions seem natural, not ideological. These assumptions have become so automatic, so given, that they are often taken as self-evident truths rather than as political assumptions. Given the importance of these assumptions, it is useful to examine the basic tenets of classical liberalism as background for our four ideological types. At this point in the discussion, we will use the term "liberalism" in its classic or historical sense. (Modern liberalism, associated with such symbols as the Democratic party or Franklin D. Roosevelt, while based on classical liberalism, is a significant modification of the classical position.)

The Foundations of Classical Liberalism

Some elements of liberalism may be found in the entire Western tradition, but we can conveniently date the immediate origin of liberalism from 16th-century England and the thought of Thomas Hobbes (1588-1679) and John Locke (1632-1704). Although Hobbes is very important to the development of basic liberal assumptions, the authoritarian conclusions of his major work, *Leviathan* (1651), place him somewhat outside the later development of liberal thought. On the other hand the foundations of liberalism are more democratically stated (although not without ambiguity) in John Locke's major work, *Two Treatises of Government* (1689). It is not without justification that Locke is called the father of the U.S. Constitution.

The work of Hobbes and Locke was the outgrowth of the breakdown of the so-called "medieval consensus." During the height of the medieval period there was basic agreement on a wide range of religious, political, and moral issues. Of course there were often differences of opinion as to specifics, but there was agreement on the basic outlines of society. God had created an orderly universe, and the traditions of the religious and secular hierarchies were reflections of this order. However, the humanism of the Italian Renaissance and the assault on the Roman church by Martin Luther (1483-1546) made it impossible to maintain consensus on these assumptions. In time it became obvious that there was a need to establish a political and social philosophy that could overcome the religious and philosophical divisions that had developed. Whatever else, this new philosophy could not be predicated on extensive agreement on questions of religion and morality. These questions would have to be left for the individual to decide—an idea that would have been shocking in the Middle Ages. Rather, this new philosophy would have to rest on a minimal basic framework of rational rules within which people could pursue their own specific ends in such areas as religion, morality, economics, and culture.

America's Liberal Consensus

Liberalism is the conventional wisdom of most Americans, but Americans are not very aware of this fact. Very few Americans would say "My ideological perspective is that of classical liberalism." But many would make such liberal assertions as "Man is by nature a competitive animal"; "Capitalism is the most efficient way of running an economy"; or "Democracy means individual freedom." Because there is now and traditionally has been a societal consensus on liberal values in the United States, political debate has occurred within this context.

Richard P. Young, *American Politics Reconsidered*, 1973.

The "social contract" was the device developed (although not originated) by Hobbes and Locke as the basis for such a philosophy of society and government. Their approach was to ask the question: What minimal rules could rational men of all beliefs agree on as the basis of government and society? These rules then would be the content of the social contract. The very idea that government could be based on rational assumptions rather than tradition and God's will was in itself revolutionary. Although the social contract was a hypothetical construct (later liberals dropped the concept altogether), it was a useful analytic device to establish the argument that government is created by individuals and must serve the interests of these individuals. The implications of viewing society as being based on social contract are far-reaching and important to understanding American thought. These implications include six basic assumptions, which are briefly reviewed below.

The Six Basic Assumptions of American Political Thought

1. Individualism. Probably the major shift from the medieval to the modern view was to make the individual rather than the community the basis for society and government. This is the most fundamental and familiar assumption of liberalism. The individual is seen as relatively discrete and autonomous. The individual is prior to society. Society is the product of individuals rather than the individual being the product of society. Individualism is so fundamental to liberalism that in some contexts the two terms are virtually interchangeable.

Not only is the individual viewed as the basic unit of society from which all else is derived, but the individual is seen as having basic motivations best described as rational self-interest. From the very beginning and particularly with the rise of capitalism, the individual was seen as striving to maximize his self-interest. Altruism and identification with the community were assumed to be absent or too tenuous to be the basis for society. In its capitalist form, though, this self-interest was seen to work for the common good through market devices. Each individual pursuing his own self-interest in a market economy ultimately benefits society by increasing overall productivity. Nevertheless self-interest should not be equated necessarily with a narrow selfishness. Although liberal thinkers vary considerably on the specifics of this point, they generally agree that man is rational enough to recognize that it is in his self-interest to support government and society, even though this support means his giving up the right to do whatever he wants whenever he wishes.

2. Instrumental View of the State. Closely tied to individualism is the view of the state as an instrument to serve individuals, not as an end or value in and of itself. The state is created for and by individuals. The state exists to serve individuals; individuals do not exist to serve the state. Of course individuals do have certain obligations to the state, and they may be punished for violating these obligations, but the obligations are incurred because as rational individuals people must agree to these obligations if the state is to exist at all. These obligations are generated by individual agreement, not by the prior claims of the state, and they primarily involve the agreement to respect the equal rights of others.

3. Limited Government. A related but distinct concept is the view that the state should play a relatively limited role in society. Its central role should be, as Locke says, the protection of "life, liberty and estate." This view of the role of the state has also been called

20

the "judicial state." These terms imply a state that protects individual rights and ensures the smooth running of society, while the initiative and energy for that society come from individuals.

It is a mistake to ascribe fully developed ideas of laissez-faire economics to early liberals, but as capitalism and industrialism developed, the liberal view of the minimal state was more and more identified with capitalism and the market economy. In the 19th century this view had developed to what Herbert Spencer called the nightwatchman theory of the state. The state should enforce contracts, provide defense and police protection, and do nothing more. This view can be contrasted with what was often called "mercantilism" in Europe. From the mercantilist point of view, the state not only controlled the individual's personal freedoms and religious practices but also directed the economy in every way so as to strengthen the nation as a whole.

Contemporary Labels

In American politics, labels like "liberal" or "conservative" apply to where politicians stand *within* the liberal consensus. Thus, so-called conservatives, like Senator Barry Goldwater, are conservative in their strict adherence to nineteenth-century *liberal* values—at least on questions of domestic economic policy. . . . "Liberals" like Senators Hubert Humphrey and Edward Kennedy are liberal in their willingness to revise traditional liberal ideas, particularly in the arena of governmental intervention in the workings of the economy. In fact, one can differentiate between contemporary "conservative" and "liberal" American politicians on the basis of *how* they depart from classical liberal thought. Conservatives diverge from the liberal tradition in their support for the expansion of government power in the areas of military and police policy; liberals depart from classical liberal thought in their call for strong government action on economic and welfare problems.

Richard P. Young, *American Politics Reconsidered*, 1973.

4. Individual Rights. A key concept in liberal thought is that each individual possesses certain fundamental rights that should not be violated by government or other individuals. The exact nature and extent of these rights has been an important issue in the development of liberal thought. Locke's phrase "life, liberty and estate" and Jefferson's derivative in the Declaration of Independence, "life, liberty, and the pursuit of happiness," generally reflect the thrust of liberal thought. The right to own and dispose of property as one wishes has been central to liberal thought from the beginning. Nevertheless rights have also included the right to free expression and behavior. Perhaps the ultimate statement of the liberal view of freedom is John Stuart Mill's *On*

21

Liberty (1859), in which he argues that society has no right to suppress ideas no matter how distasteful and that individuals should be allowed to do as they wish (even self-destructive acts) so long as they do no substantial harm to others.

5. *Equality Under the Law.* Equality is also a central concept in liberal thought, but one that is often misunderstood. Equality is best considered as a legal equality in which all individual claims to rights and legal standing are to be the same. There are to be no special privileges attached to classes or castes based on heredity. In more modern times this idea of equal standing developed into the ideal of "equality of opportunity." This implied that birth should place no one at disadvantage not only in a relatively narrow sense of legal standing but in the larger sense of economic, educational, and other opportunities for development. Historically, however, equality has not meant equality of property or substance. In fact the major thrust of liberalism has been that the abolition of hereditary privileges and inequalities means that whatever inequalities develop in liberal society are the result of effort and ability and therefore are natural. Not only are these differences justified but it is a major task of government to protect them. As James Madison says in *The Federalist,* no. 10:

> The diversity in the faculties of men, from which the rights of property originate, is not less an insuperable obstacle to a uniformity of interests. The protection of these faculties is the first object of government. From the protection of different and unequal faculties of acquiring property, the possession of different degrees and kinds of property immediately results; and from the influence of these on the sentiments and views of the respective proprietors, ensues a division of the society into different interests and parties [pp. 17-18].

6. *Representative Government.* It may seem strange initially that representative government has not been treated more centrally in a discussion of liberal thought, but this relationship is in fact quite problematic. The two concepts are analytically and historically distinct, in that one can have a liberal system without representative institutions or vice versa. Most but not all early liberals favored some type of representative government. Early liberals, however, did not favor full adult suffrage. They assumed that universal suffrage would be a threat to property and other rights. In time it became increasingly difficult for liberals to support the idea of equality and at the same time resist pressures for extension of the franchise. By the end of the 19th century most liberals supported adult male suffrage, although the franchise was not achieved by women until well into the 20th century and effectively even later by blacks. Over time, then, liberalism came to include at least some degree of acceptance of institutions, such as a Congress or House of Commons, that allowed most citizens to express their views through government, although most liberals

still demanded limits on how much influence the masses could have.

Conclusion

These then are the central assumptions of classical liberalism, which have provided the basis and context for most political thought and public opinion in the United States. At both the philosophical and mass levels, there has been a consensus on most of these assumptions. One consequence of this agreement is that ideological differences in the United States fall within a relatively narrow range. Rarely are these basic assumptions totally rejected by a political movement or leader. This is in contrast to many other Western nations where basic liberal assumptions are often rejected, for example by socialists who wish to give greater precedence to community or by conservatives who wish to return to a society based on rank and privilege. From a European perspective, American ideological disputes seem relatively confined. Nonetheless within the American consensus there have been important disagreements as to the proper emphasis, interpretation, and application to be given to these liberal principles. Two general areas of disagreement have in fact been central to modern American politics. One area is the extent to which government should or should not intervene in economic affairs, and the other is the extent to which government should or should not regulate individual behavior in matters of morality and conscience.

"Our Government . . . was no type of an experiment in advanced democracy . . . it was simply an adaptation of English constitutional government."

English Constitutional Government Is the Basis of American Democracy

Woodrow Wilson

Woodrow Wilson, the only political scientist to hold the office of President of the United States, taught at several universities before serving as President of Princeton University from 1902 to 1910. He also held the governorship of New Jersey for the two years before his election to the presidency in 1912. The following viewpoint, taken from a speech in 1889, argues that the American government established 100 years earlier was not a revolutionary experiment in democracy. It was merely an adaptation of English Constitutional government. We Americans, he claims, are not revolutionary democrats, merely progressive Englishmen.

As you read, consider the following questions:

1. According to Wilson, Americans, including the framers of the Constitution, have had what mistaken idea about the origins of American government?
2. What point does he make when he claims that "we founded, not democracy, but Constitutional government, in America"?

From a speech by Woodrow Wilson, "The Nature of Democracy in the United States" given on May 17, 1889.

There is one thought which must, I am sure, have been common to all serious minds during the past few weeks, namely, *That it is a long time since 1789,*—if time is to be measured by change. Everything apprises us of the fact that we are not the same nation now that we were then. And I suppose that in looking back to the time in which our government was formed you have gotten the same impression that has for some time been fixing itself upon my mind, and that is, that we started with sundry wrong ideas about ourselves. We thought ourselves rank democrats, whereas we were in fact only progressive Englishmen. Turn the leaves of that sage manual of constitutional interpretation and advocacy, the *Federalist*, and note the perverse tendency of its writers to refer to *Greece and Rome* for precedents.—that Greece and Rome which haunted all our earlier and even some of our more mature years. . . . The truth is that we long imagined ourselves related in some unexplained way to all ancient republicans. Strangely enough, too, we at the same time accepted the quite incompatible theory that we were related also to the French philosophical radicals. We claimed kinship with democrats everywhere—with all democrats. . . .

Almost equally incredible to us is the ardour of revolution that then filled the world—the fact that one of the rulers of the world's mind in that generation was *Rousseau*, the apostle of all that is fanciful, unreal, and misleading in politics. . . .

American Government Is an Adaptation of English Constitutional Government

It is common to say, in explanation of our regret that that dawn and youth of democracy's day is past; that our principles are cooler now and more circumspect, with the coolness and circumspection of advanced years. It seems to some that as our sinews have hardened our enthusiasms have become tamer and more decorous: that as experience has grown idealism has declined.

But to speak thus is to speak with old self-deception as to the character of our politics. If we are suffering disappointment, it is the disappointment of an awakening: we were dreaming. For we never had any business harkening to Rousseau or consorting with Europe in revolutionary sentiment. Our Government, founded one hundred years ago, was no type of an experiment in advanced democracy, as we allowed Europe and even ourselves to suppose; it was simply an adaptation of English constitutional government. If we suffered Europe to study our institutions as instances in point touching experimentation in politics *she was the more deceived.* If we began the *first* century of our national existence under a similar impression ourselves, there is the greater reason why we should start out upon a *new* century of national life with accurate conceptions about our place in history. It is my modest purpose to make such contribution as I may to this end. I shall, therefore, ask you to note:

(1) That there are certain influences astir in this century which make for democracy the world over, and that these influences owe their origin in part to the radical thought of the last century; but that it was not such forces that made us democratic, nor are we responsible for them.

(2) That, so far from owing our governments to these general influences, we began, not by carrying out any theory, but by simply carrying out a history, inventing nothing, only establishing a specialized species of English government. That we founded, not Democracy, but Constitutional government, in America.

(3) That the government which we set up thus in a quite normal manner has nevertheless *changed greatly* under our hands by reason both of growth and of the operation of the general democratic forces,—the European or rather world-wide democratic forces, of which I have spoken; and

---

Acceptance of English Traditions

The Mission of colonial America was to carry a great political tradition to conclusion, not to create a great tradition of its own.

Political thought in the colonies was a proudly conscious extension of political thought in England. The more independent and self-assertive the colonists became the more anxious they seemed to sound like true-born Englishmen. The prophets to whom appeals for support were most often and confidently directed were John Locke, Algernon Sidney, Bolingbroke, John Somers, Benjamin Hoadly, Henry Care, James Burgh, Joseph Addison, Alexander Pope, and the estimable team of Thomas Gordon and John Trenchard.

Clinton Rossiter, *Seedtime of the Republic*, 1953.

---

(4) That the very *size* to which our governmental organism has attained, and more particularly this new connection of its character and destiny with the character and destiny of the common democratic forces of the age of steam and electricity have created new *problems of organization* which it behooves us to meet in such spirit and with such measures as I shall briefly indicate before closing. If you will vouchsafe me much kind patience, I will make such expedition as I may in this large undertaking.

The Forces Behind Democracy

First, then, for the forces which are bringing in democratic temper and method the world over. You familiarly know what these forces are, but it will be profitable to our thought to pass them once more in review. They are freedom of thought and the diffusion of enlightenment among the people. Steam and electricity have cooperated with systematic popular education to accomplish this diffusion. The process of popular education and the progress of democracy have been inseparable. The publication of their great *Encyclopaedia* by Diderot and his associates in France in the last century was the sure sign of the change that was setting in. Learning was turning its face away from the studious few to the curious many. The intellectual movement of the modern time was emerging from the narrow courses of scholastic thought and beginning *to spread itself abroad* over the extended, if shallow, levels of the common mind. The serious forces of democracy will be found, upon analysis, to reside, not in the disturbing doctrines of eloquent revolutionary writers, not in the turbulent discontent of the pauperized and oppressed, but in the educational forces of the last hundred and forty years which have elevated the masses in many countries to a plane of understanding and of orderly, intelligent purpose more nearly on a level with the average man of the hitherto governing classes. The movements towards democracy which have mastered all the other political tendencies of our own day are not older than the middle of the last century: and that is just the age of the now ascendent movement towards systematic popular education.

Organized popular education is, after all, however, only *one* of the quickening influences which have been producing the general enlightenment which is everywhere becoming the promise of general liberty: or, rather, it is only part of a great whole vastly larger than itself. Schools are but separated seedbeds in which only the staple thoughts of the steady and stay-at-home people are prepared and nursed. Not much of the world, after all, goes to school in the school-house. But through the mighty influences of commerce and the press *the world itself has become a school*. The air is alive with the multitudinous voices of information. . . .

General Forces Do Not Explain American Democracy

These are the forces which have established the drift towards democracy. When all sources of information are accessible to all men alike, when the world's thought and the world's news are scattered broadcast where the poorest may find them, the nondemocratic forms of government find life a desperate venture. Exclusive privilege needs privacy, but cannot have it. Kingship of the elder patterns needs sanctity, but we can find it nowhere obtainable in a world of news items and satisfied curiosity. The many will no longer receive submissively the thought of a ruling few, but insist upon having opinions of their own. The reaches of public opinion have been infinitely extended: the number of voices that must be heeded in legislation and in executive policy has been infinitely multiplied. Modern influences have inclined every man to clear his throat for a word in the world's debates. They have popularized everything they have touched. . . .

But, mighty as such forces are,—democratic as they are,—no one can fail to see that they are inadequate to *produce of themselves* such a government as ours. There is little in them of *constructive* efficacy. They could not of themselves build any government at all. They are critical, analytical, questioning, quizzing forces;— but not architectural, not powers that devise and build. The influences of popular education, of the press, of travel, of commerce, of the innumerable agencies which nowadays send knowledge and thought in quick pulsations through every part and member of society, do not necessarily mould men for effective endeavour. They may only confuse and paralyze the mind with their myriad stinging lashes of excitement. They may only strengthen the impression that "the world's a stage" and that no one need do more than sit and look on through his ready glass, the newspaper. They overwhelm one with impressions, but do they give stalwartness to his manhood; do they make his hand any steadier on the plow, or his purpose any clearer with reference to the duties of the moment? They stream light about him, it may be, but do they clear his vision? Is he better able to see because they give him countless things to look at? Is he better able to judge because they fill him with a delusive sense of knowing everything? Activity of mind is not necessarily strength of mind. It may manifest itself in mere dumb show; it may run into jigs as well as into strenuous work at noble tasks. A man's farm does not yield its fruit the more abundantly in its season because he reads the world's news in the papers. A merchant's shipments do not multiply because he studies history. Banking is none the less hazardous to the banker's capital or taxing to his powers because the best writing of the best essayists is to be bought cheap.

The Origins of American Politics

Having thus expanded my first point by exhibiting the general forces of that democracy which we recognize as belonging to the age and to the world at large, rather than exclusively or even characteristically to ourselves, I now ask you to turn to view by contrast our origins in politics.

How different were the forces back of us! Nothing establishes the republican state save trained capacity for self-government, practical aptitude for public affairs, habitual soberness and temperateness of united action. When we look back to the moderate sagacity and steadfast, self-contained habit in self-government of the men to whom we owe the establishment of our institutions in the United States we are at once made aware that there is no communion between their democracy and the radical thought and restless spirit called by that name in Europe. There is almost nothing in common between popular outbreaks such as took place in France at her great Revolution and the

28

establishment of a government like our own. Our memories of the year 1789 are as far as possible removed from the memories which Europe retains of that pregnant year. We *manifested* one hundred years ago what Europe *lost*, namely self-command, self-possession. Democracy in Europe, outside of closeted Switzerland, has acted always *in rebellion* as a *destructive* force: it can scarcely be said to have had, even yet, any period of organic development. It has built such temporary governments as it has had opportunity to erect on the old foundations and out of the discredited materials of centralized rule, elevating the people's representatives for a season to the throne, but securing almost as little as ever of that every-day local self-government which lies so near to the heart of liberty. Democracy in America, on the other hand, and in the English colonies, has had, almost from the first, a truly organic growth. There was nothing revolutionary in its movements: it had not to overthrow other polities; it had only to organize itself. It had, not to create, but only to expand self-government. It did not need to spread propaganda: it needed nothing but to methodize its ways of living.

The US Government Follows England's Model

It was not necessary to begin altogether afresh in 1776. Americans believed that their ancestors, coming from England, had not brought with them laws adapted to a *people grown old in the habits of vice*, but had very early established a constitution of government by their own authority, with virtue for its principle and the public good as its object. It remained only to adjust that system to new conditions.

Oscar Handlin, *The Americans*, 1963.

In brief, we were doing nothing essentially new a century ago. Our politics and our character were derived from a

> land that freemen till,
> That sober-suited Freedom chose.
> The land, where girt with friends or foes
> A man may speak the thing he will;
>
> A land of settled government,
> A land of just and old renown,
> Where freedom broadens slowly down
> From precedent to precedent:
>
> Where faction seldom gathers head,
> But by degrees to fulness wrought,
> The strength of some diffusive thought
> Hath time and space to work and spread.

Our strength and our facility alike inhered in our traditions; those traditions made our character and shaped our institutions. Liberty is not something that can be created by a document;

neither is it something which, when created, can be laid away in a document, a completed work. It is an *organic* principle, a principle of *life*, renewing and being renewed. Democratic institutions are never done; they are like living tissue, always a-making. It is a strenuous thing, this of living the life of a free people; and our success in it depends upon training, not upon clever invention.

American Democracy Came from a Stage of Development

Our democracy, plainly, was not a body of doctrine: it was a stage of development. Our democratic state was not a piece of developed theory, but a piece of developed habit. It was not created by mere aspirations or by new faith; it was built up by slow custom. Its process was experience, its basis old wont, its meaning national organic oneness and effective life. It came, like manhood, as the fruit of youth. An immature people could not have had it, and the maturity to which it was vouchsafed was the maturity of freedom and self-control. Such government as ours is a form of conduct, and its only stable foundation is character. A particular form of government may no more be *adopted* than a particular type of character may be adopted: both institutions and character must be developed by conscious effort and through transmitted aptitudes.

Governments such as ours are founded upon discussion and government by discussion comes as late in political as scientific thought in intellectual development. It is a habit of state life created by long-established circumstance, and possible for a nation only in the adult age of its political life. The people which successfully maintains it must have gone through a period of political training which shall have prepared it by gradual steps of acquired privilege for assuming the entire control of its affairs. Long and slowly widening experience in local self-direction must have prepared them for national self-direction. They must have acquired adult self-reliance, self-knowledge, and self-control, adult soberness and deliberateness of judgment, adult sagacity in self-government, adult vigilance of thought and quickness of insight. When practiced, not by small communities, but by wide nations, democracy, far from being a crude form of government, is possible only amongst peoples of the highest and steadiest political habit. It is the heritage of races purged alike of hasty barbaric passions and of patient servility to rulers, and schooled in temperate common counsel. It is an institution of political noon-day, not of the half light of political dawn. It can never be made to sit easily or safely on *first generations*, but strengthens through long heredity. It is poison to the infant, but tonic to the man. Monarchies may be made, but democracies must grow.

It is a deeply significant fact, . . . again and again to be called to mind, that only in the United States, in a few other governments begotten of the English race and in Switzerland where old Teutonic habit has had the same persistency as in England, have examples yet been furnished of successful democracy of the modern type. England herself is close upon democracy. Her backwardness in entering upon its full practice is no less instructive as to the conditions prerequisite to democracy than is the forwardness of her offspring. She sent out to all her colonies which escaped the luckless beginning of being made penal settlements comparatively small, homogeneous populations of pioneers with strong instincts of self-government and with no social materials out of which to build government otherwise than democratically. She herself, meanwhile, retained masses of population never habituated to participation in government, untaught in political principle either by the teachers of the hustings or of the school house. She has had to approach democracy, therefore, by slow and cautious extensions of the franchise to those prepared for it: while her better colonies, born into democracy, have had to receive all comers into its pale. She has been paring down exclusive privileges and levelling classes; they have from the first been asylums of civil equality. They have assimilated new, she has prepared old, populations.

Erroneous as it is to represent government as only a commonplace sort of business, little elevated in method above merchandizing, and to be regulated by counting-house principles, the favour easily won for such views among our own people is very significant. It means self-reliance in government. It gives voice to the eminently modern democratic feeling that government is no hidden cult to be left to a few specially prepared individuals, but a common everyday concern of life, even if the biggest such concern. It is this self-confidence, in many cases mistaken, which is gradually spreading among other peoples, less justified in it than are ours.

One cannot help marvelling that facts so obvious as these should have escaped the perception of some of the sagest thinkers and most thorough historical scholars of our day. And yet so it is. Sir Henry Maine even, the great interpreter to Englishmen of the historical forces operative in law and social institutions, has utterly failed, in his plausible work on Popular Government to distinguish the democracy, or rather the popular government, of the English race, which is bred by slow circumstance and founded upon habit, from the democracy of other peoples, which is bred by discontent and founded upon revolution. He has missed that most obvious teaching of events, that successful democracy differs from unsuccessful in being a product of history, a product of forces not suddenly become operative, but slowly working upon whole peoples for generations together. The level of democracy is the level of everyday habit, the level of common national experiences, and lies far below the elevations of ecstasy to which the revolutionist climbs.

"In 1787, classical republicanism was the basic premise of American thinking."

Republicanism Is the Basis of American Democracy

Gordon S. Wood

Gordon S. Wood is chairman of the department of history at Brown University. The author of numerous books on American history, he won the Bancroft Prize in 1969 for his book, *The Creation of the American Republic*. In the following viewpoint, he claims that republicanism formed the presuppositions of American thinking in 1787. Although he would agree with Woodrow Wilson's arguments for the importance of the English heritage, as expressed in the preceding viewpoint, he would argue that the American system is not the English system. Americans, he claims, have fashioned a unique government, and the foundation stone is republicanism.

As you read, consider the following questions:

1. In the author's opinion, how did ancient Rome and classical literature influence the framers of the Constitution?
2. Why did the framers' enthusiasm for republicanism wane somewhat between 1776 and 1787?
3. How did the framers make American republicanism unique?

Gordon S. Wood, "The Intellectual Origins of the American Constitution," *National Forum*, Fall 1984. Reprinted by permission.

Searching for one key person in order to explain the Constitution is doomed to futility. Influence on something as monumental and as collectively created as the Constitution does not work in such a simple and direct way. The writings of Locke, Montesquieu, Hume, Burlamaqui, and even Polybius were all important to the creation of the mental world of Americans in the 1780s. But so too were the works of countless other thinkers. All formed virtually inseparable aspects of the Americans' political culture. To be sure, the Founders often referred to this book or that philosopher in their speeches and writings; indeed, they cited and quoted from every conceivable source available to an educated man in the eighteenth century—from Plutarch to Pufendorf, from Cicero to Blackstone, from Plato to Rousseau. But so many sources were cited so promiscuously, it is difficult to perceive the dominant influence of any one.

This does not mean, however, that there were no intellectual influences affecting the thinking and actions of the Framers of the Constitution. Although isolating the influence of any one thinker on the Founding Fathers may be impossible, describing the currents of the political culture in which they were immersed in 1787 is not. The Founders were experienced, pragmatic political leaders, but they were not such practical, down-to-earth men that they could not be bothered by questions of political philosophy and theory. On the contrary, they were men intensely interested in ideas and especially concerned with making theoretical sense of what they were doing. They were participants in a rich, dynamic political culture that helped determine the nature of the Constitution they created. Understanding the Constitution requires an understanding of that political culture.

Republicanism Was the Ideology of the Day

The most pervasive characteristic of that political culture was republicanism, a body of ideas and values so deeply rooted that it formed the presuppositions of American thinking. This body of thought not only determined the elective political system the Founders believed in; it also determined their moral and social goals. To become republican was what the American Revolution had been about.

It is difficult for us today to appreciate the revolutionary character of this civic culture. We live in a world in which almost all states purport to be republican; even those few states such as Britain or Sweden that remain monarchies are more republican in fact than some others that claim to be in theory. But in the monarchy-dominated world of the eighteenth century, republicanism was not so widespread or acceptable. It was then a radical ideology; indeed, this body of civic thought was to the eighteenth century what Marxism was to be for the nineteenth

33

century. For the eighteenth century republicanism was a counter-cultural ideology of protest, an intellectual means by which dissatisfied people could criticize the luxury, selfishness, and corruption of monarchical culture.

It is not surprising, therefore, when eighteenth-century Americans and Frenchmen alike decided upon revolution that they should have repudiated royal authority and erected republics in its place. Republicanism was the ideology of the democratic revolutions of the late eighteenth century; it was the ideology of the people against monarchs and hereditary aristocracies. Even the English who held on to their king and their House of Lords through the upheavals of this period nevertheless felt compelled to claim that, because of the power of the House of Commons, their constitution was already greatly republicanized. By the last quarter of the eighteenth century, being enlightened in the Western world, it seemed, was nearly equivalent to believing in republican values.

Intellectual Heirs of English Republicanism

The men who drew up the Constitution in Philadelphia during the summer of 1787 had a vivid Calvinistic sense of human evil and damnation and believed with Hobbes that men are selfish and contentious. . . .

To them a human being was an atom of self-interest. They did not believe in man, but they did believe in the power of a good political constitution to control him. . . .

And yet there was another side to the picture. The Fathers were intellectual heirs of seventeenth-century English republicanism with its opposition to arbitrary rule and faith in popular sovereignty. If they feared the advance of democracy, they also had misgivings about turning to the extreme right. Having recently experienced a bitter revolutionary struggle with an external power beyond their control, they were in no mood to follow Hobbes to his conclusion that any kind of government must be accepted in order to avert the anarchy and terror of a state of nature.

Richard Hofstadter, *The American Political Tradition*, 1948.

The deepest origins of these civic and moral values went all the way back to ancient Rome and the great era of the Roman Republic. The modern world found most of what it wanted to know about the Roman Republic from the writings of the period that Peter Gay has called the Roman Enlightenment—the golden age of Latin literature between the breakdown of the republic in the middle of the first century B.C. to the establishment of the empire in the middle of the second century A.D. The celebrated

Latin writers of this time—Cicero, Sallust, Tacitus, and Plutarch among others—lived when the greatest days of the republic were fading or already passed; and thus they contrasted the growing stratification, corruption, and disorder they saw around them with an imagined earlier world of rustic simplicity and pastoral virtue. Roman farmers had once been hardy soldiers devoted to their country. But they had become selfish, corrupted by luxury, torn by struggles between rich and poor, and had lost their capacity to serve the public good. So went these Latin writers' pessimistic explanation of the republic's decline. They left a collection of writings embodying beliefs and values—about the good life, about citizenship, about political health, about social morality—that have had an enduring effect on Western culture. Their work is Rome's greatest legacy to us.

Civic Humanism and Republican Values

This great body of classical literature was revived and updated by the Renaissance, especially in the writings of the Italian philosopher Machiavelli. All was blended into a tradition of what has been called "civic humanism." This tradition stressed the moral character of the independent citizen as the prerequisite to good politics and disinterested service to the country. To be good citizens, men had to be independent, property-holding farmers free of control by other men, and free of the influence of selfish interests. The importance of this classical conception of political morality can scarcely be exaggerated. Among educated people it rivaled Christianity for dominance.

This tradition of civic humanism passed into the culture of northern Europe. In English culture it inspired the writings of the great seventeenth-century republicans, Milton, Harrington, and Sidney. And it was carried into the eighteenth century by scores of popularizers and translators. It was not so much the treatises of philosophers like John Locke as it was the essays of coffee-house journalists like John Trenchard and Thomas Gordon that spread republican values throughout the eighteenth-century, English-speaking world. Gordon, for example, in addition to writing about the importance of free speech and religious liberty, also translated editions of Sallust and Tacitus. But these classical republican values were confined neither to the radical fringes of British thought nor to the British world. They permeated the thinking of educated people throughout the West. . . .

What precisely did this body of ideas mean? It meant most obviously the elimination of a king and the institution of an electoral system of government. But these were just incidental means to a larger end. Republicanism really meant creating a political system concerned with the *res publica*, public things, the welfare of the people. Liberal critics of eighteenth-century monarchism believed that kings had become too wrapped up in their own selfish dynastic purposes and were ignoring the good of their people. By eliminating hereditary kings and instituting governments in which the people themselves would elect their political leaders, liberal reformers hoped that governments at last would promote only the public's welfare.

Democracy and Freedom

Unwilling to turn their backs upon republicanism, the Fathers wished to avoid violating the prejudices of the people. "Notwithstanding the oppression and injustice experienced among us from democracy," said George Mason, "the genius of the people is in favor of it, and the genius of the people must be consulted." Mason admitted "that we had been too democratic," but feared that "we should incautiously run into the opposite extreme." James Madison, who has quite rightfully been called the philosopher of the Constitution, told the delegates: "It seems indispensable that the mass of citizens should not be without a voice in making the laws which they are to obey, and in choosing the magistrates who are to administer them.". . . There was no better expression of the dilemma of a man who has no faith in the people but insists that government be based upon them than of Jeremy Belknap, a New England clergyman, who wrote to a friend: "Let it stand as a principle that government originates from the people; but let the people be taught . . . that they are not able to govern themselves."

Richard Hofstadter, *The American Political Tradition*, 1948.

This civic culture, however, had more than political significance; it had social and moral significance as well. Republics required a particular sort of egalitarian and virtuous people: independent, property-holding citizens without artificial hereditary distinctions who were willing to sacrifice many of their private, selfish interests for the good of the whole community. This dependence on a relatively equal and virtuous populace was what made republics such fragile and often short-lived polities. Monarchies were long-lasting; they could maintain order from the top down over large, diverse, and stratified populations through their use of hereditary privilege, executive power, standing armies, and religious establishments. But republics had to be held together from below, from the consent and sacrifice of the people themselves; and therefore, as Montesquieu and other theorists had warned, republics necessarily had to be small in territory and homogeneous and moral in character. The only republics left in the eighteenth century—the Netherlands and the city-states of Italy and Switzerland—were small and compact. Large, class-ridden states that had tried to establish republics—as England had in the seven-

36

teenth century—were bound to end up in some sort of military dictatorship, such as that of Oliver Cromwell. It was little wonder that Americans in 1776 embarked on their experiment in republicanism in a spirit of great risk and high adventure. There had been nothing to resemble their confederation of republics since the fall of Rome. By 1787, however, Americans had become increasingly anxious about what they were attempting.

Americans of 1787 were not the republican enthusiasts they had been in 1776. In a decade's time many of them had had their earlier dreams and illusions about republicanism considerably dampened. Experience with popular government, especially in the state legislatures, had cast doubt on the American people's capacity for virtue and disinterestedness. By 1787 many leaders, therefore, were ready for what James Madison called a "systematic change" of government, a change that resulted in the creation of the federal Constitution. But dissatisfied as many American leaders were with the Confederation and with the state legislatures, none of them—not even Alexander Hamilton who was the most monarchically minded among them—was prepared to give up on republican government. They knew, as Madison said, that "no other form would be reconcilable with the genius of the people of America; with the fundamental principles of the revolution; or with that honorable determination, which animates every votary of freedom, to rest all our political experiments on the capacity of mankind for self-government." Hence in the new Constitution, the Framers provided for periodically elected officers of the executive and legislative branches, and they made the federal government guarantee a republican form of government for each state (Article IV, Section 4), and forbade the United States from granting any titles of nobility (Article I, Section 9). . . .

The Theory of Balanced Government

In 1787, classical republicanism was the basic premise of American thinking—the central presupposition behind all other ideas. However, it alone was not responsible for the peculiar structure of the revolutionary governments, including that of the federal government created by the Constitution. There was another set of ideas encapsulated in the theory of balanced or mixed government. It came likewise out of antiquity and was closely if not inextricably entwined with the tradition of classical republicanism. The classical theory of balanced government provided much more than the foundational ideas for the structures of the several state governments. The classical theory also included the notion of an independent president, the aristocratic Senate, and the popular House of Representatives.

Since at least the time of Aristotle, theorists had categorized forms of government into three ideal types—monarchy, aristocracy, and democracy. These types were derived from the number of rulers in each: for monarchy, one person; for aristocracy, a few nobles; for democracy, all the people. Aristotle and others believed that each of these rulers when alone entrusted with political power tended to run amok and to become perverted. By itself monarchy became tyranny; aristocracy became oligarchy; and democracy became anarchy. Only by mixing each of these types together in the same constitution, only by balancing the tendencies of each of them, could order be maintained and the perfections of each type of simple government be achieved. The result would be a governmental system in equilibrium—the very kind of static model that the eighteenth-century Enlightenment admired. . . .

The Separation of Powers

Members of America's executive branch, unlike those of most of the democracies in the world, cannot at the same time hold seats in the legislatures. The separation of the legislature from what was thought to be the perverse, corrupting influence of the executive was written into the revolutionary state constitutions of 1776-77. This division was instituted for the sake of maintaining the independence of the ruling parts and the balance that an ideal government ought to have. Since separation of powers was often used to justify the maintenance of this independence and balance, there was the likelihood that separating powers and balancing parts of the government would blend in people's minds.

By the time Americans came to form the federal Constitution in 1787-88, the two sets of ideas had become thoroughly confused. Undoubtedly most of the Framers at Philadelphia thought they were creating a balanced government much in the form of the several state governments—only with a stronger chief executive and senate than in most of the states. Although the ultimate source of this structure was the ideal English constitution, by 1787 few American political leaders felt comfortable any longer saying so in public. (John Adams was a conspicuous exception.) Referring to the chief executive as the monarchical element and the Senate as the aristocracy in a balanced government was politically impossible in the popular atmosphere of the 1780s. Thus the Framers had to find justifications for their two-house legislature and their strong, independent president in some place other than the English constitution and the classical ideal of mixed government.

What they did was blend the notion of separating the functional powers of government—executive, legislative, and judicial—with the older theory of balanced government; and they used both indiscriminately to describe the now incredibly fragmented and countervailing character of America's political system.

"The causes of faction cannot be removed, and . . . relief is only to be sought in the means of controlling its effects."

Controlling Factions Are the Basis of American Democracy

James Madison

Americans have never been accused of having a surplus of political theorists or theories. The reason may be the effectiveness of our Constitution. There is no need to speculate about an ideal form of government when the existing system works so well. James Madison, as the Constitution's main architect, has been referred to as its father. The viewpoint that follows is excerpted from his tenth essay of *The Federalist*, which originally appeared as a newspaper article in 1787, advocating the adoption of the new constitution. If America does have a political theory, it may be best exemplified in this persuasive argument for a practical and workable government.

As you read, consider the following questions:

1. How does Madison define the term faction?
2. Why does he claim that pure democracy is not effective in dealing with the mischief created by conflicting factions?
3. Why does he argue that republics can control conflicting factions more effectively, and large republics more easily than small republics?

James Madison, *The Federalist*, Number 10, 1787.

Among the numerous advantages promised by a well-constructed Union, none deserves to be more accurately developed than its tendency to break and control the violence of faction. The friend of popular governments never finds himself so much alarmed for their character and fate as when he contemplates their propensity to this dangerous vice. He will not fail, therefore, to set a due value on any plan which, without violating the principles to which he is attached, provides a proper cure for it. The instability, injustice, and confusion introduced into the public councils, have, in truth, been the mortal diseases under which popular governments have everywhere perished. . . .

The Nature and Mischief of Factions

By a faction, I understand a number of citizens, whether amounting to a majority or minority of the whole, who are united and actuated by some common impulse of passion, or of interest, adverse to the rights of other citizens, or to the permanent and aggregate interests of the community.

There are two methods of curing the mischiefs of faction: the one, by removing its causes; the other, by controlling its effects.

There are again two methods of removing the causes of faction: the one, by destroying the liberty which is essential to its existence; the other, by giving to every citizen the same opinions, the same passions, and the same interests.

It could never be more truly said than of the first remedy, that it was worse than the disease. Liberty is to faction what air is to fire, an aliment without which it instantly expires. But it could not be less folly to abolish liberty, which is essential to political life, because it nourishes faction, than it would be to wish the annihilation of air, which is essential to animal life, because it imparts to fire its destructive agency.

The second expedient is as impracticable as the first would be unwise. As long as the reason of man continues fallible, and he is at liberty to exercise it, different opinions will be formed. As long as the connection subsists between his reason and his self-love, his opinions and his passions will have a reciprocal influence on each other; and the former will be objects to which the latter will attach themselves. The diversity in the faculties of men, from which the rights of property originate, is not less an insuperable obstacle to a uniformity of interests. The protection of these faculties is the first object of government. From the protection of different and unequal faculties of acquiring property, the possession of different degrees and kinds of property immediately results; and from the influence of these on the sentiments and views of the respective proprietors, ensues a division of the society into different interests and parties.

The latent causes of faction are thus sown in the nature of man;

and we see them everywhere brought into different degrees of activity, according to the different circumstances of civil society. A zeal for different opinions concerning religion, concerning government, and many other points, as well of speculation as of practice; and attachment of different leaders ambitiously contending for pre-eminence and power; or to persons of other descriptions whose fortunes have been interesting to the human passions, have, in turn, divided mankind into parties, inflamed them with mutual animosity, and rendered them much more disposed to vex and oppress each other than to co-operate for their common good. So strong is this propensity of mankind to fall into mutual animosities, that where no substantial occasion presents itself, the most frivolous and fanciful distinctions have been sufficient to kindle their unfriendly passions and excite their most violent conflict.

The Variety of Factions

But the most common and durable source of factions has been the various and unequal distribution of property. Those who hold and those who are without property have ever formed distinct interests in society. Those who are creditors, and those who are debtors, fall under a like discrimination. A landed interest, a manufacturing interest, a mercantile interest, a moneyed interest, with many lesser interests, grow up of necessity in civilised nations, and divide them into different classes, actuated by different sentiments and views. The regulation of these various and interfering interests forms the principal task of modern legislation, and involves the spirit of party and faction in the necessary and ordinary operations of the government.

America's Dominant Political Theory

Madison's political theory, which I suggest has been the dominant political theory in our history, was in part the inevitable product of past political history and past political theory. The values implicit and explicit in Madison's theory of the extensive republic were . . . orthodox republican values: rule by the great body of the people, majority rule, limited government dedicated to life, liberty, property, happiness, and safety.

Neal Riemer, *The Journal of Politics*, November 1958.

No man is allowed to be a judge in his own cause, because his interest would certainly bias his judgment, and, not improbably, corrupt his integrity. With equal, nay, with greater reason, a body of men are unfit to be both judges and parties at the same time; yet what are many of the most important acts of legislation but so many judicial determinations, not indeed concerning the rights

41

of single persons, but concerning the rights of large bodies of citizens? And what are the different classes of legislators but advocates and parties to the causes which they determine? Is a law proposed concerning private debts? It is a question to which the creditors are parties on one side and the debtors on the other. Justice ought to hold the balance between them. Yet the parties are, and must be, themselves the judges; and the most numerous party, or, in other words, the most powerful faction must be expected to prevail. Shall domestic manufactures be encouraged, and in what degree, by restrictions on foreign manufactures? are questions which would be differently decided by the landed and the manufacturing classes, and probably by neither with a sole regard to justice and the public good. The apportionment of taxes on the various descriptions of property is an act which seems to require the most exact impartiality; yet there is, perhaps, no legislative act in which greater opportunity and temptation are given to a predominant party to trample on the rules of justice. Every shilling with which they overburden the inferior number is a shilling saved to their own pockets. . . .

Controlling the Effects of Factions

The inference to which we are brought is, that the *causes* of faction cannot be removed, and that relief is only to be sought in the means of controlling its *effects*.

If a faction consists of less than a majority, relief is supplied by the republican principle, which enables the majority to defeat its sinister views by regular vote. It may clog the administration, it may convulse the society; but it will be unable to execute and mask its violence under the forms of the Constitution. When a majority is included in a faction, the form of popular government, on the other hand, enables it to sacrifice to its ruling passion or interest both the public good and the rights of other citizens. To secure the public good and private rights against the danger of such a faction, and at the same time to preserve the spirit and the form of popular government, is then the great object to which our inquiries are directed. Let me add that it is the great desideratum by which this form of government can be rescued from the opprobrium under which it has so long laboured, and be recommended to the esteem and adoption of mankind.

By what means is this object obtainable? Evidently by one of two only. Either the existence of the same passion or interest in a majority at the same time must be prevented, or the majority, having such co-existent passion or interest, must be rendered, by their number and local situation, unable to concert and carry into effect schemes of oppression. If the impulse and the opportunity be suffered to coincide, we well know that neither moral nor religious motives can be relied on as an adequate control. They are not found to be such on the injustice and violence of individuals, and lose their efficacy in proportion to the number combined together, that is, in proportion as their efficacy becomes needful.

Pure Democracy Cannot Control Factions

From this view of the subject it may be concluded that a pure democracy, by which I mean a society consisting of a small number of citizens, who assemble and administer the government in person, can admit of no cure for the mischiefs of faction. A common passion or interest will, in almost every case, be felt by a majority of the whole; a communication and concert result from the form of government itself; and there is nothing to check the inducements to sacrifice the weaker party or an obnoxious individual. Hence it is that such democracies have ever been spectacles of turbulence and contention; have ever been found incompatible with personal security or the rights of property; and have in general been as short in their lives as they have been violent in their deaths. . . .

A Republic Can Control Factions

A republic, by which I mean a government in which the scheme of representation takes place, opens a different prospect, and promises the cure for which we are seeking. Let us examine the points in which it varies from pure democracy, and we shall comprehend both the nature of the cure and the efficacy which it must derive from the Union.

Madison's Contribution

Between 1781 and 1787 this country was groping its way painfully toward a theory of a more perfect union. The theory that emerged in 1787 in James Madison's concept of the extensive republic crystalized the nature of that more nearly perfect union under which we have lived ever since. . . .

Madison's theory was articulated before, during, and after the Constitutional Convention. It was embodied, however incompletely, in what is perhaps the most widely read and most influential work on political theory that America has yet produced, *The Federalist.*

Neal Riemer, *The Journal of Politics,* November 1958.

The two great points of difference between a democracy and a republic are: first, the delegation of the government, in the latter, to a small number of citizens elected by the rest; secondly, the greater number of citizens, and greater sphere of country, over which the latter may be extended.

The effect of the first difference is, on the one hand, to refine and enlarge the public views, by passing them through the medium of a chosen body of citizens, whose wisdom may best discern the true interest of their country, and whose patriotism and love of justice will be least likely to sacrifice it to temporary or partial considerations. Under such a regulation, it may well happen that the public voice, pronounced by the representatives of the people, will be more consonant to the public good than if pronounced by the people themselves, convened for the purpose. On the other hand, the effect may be inverted. Men of factious tempers, of local prejudices, or of sinister designs, may, by intrigue, by corruption, or by other means, first obtain the suffrages, and then betray the interests, of the people. The question resulting is, whether small or extensive republics are more favourable to the election of proper guardians of the public weal; and it is clearly decided in favour of the latter by two obvious considerations:

A Large Republic Can Better Control Factions

In the first place, it is to be remarked that, however small the republic may be, the representatives must be raised to a certain number, in order to guard against the cabals of a few; and that, however large it may be, they must be limited to a certain number, in order to guard against the confusion of a multitude. Hence the number of representatives in the two cases not being in proportion to that of the two constituents, and being proportionally greater in the small republic, it follows that, if the proportion of fit characters be not less in the large than in the small republic, the former will present a greater option, and consequently a greater probability of a fit choice.

In the next place, as each representative will be chosen by a greater number of citizens in the large than in the small republic, it will be more difficult for unworthy candidates to practise with success the vicious arts by which elections are too often carried; and the suffrages of the people being more free, will be more likely to centre in men who possess the most attractive merit and the most diffusive and established characters. . . .

Republics Are More Effective in Larger Countries

The other point of difference is, the greater number of citizens and extent of territory which may be brought within the compass of republican than of democratic government; and it is this circumstance principally which renders factious combinations less to be dreaded in the former than in the latter. The smaller the society, the fewer probably will be the distinct parties and interests composing it; the fewer the distinct parties and interests, the more frequently will a majority be found of the same party; and the smaller the number of individuals composing a majority, and the smaller the compass within which they are placed, the more easily will they concert and execute their plans of oppression. Extend the sphere, and you take in a greater variety of parties and interests; you make it less probable that a majority of the whole will have a common motive to invade the rights of other citizens; for if such a common motive exists, it will be more difficult for all who feel it to discover their own strength, and to act in unison with each other. Besides other impediments, it may be remarked that, where there is a consciousness of unjust or dishonourable purposes, communication is always checked by distrust in proportion to the number whose concurrence is necessary.

The Union Has the Advantage of a Large Republic

Hence, it clearly appears, that the same advantage which a republic has over a democracy, in controlling the effects of faction, is enjoyed by a large over a small republic—is enjoyed by the Union over the States composing it. Does the advantage consist in the substitution of representatives whose enlightened views and virtuous sentiments render them superior to local prejudices and to schemes of injustice? It will not be denied that the representation of the Union will be most likely to possess these requisite endowments. Does it consist in the greater security afforded by a greater variety of parties, against the event of any one party being able to outnumber and oppress the rest? In an equal degree does the increased variety of parties, parties comprised within the Union increase this security? Does it, in fine, consist in the greater obstacles opposed to the concert and accomplishment of the secret wishes of an unjust and interested majority? Here, again, the extent of the Union gives it the most palpable advantage.

The influence of factious leaders may kindle a flame within their particular States, but will be unable to spread a general conflagration through the other States. A religious sect may degenerate into a political faction in a part of the Confederacy; but the variety of sects dispersed over the entire face of it must secure the national councils against any danger from that source. A rage for paper money, for an abolition of debts, for an equal division of property, or for any other improper or wicked project, will be less apt to pervade the whole body of the Union than a particular member of it; in the same proportion as such a malady is more likely to taint a particular county or district, than an entire State.

In the extent and proper structure of the Union, therefore, we behold a republican remedy for the diseases most incident to republican government. And according to the degree of pleasure and pride we feel in being republicans, ought to be our zeal in cherishing the spirit and supporting the character of Federalists.

"The American philosophy of politics is not a speculative entity. . . . It is rather a pragmatic method of solving problems."

America's Genius Is Its Practice of Pragmatism

David L. Bender

David L. Bender is the editor of this book and the publisher and originator of the Opposing Viewpoints Series. He has edited numerous titles in the series, most recently *Constructing a Life Philosophy* and *The Political Spectrum*. In the following viewpoint, he suggests that America does have a blueprint for its political actions. He argues that although it may not be recognized as an identifiable political theory, it is a practical way of dealing with concrete issues and has developed because of unique circumstances in America's past. He refers to it as America's pragmatic method.

As you read, consider the following questions:

1. What does the author mean when he claims American political life is guided by a "pragmatic method"?
2. In describing America's pragmatic method, what three factors does he identify as its cause?

This viewpoint was written for this book. An earlier version was written by David Bender in 1965 titled, "The Pragmatic Method and American Political Thought."

For years the early critics of America complained of its lack of an underlying philosophy and its small contribution to history's deposit of philosophical knowledge. Then someone noticed that America was not a hopeless case, and that it did have something new to offer. Alexis de Tocqueville, a foreign observer in America, pointed out that Americans, although never having discovered a general law of mechanics, did introduce an engine, which as he put it, "changes the aspect of the world."

Americans, it was discovered, although not adept at withdrawing into the sanctuaries of their oak-panelled studies to meditate on abstract subjects, were extremely proficient at solving concrete problems. They had a practical way of looking at things that produced results. Eventually this trait found expression in the philosophy of pragmatism advanced by C.S. Pierce, William James, and John Dewey. The philosophy was described by James as being "the attitude of looking away from first things, principles, categories, supposed necessities; and of looking toward last things, fruits, consequences, facts."

Americans in general did not then, and do not now, subscribe to the philosophy of pragmatism as one would to a favorite theory. However, this philosophy is symptomatic of the American mind. It is the expression of the American creed, a creed that Americans may not be able to articulate or expound on readily, but one that they profess by practice. The thesis of this essay is that the American philosophy of politics is not a speculative entity. It is not the result of philosophical meditation and spelled out in metaphysical terms. It is rather a pragmatic method of solving problems that, as Tocqueville observed, is constructed "to tend to results without being bound to means."

America's Lack of an Explicit Philosophy and Its Pragmatism

The pragmatic bent of the American mind, a "philosophical method" that is not really a philosophy, fills the vacuum created by the absence of an American political theory. When Daniel Boorstin, the author of the following viewpoint, wrote that Americans "have not been much interested in the grammar of politics," but rather, "have been more interested in the way it works than in the theory behind it," he was not only describing America's lack of a political philosophy, but was also pointing out the practical political method it does possess.

George Sabine, in an essay titled "What Is a Political Theory?" claims that

> a political theory . . . covers three kinds of factors: it includes factual statements about the posture of affairs that gave rise to it; it contains statements of what may be roughly called a causal nature, to the effect that one kind of thing is more likely to hap-

pen, or may be more easily brought about than another; and it contains statements that something ought to happen or is the right and desirable thing to have happen.

The pragmatist, Sabine indicates, would generalize this description, claiming that "the joint reference to past and future, and the joint reference to causes and values, are characteristic of every complete act of thought." The pragmatist holds that the three elements of a political theory, the factual, the causal, and the valuational, "occur in the same psychological situation, they must therefore be united in some logical form of synthesis." Americans, although they make political judgements with one sweep of the mind, compressing factual, causal, and valuational considerations into one pragmatic overview, do not see the necessity of devising some logical form of synthesis.

Americans Are Pragmatists

Americans are pragmatists. Pragmatists believe that whatever works must be right. If big government worked during the New Deal, then it must have been right, at least for that time. If Reagan's conservative policies are working—and most people still think they are—then they must be right for our time.

William Schneider, *The Atlantic Monthly,* January 1987.

This is the American method, one that operates within the framework laid out by the philosophers of pragmatism, yet it does so on instinct and not deduction. It sees a contradiction between theory and practice and automatically rejects theory as being useless. It is a theory without thought, a philosophy that is not a philosophy. It is a common method of solving problems that is eminently utilitarian. It is the habit of relying on experience and doing what works, and it is the genius of American political thought.

The Causes of American Pragmatism

Arthur Schlesinger, in answering Crevecoeur's famous question, "What then is the American, this new man?" claims that "This 'new man' is the product of the interplay of his Old World heritage and New World conditions. Real understanding dawns only when the nature of these two factors is properly assessed." The interplay of forces producing America's pragmatic method can be identified by three forces: the acceptance of a general consensus, the political realism of the founding fathers, and the impact of the American frontier.

1. Acceptance of a General Consensus

Louis Hartz has observed that "American pragmatism has

always been deceptive because glacier-like, it has rested on miles of submerged conviction. . . . The American deals with concrete cases because he never doubts his general principles." It is this common consensus, this "oneness" of the American mind, that explains the lack of an American political philosophy and the pragmatic method that takes its place. If everyone is in agreement on the ends of society there is no need for theorizing, rather the need is to discover the proper means to arrive at agreed upon ends.

Clinton Rossiter, in an attempt to reconstruct the political consensus at the time of the American Revolution, has described in a 1953 article in *The Review of Politics*, a mythical revolutionary who concisely expresses this consensus. On the subject of equality the imaginary individual had this to say:

> Men may be grossly unequal in appearance, talents, intelligence, virtue, and fortune, but to this extent at least they are absolutely equal: no man has any natural right of dominion over any other; every man is free in the sight of God and plan of nature.

The individual's opinion of governmental control versus individualism was the following:

> Every man must surrender enough control over his original rights to permit government to maintain an organized, stable, peaceful pattern of human relations. No man should surrender so much that government dictates his every action. Between these two self-evident extremes the balance of liberty and authority must ever be in constant motion. In a free state the balance tips decisively in the direction of liberty.

He believed that a

> true constitution has three sound claims to obedience and even adoration: it is the command of the people, an original compact expressing their unalienable sovereignty; the handiwork of the wisest men in the community; and an earthly expression of the eternal principles of the law of nature.

These are some of the basic principles that constituted the consensus of revolutionary America. They are worth mentioning for they still apply. Americans today subscribe to almost the same political creed. As Gunnar Myrdal, the astute Swedish observer of America has phrased it, "America is . . . conservative. . . . But the principles conserved are liberal and some, indeed, are radical." Americans are still championing the principles of a liberal cause that is two centuries old. This system of beliefs still characterizes the American people and still accounts for its common consensus. Because Americans agree on first principles, they have no need to theorize about politics. Instead, Americans occupy themselves with the practical application of this consensus to issues of the day.

2. The Political Realism of the Founding Fathers

Another factor which helped to account for America's pragmatic method taking the place of a full-blown philosophy was the political realism of the founding fathers. In a paper titled, "Political Realism and the Age of Reason: The Anti-Rationalist Heritage in America," Norman Jacobson argues that the founding fathers were realists with a pessimistic view of human nature. He claims they were adversely stimulated by the Age of Reason, and had a profound skepticism concerning the ability of human reason or political theories maintaining a stable and enduring society.

America's Contribution to Political Theory

America has been criticized for contributing little or nothing to the cultural progress of humanity. It has been pointed out that there are no American Bachs, Michelangelos, or Miltons, and that in political theory there have been no Edmund Burkes or John Lockes. However, America has made a substantial contribution, not in the world of philosophy, but rather in the daily world of reality. America has produced a Henry Ford, a Thomas Edison, and two Wright brothers. In political theory America has not produced individuals who have been masters at speculating on how the good life should be ordered. Instead, it has constructed a pragmatic method that actually puts into practice the good life for citizens. Americans, rather than sitting back and plaintively musing the difficulty, if not impossibility, of treading the narrow line between the necessity of a strong government that can provide for citizens' needs and one that will not abridge civil rights, have instead walked this tightrope with an ever increasing degree of skill. This is America's gift to humanity, a handbook of directions rather than a tome of skillfully phrased and profound reflections on the nature of government.

David L. Bender, 1965.

The founding fathers placed great importance on experience gained in the past and had little time for innovation based on speculation. As they saw it, an important lesson to be learned from history was the irrational tendency of human nature. Hamilton was perhaps their best spokesman on this point. He wrote in number fifteen of *The Federalist*, "Why has government been instituted at all? Because the passions of men will not conform to the dictates of reason and justice, without constraint." In number fifty-one Madison added his famous observation, "But what is government itself, but the greatest of all reflections on human nature? If men were angels, no government would be necessary."

Not all of the founding fathers shared this anti-rational sentiment. Jefferson and his followers were convinced of the rationality of human nature and the ability of people to control their leaders and guide their own affairs. However, as numerous as Jefferson and his followers might have been, they were a minority. The majority of the fathers shared Hamilton's view. Concerning the Constitutional Convention, Jacobson wrote: "There was general agreement among the delegates at Philadelphia in 1787 that 'Experience must be [the] only guide.' 'Reason,' it was feared, might 'mislead them.'"

Considering the common anti-rational viewpoint of the founding fathers it is not surprising that they looked on political theorizing as the pastime of those who specialized in parlor games. America's lack of interest in political theory can be traced partially to this factor. It also helps to explain America's pragmatic method and its reliance on experience rather than theory.

3. The Impact of the American Frontier

Frederick Jackson Turner, in *The Frontier in American History*, has observed that "American democracy was born of no theorist's dream, it was not carried in the Sarah Constant to Virginia, nor in the Mayflower to Plymouth. It came out of the American forest, and it gained new strength each time it touched a new frontier." Turner claimed that physical America determined the American philosophy, or more correctly, the lack of a philosophy. There is much truth in this consideration. The frontier proposition was an important factor, but it was not, as Turner would have his reader believe, the only factor. One cannot say with Turner that "this forest philosophy is the philosophy of American democracy." However, Turner's book brings to light an important contributing factor in accounting for American pragmatism.

Perhaps the best example of the frontier fostering pragmatism at the expense of philosophical speculation is the experience of the Puritans in the new world. They were probably the only sizable segment of Americans who brought to this country a specific social and religious doctrine that governed almost all phases of life. However, physical America changed the direction of the Puritan approach from the normative to the empirical. When the Puritans first landed on the American shore, they looked upon the country as a promised land where they could live to perfection their intricately thought out and highly regimented play of life. But they were to discover that the reality of life in America did not correspond to the dream life they anticipated. The wilderness of America demanded practical energy, such as clearing land and fighting Indians.

The Puritan's providential outlook on life, where everything was classified as being either an agent of God or of the devil, and subject to supernatural causality, was altered by the frontier. The Puritans came to realize that, though God's directing hand may always be present, people were the real protagonists in life. They discovered that it was necessary to devote most of their energies to the practical necessities of life. As they became more caught up in the everyday act of living in America, they tended "to make

51

the 'is' the guide to the 'ought.'"

An example of the "ought" giving way to the "is," was the reaction of the Puritans to the availability of land in the new world. Their initial plan, according to Thomas J. Wertenbaker in *The Puritan Oligarchy,* called for the founding of a central area in town "in which all should have their dwellings, and so live under the watchful eyes of the minister and the elder, within walking distance of the meeting-house, the school and the parsonage." But the temptation for individuals to leave the village and carve their own farms out of the forest was irresistible. The result was a far-flung inhabitation of the land that had a disintegrating effect on the closely-knit Puritan blueprint. Their theoretical approach gradually became a practical one. The American frontier forced the Puritans to discard, or at least revise, their speculative approach in favor of a more pragmatic one.

Turner argued that the history of our political institutions and our unique form of democracy was the result of adapting to a continually changing environment. The same can be said for our political theory. The impact of the American frontier is to some degree responsible for the pragmatic method that has evolved in America.

Conclusion

Because of the peculiar circumstances that have made their weight felt on American society, even before it became a nation-state, its members have been little disposed to either construct a philosophy or to reflect deeply on the relationship between society's stated goals and the means for attaining them. Rather, the goals have been taken for granted. The result has been a practical approach to politics, a pragmatic method that takes the place of an American political philosophy. This pragmatic method is the genius of American politics.

"No nation has ever been less interested in political philosophy or produced less in the way of theory."

America's Genius Is Its Absence of a Political Theory

Daniel Boorstin

Daniel Boorstin, the Librarian of Congress, is also one of America's leading historians. A Rhodes Scholar and worldwide educator, he has authored numerous books on American history and culture. In 1974 he won the Pulitzer Prize for his trilogy, *The Americans*. In the following viewpoint, excerpted from his influential book, *The Genius of American Politics*, Boorstin claims America's lack of interest in political theory is based on a broad consensus that he labels "givenness." He argues that American acceptance of common values is so pervasive that an explicit political philosophy is superfluous.

As you read, consider the following questions:

1. What phenomenon does the author describe with the term "givenness"?
2. What are the three axioms of "givenness"?

Daniel J. Boorstin, *The Genius of American Politics.* The University of Chicago Press, 1953. © 1953 by the University of Chicago. Subheads were added by the publisher.

The genius of American democracy comes not from any special virtue of the American people but from the unprecedented opportunities of this continent and from a peculiar and unrepeatable combination of historical circumstances. These circumstances have given our institutions their character and their virtues. The very same facts which explain these virtues, explain also our inability to make a "philosophy" of them. They explain our lack of interest in political theory, and why we are doomed to failure in any attempt to sum up our way of life in slogans and dogmas. They explain, therefore, why we have nothing in the line of a theory that can be exported to other peoples of the world. . . .

My argument is simple. It is based on forgotten commonplaces of American history—facts so obvious that we no longer see them. I argue, in a word, that American democracy is unique. It possesses a "genius" all its own. . . .

US Has Produced No Philosophers

We have not been much interested in the grammar of politics. We have been more interested in the way it works than in the theory behind it. Our unique history has thus offered us those benefits which come (in Edmund Burke's words) "from considering our liberties in the light of an inheritance" and has led us away from "extravagant and presumptuous speculations."

The great political theorists—men like Plato, Aristotle, Augustine, Hobbes, Locke, and Rousseau—even when not guilty of "extravagant and presumptuous speculations," have been primarily interested in discovering and systematizing general truths about society, regardless of time and place. However much they may have differed in other matters, they have all had in common an attempt to *abstract*, to separate the universal principles of all societies and governments from the peculiar circumstances of their own society and government. Much of what we understand comes from the light which they have thrown, from their different vantage points, on the problem of government. The United States has never produced a political philosopher of their stature or a systematic theoretical work to rank with theirs. . . .

One of the many good fortunes of American civilization has been the happy coincidence of circumstances which has led us away from such idolatry. It is my belief that the circumstances which have stunted our interest in political philosophy have also nourished our refusal to make our society into the graven image of any man's political philosophy. In other ages this refusal might have seemed less significant; in ours it is a hallmark of a decent, free, and God-fearing society. . . .

The American must go outside his country and hear the voice of America to realize that his is one of the most spectacularly lopsided cultures in all history. The marvelous success and vitality

54

of our institutions is equaled by the amazing poverty and inarticulateness of our theorizing about politics. No nation has ever believed more firmly that its political life was based on a perfect theory. And yet no nation has ever been less interested in political philosophy or produced less in the way of theory. If we can explain this paradox, we shall have a key to much that is characteristic—and much that is good—in our institutions.

I shall attempt an explanation. I start from the notion that the two sides of the paradox explain each other. The very same facts which account for our belief that we actually possess a theory also explain why we have had little interest in political theories and have never bothered seriously to develop them.

"Givenness"

For the belief that an explicit political theory is superfluous precisely because we already somehow possess a satisfactory equivalent, I propose the name "givenness." "Givenness" is the belief that values in America are in some way or other automatically defined: *given* by certain facts of geography or history peculiar to us. The notion, as I shall outline it, has three faces, which I shall describe in turn. First is the notion that we have received our values as a gift from the *past*; that the earliest settlers or Founding Fathers equipped our nation at its birth with a perfect and complete political theory, adequate to all our future needs.

America's Unchanging Political Culture

The American political culture can be referred to as the liberal tradition . . . the values of Locke, Madison, and the other liberals of the seventeenth and eighteenth centuries represent essentially the same values which comprise the American political culture at the present. Although it has changed, the remarkable phenomenon is that American political culture has survived so unchanged under substantial environmental pressure.

Donald J. Devine, *The Political Culture of the United States*, 1972.

The second is the notion that in America we receive values as a gift from the *present*, that our theory is always implicit in our institutions. This is the idea that the "American Way of Life" harbors an "American Way of Thought" which can do us for a political theory, even if we never make it explicit or never are in a position to confront ourselves with it. It is the notion that to Americans political theory never appears in its nakedness but always clothed in the peculiar American experience. We like to think that, from the shape of the living experience, we can guess what lies underneath and that such a guess is good enough—perhaps actually better than any naked theory. While according to the first axiom of "givenness" our values are the gift of our history, according to the second they are the gift of our landscape.

The third part of "givenness" is a belief which links these two axioms. It is a belief in the *continuity* or homogeneity of our history. It is the quality of our experience which makes us see our national past as an uninterrupted continuum of similar events, so that our past merges indistinguishably into our present. This sense of continuity is what makes it easy for us to accept the two first axioms at the same time: the idea of a preformed original theory given to us by the Founding Fathers, and the idea of an implicit theory always offered us by our present experience. Our feeling of continuity in our history makes it easy for us to see the Founding Fathers as our contemporaries. It induces us to draw heavily on the materials of our history, but always in a distinctly nonhistorical frame of mind.

I. Values Given by the Past: The Preformation Ideal

Now I shall begin by trying to explain what I have called the first axiom of "givenness": the idea that values are a gift from our past. Here we face our conscious attitude toward our past and toward our way of inheriting from it. This particular aspect of the "givenness" idea may be likened to the obsolete biological notion of "preformation." That is the idea that all parts of an organism pre-exist in perfect miniature in the seed. Biologists used to believe that if you could look at the seed of an apple under a strong enough microscope you would see in it a minute apple tree. Similarly, we seem still to believe that if we could understand the ideas of the earliest settlers—the Pilgrim Fathers or Founding Fathers—we would find in them no mere seventeenth- or eighteenth-century philosophy of government but the perfect embryo of the theory by which we now live. We believe, then, that the mature political ideals of the nation existed clearly conceived in the minds of our patriarchs. The notion is essentially static. It assumes that the values and theory of the nation were given once and for all in the very beginning. . . .

Our firm belief in a perfectly performed theory helps us understand many things about ourselves. In particular, it helps us see how it has been that, while we in the United States have been unfertile in political theories, we have at the same time possessed an overweening sense of orthodoxy. The poverty of later theorizing has encouraged appeal to what we like to believe went before. In building an orthodoxy from sparse materials, of necessity we have left the penumbra of heresy vague. The inarticulate character of American political theory has thus actually facilitated heresy-hunts and tended to make them indiscriminate. The heresy-hunts which come at periods of national fear—the Alien and Sedition Acts of the age of the French Revolution, the Palmer raids of the

56

age of the Russian Revolution, and similar activities of more recent times—are directed not so much against acts of espionage as against acts of irreverence toward that orthodox American creed, believed to have been born with the nation itself. . . .

America's Disinterest in Philosophy

I think that in no country in the civilized world is less attention paid to philosophy than in the United States. The Americans have no philosophical school of their own; and they care but little for all the schools into which Europe is divided, the very names of which are scarcely known to them.

Alexis de Tocqueville, *Democracy in America*, 1835.

The fact that we have had a written constitution, and even our special way of interpreting it, has contributed to the "preformation" notion. Changes in our policy or our institutions are read back into the ideas, and sometimes into the very words, of the Founding Fathers. Everybody knows that this had made of our federal Constitution an "unwritten" document. What is more significant is the way in which we have justified the adaptation of the document to current needs: by attributing clarity, comprehensiveness, and a kind of mystical foresight to the social theory of the founders. In Great Britain, where there is an "unwritten" constitution in a very different sense, constitutional theory has taken for granted the *gradual* formulation of a theory of society. No sensible Briton would say that his history is the unfolding of the truths implicit in Magna Charta and the Bill of Rights. Such documents are seen as only single steps in a continuing process of definition. . . .

II. Values Given by the Landscape: The Land of the Free

The first axiom is the one which I have just described and called by the name of the "preformation" ideal. It is the notion that, in the beginning and once and for all, the Founding Fathers of the nation gave us a political theory, a scheme of values, and a philosophy of government. As we have seen, it is an ideal, a static kind of "givenness"—a gift of orthodoxy, the gift of the past.

The second axiom is similar, in that it, too, is an excuse or a reason for not philosophizing. It is the notion that a scheme of values is given, not by traditions, theories, books, and institutions, but by present experience. It is the notion that our theory of life is embodied in our way of life and need not be separated from it, that our values are given by our condition. If this second part of the idea of "givenness" seems, in strict logic, contradictory to the first, from the point of view of the individual believer it is

57

actually complementary. For, while the first axiom is ideal and static in its emphasis, the second is practical and dynamic. "Preformation" means that the theory of community was given, once and for all, in the beginning; the second sense of "givenness" means that the theory of community is perpetually being given and ever anew.

Taken together with the idea of preformation, this second "givenness" makes an amazingly comprehensive set of attitudes. The American is thus prepared to find in *all* experience—in his history and his geography, in his past and his present—proof for his conviction that he is equipped with a hierarchy of values, a political theory. Both axioms together encourage us to think that we need not invent a political theory because we already possess one. The idea of "givenness" as a whole is, then, both as idealistic as a prophet's vision and as hardheaded as common sense.

This second face of "givenness" is at once much simpler and much more vague than the concept of preformation. It is simply the notion that values are implicit in the American experience. The idea that the American landscape is a giver of values is, of course, old and familiar. It has long been believed that in America the community values would not have to be sought through books, traditions, the messianic vision of prophets, or the speculative schemes of philosophers but would somehow be the gift of the continent itself. . . .

We have been told again and again, with the metaphorical precision of poetry, that the United States is the *land* of the free. Independence, equality, and liberty, we like to believe, are breathed in with our very air. No nation has been readier to identify its values with the peculiar conditions of its landscape: we believe in *American* equality, *American* liberty, *American* democracy, or, in sum, the *American* way of life. . . .

III. The Continuity of American History

The third part of the idea of "givenness," as I have said, is actually a kind of link between the two axioms which I have already described: the notion that we have an ideal given in a particular period in the past (what I have called the idea of "preformation") and the idea that the theory of American life is always being given anew in the present, that values are implicit in the American experience. The third aspect to which I now turn helps us understand how we can at once appeal to the past and yet be fervently unhistorical in our approach to it.

By this I mean the remarkable continuity or homogeneity of American history. . . .

The impression which the American has as he looks about him is one of the inevitability of the particular institutions, the particular kind of society in which he lives. The kind of acceptance of institutions as proper to their time and place which tyrants have labored in vain to produce has in the United States been the result of the accidents of history. The limitations of our history have perhaps confined our philosophical imagination; but they have at the same time confirmed our sense of the continuity of our past and made the definitions of philosophers seem less urgent. We Americans are reared with a feeling for the unity of our history and an unprecedented belief in the normality of our kind of life to our place on earth.

We have just been observing that our history has had a continuity: that is, that the same political institutions have persisted throughout our whole national career and therefore have acquired a certain appearance of normality and inevitableness. No less important is the converse of this fact, namely, that our history has *not* been *dis*continuous, has not been punctuated by the kind of internal struggles which have marked the history of most of the countries of western Europe, and which have fed their awareness that society is shaped by men.

Discriminating Between Factual and False Statements

Usually difficult situations and propositions do not present easy choices. Real life problems are often too complex to permit simple choices between absolute right and wrong. This uncertainty is particularly true when dealing with philosophical propositions. This activity will exercise your ability to discriminate between degrees of truth or falsehood about statements concerning the basis of American democracy. The statements that follow are taken from the viewpoints in this chapter. Using the continuum at the beginning of the statements as a model, evaluate each statement's degree of truth or falsehood.

If you are doing this activity as a member of a group or class, work in small groups of four to six. Compare your group's results with those of the other groups.

+	5	4	3	2	1	0	1	2	3	4	5	−
	completely true			partially true			partially false			completely false		

1. There is now and traditionally has been a societal consensus of liberal values in the United States.

2. The political theory of James Madison has been the dominant political theory in our history.

3. More so than most other peoples, Americans are pragmatists.

4. In no country in the civilized world is less attention paid to philosophy than in the United States.

5. From a global perspective the most striking thing about American thought is the degree of consensus rather than conflict.

6. Our Government was no type of an experiment in advanced democracy; it was simply an adaptation of English constitutional government.

7. As long as the reason of man continues fallible, and he is at liberty to exercise it, different opinions will be formed.

8. The most common and durable source of factions has been the various and unequal distribution of property.

9. A pure democracy, by which I mean a society consisting of a small number of citizens, who assemble and administer the government in person, can admit of no cure for the mischiefs of factions.

10. No nation (other than America) has ever believed more firmly that its political life was based on a perfect theory.

11. Americans do not have a political philosophy, but rather have a pragmatic method of solving problems.

Periodical Bibliography

The following periodical articles deal with the subject matter of this chapter.

Daniel J. Boorstin	"Our Unspoken National Faith," *Commentary*, June 12, 1953.
Henry Steele Commager	"The Revolution as a World Ideal," *Saturday Review*, December 13, 1975.
J.W. Fulbright	"The American Character," *Vital Speeches of the Day*, January 1, 1964.
Max Gordon	"Reclaiming the American Ideal," *The Nation*, April 5, 1975.
Jeffrey R. Hummel and William Marina	"Did the Constitution Betray the Revolution?" *Reason*, April 1987. Two separate articles debating the issue.
Harry V. Jaffa	"The Constitution: An Application of Natural Law," *The Center Magazine*, July/August 1986.
Dwight R. Lee	"The Political Economy of the US Constitution," *The Freeman*, February 1987.
Daniel L. Marsh	"The American Canon," *Vital Speeches of the Day*, June 15, 1942.
George W. Maxey	"The Qualities of the Early Americans," *Vital Speeches of the Day*, January 1, 1944.
Robert Nisbet	"America as Utopia," *Reason*, March 1987.
Jeffrey St. John	"Reviving America's Revolutionary Principles of Liberty," *Vital Speeches of the Day*, October 1, 1976.
George Weigel	"John Courtney Murray & the American Proposition," *Catholicism in Crisis*, November 1955.

2 CHAPTER

What Is the Role of American Government?

American GOVERNMENT

Chapter Preface

In 1913 Walter Lippman, an eminent American political philosopher, observed that "It is perfectly true that that government is best which governs least. It is equally true that that government is best which provides most." This observation highlights the essence of the continual debate over the role and size of government. Does a large government more easily "promote the general welfare" that the Constitution calls for? Or does it instead become too intrusive and lessen the freedom and liberty of its citizens? It is this issue that is debated in the four following viewpoints.

Richard B. McKenzie, in the first viewpoint, claims large government erodes democracy. He argues that the history of tyranny is the history of the garnering of rights and powers by the state. Henry Steele Commager takes an opposite tack. He details many of the ways a strong American government has improved the lot of its citizens, concluding that those who decry a strong national government are ignorant of America's history. Edward H. Crane, the president of a think tank dedicated to controlling governmental growth, counters Commager, giving examples of the ways a bureaucratic American government has lessened the liberties of all Americans. In the last viewpoint, the president of another foundation that is dedicated to accommodating "inevitable change," presents an opposing opinion. Alan Pifer claims that it would be a mistake to reduce the increasing social role of the federal government. He describes the ways the enlarged social role of government has improved the lot of citizens.

"The history of tyranny is the history of the garnering of rights and power by the state."

Large Government Erodes Democracy

Richard B. McKenzie

Richard B. McKenzie is professor of economics at Clemson University. A syndicated radio commentator on economics issues, he has published numerous scholarly articles on economics. His book, *The New World of Economics*, has been used in over 500 colleges and universities. The viewpoint that follows is taken from his book *Bound To Be Free*. In the book he identifies the government forces that are destroying American democracy, and he provides a program of action to limit those forces. This viewpoint presents some of McKenzie's arguments, demonstrating how large government erodes democracy.

As you read, consider the following questions:

1. What point does the author make in claiming the framers of the Constitution "largely failed to accomplish their goal"?
2. How does McKenzie support his claim that individual freedom is being lessened by the growth of government? How is individual dishonesty increased?
3. What are his conclusions? Do you agree?

Reprinted from BOUND TO BE FREE by Richard B. McKenzie with permission of Hoover Institution Press. © 1982 by the Board of Trustees of the Leland Stanford Jr. University.

The American political system has often been characterized as a grand social experiment in self-government. The framers of the Constitution constructed a republican system for the express purpose of dispersing, not concentrating, political power and, thereby, economic power. Their motto was, effectively, "the government which governs least, governs best," and they set about establishing a new political order with strict constitutional limitations on the "centres" of governmental decision making and political power. A *federal* republic made up of largely independent states, loosely coordinated by a central administration, was delegated limited responsibilities and powers. At the national level they established a political obstacle course, composed of two houses, a president, and judiciary, through which legislation had to pass before it could become law; they thought few legislative proposals would make their way through this maze.

The founders of this country's social experiment were willing to rely on majority rule not because it was a way of facilitating collective decisions and the control of people by government but because it was a means of restricting the range of issues decided and controlled by politics. . . .

In short, the framers wanted the power given up by people to government to be dispersed among many different and competing governments—at the federal, state, and local levels. No one level of government would be allowed to have much say over anything. Further, they thought majority rule would restrain government simply because there were few issues on which a majority of the "multiplicity of interests" and "multiplicity of sects" could and would agree. Therefore, few collective decisions usurping the rights of individuals could be expected.

Freedom Is Maximized by Containing Government

The presuppositions most of the framers took with them to Philadelphia are fairly evident in what they said and did. Rights ultimately spring from individuals, not government. The history of tyranny is the history of the garnering of rights and power by the state. Freedom can be maximized only by the strict containment of the state, by the minimization of the scope and influence of government. The framers were not interested in using government to constrain an otherwise free market; rather, they were interested in fostering the freedom of individuals within the market and political systems as a means of restricting and controlling government. . . .

The experience of the past two centuries has, unfortunately, revealed that the framers largely failed to accomplish their goal: to control for their time and future generations the power of government. We have come full circle to the point where individual freedom and individual decision making are gradually being eroded by the encroachment of "governmental freedom" and "collective decision making." Today's government is neither insignificant in terms of resource use nor unimportant in terms of its influence over people's welfare. It has grown and continues to grow. More important, the propensity of people to seek governmental solution of their individual problems seems unbounded. The government is now the "maker" and the "breaker" of economic and political lives. We see all around us the mercantilist controls that . . . were explicitly rejected by the Founding Fathers: "the fixing of prices, wages, and interest rates; the outlawing of forestalling and engrossing; the regulating of the quality of goods; the licensing of labor; the chartering of corporations; and the establishment of state enterprises." Data on growth in government and in its economic influence clearly demonstrate this point. . . .

The trends in governmental economic activity are alarming. This growth in government means that decisions regarding resource use are now made by collective, political institutions. The realm

Jeff MacNelly. Reprinted by permission: Tribune Media Services.

of private decision making—and private responsibility for decisions made—is seriously constricted. As an affront to freedom, this is in itself bad. However, there are other reasons for concern. Many production and distribution decisions are now channeled through the slow, tedious, and inefficient political process. Indeed, we have overburdened the political process with far more decisions than that process can make with any reasonable degree of responsiveness and flexibility. We are using a scarce resource—democracy—as though it were a free good, inexhaustible in supply, and as though the assumption of more responsibility by government has little or no impact on the government's ability to perform its basic functions of providing for defense, law enforcement, and education.

When people make private decisions to engage in private trades, they do so voluntarily—because they choose to do so. Presumably, both parties to a trade gain because of their private decisions. Neither exerts coercion over the other because the gain is mutual. Each party to a potential trade has a private incentive, when decisions are private and voluntary, to seek ways to help the other; that is the only way to achieve the unanimous consent necessary for trades to occur.

Collective, democratic decisions made through government do not, on the other hand, require unanimity. Most of the time democratic decisions require agreement among a simple majority of voters; much of the time, because of reliance on representatives and the committee process and the undue political influence of special interest groups, democratic decisions are made with much less than majority agreement. Indeed, given the reliance on bureaucracy in modern government, many public decisions are made by a handful of unelected government workers.

Growth in government means a movement away from private decisions, which require unanimous agreement but affect relatively few people, to collective decisions, which, although they affect many, can be made by a small group. Growth in government can mean and has meant a growth in the ability of some people—those in agreement and with political clout—to impose their will on others who may or may not be in the minority. John Stuart Mill, in his *Essay on Liberty*, was understandably concerned about the "tyranny of the majority"; former Senator Eugene McCarthy has expressed many of the same sentiments, arguing that government restrictions on political campaigns are "the ultimate tyranny of the majority."[1]

Vested Interest in Governmental Growth

Further, growth in government means a growth in the number of people whose livelihood depends directly on government and its programs. The government has created its own constituency to whom it can turn for the political support it needs for its own growth. Farmers definitely have an interest in the growth of the Department of Agriculture and the subsidies it provides them. University professors would like an expansion of state and federal budgets for education and research. Social security recipients concern themselves with expanded benefits and increased taxes on those who are working and supplying the funds for that system. Workers at Lockheed watch the defense budget. Many, if not most, government employees, of course, have an interest in the growth of virtually all governmental programs: further expansion means an increase in the demand for their services, higher wages, and greater job security.

Governmental expansion can start as a small snowball, with a few people who have a direct interest, and end up as an avalanche of all-encompassing government activity, with a constituency for governmental growth that spans the political spectrum. When government becomes ''large,'' it is very difficult to contract it, to eliminate or significantly reduce programs riddled with waste, inefficiency, and corruption. Each program develops its own constituency that will, when its ox is gored, vocally oppose any cutbacks in the program. Furthermore, a constituency adversely affected by proposed cuts can be expected to use its money in the political arena, buying by campaign contributions and outright bribes the legislative support it needs. We may now be unable to return to a condition of restricted state responsibility. We can only hope not.

The Growth of Local Governments

Statistics suggest that government in recent decades has grown faster at the local and state levels than it has at the federal level. Some observers have concluded that governmental growth has been accompanied by a relative, if not absolute, dispersion of political power. These statistics, however, hide a general tendency toward greater centralization of power. One of the reasons for the rapid growth of state and local governments is the enormous increase in federal grants, restricted and unrestricted, to state and local governments. In 1902 federal grants represented only 0.7 percent of total state and local revenues. In the late 1970s, federal grants made up about 15 percent of their total revenues. Similarly, federal and state grants to local governments accounted for only 6 percent of local government revenues in 1902. Now, such grants constitute about 35 percent of local government budgets. It follows that much of the growth in state and local government employment is attributable to the growing influence of the federal government. State and local governments have become, to a great extent, arms (or dependent agencies) of the federal government. . . .

Government regulation is without question the number-one

69

growth industry in the country. Rules on what we shall wear, how we should work and under what conditions, what we can eat and drink, where we should live and in what kind of houses, and what we can drive flow from the seats of government like lava from an erupting volcano. Because of the growth in regulation, we are now a nation of criminals; no mortal can read, much less comprehend, all of the rules that emanate from the halls of government. Each person daily violates some rule that he does not know even exists.[2] With considerable naiveté, President Jimmy Carter, during his first year in office, asked his cabinet members to read over the rules of their own departments before imposing them on the public. Most of the secretaries did not even try to follow this directive. Those who tried did nothing else but read; and still they fell behind.

Balance Destroyed

The Constitution our founding fathers gave us was indeed good. The fact that it stands today as the oldest surviving written Constitution in the world attests to their ability to construct a perfect balance between governmental power and personal liberty. Over the years, however, that balance has been largely destroyed by the steady growth of governmental power, a trend that Robert Welch once termed "the greatest tragedy" of our time.

Warren L. McFerran, *The New American*, March 30, 1987.

No matter how inconsequential, no social or economic ill seems to escape the attention of social reformers in their missionary quest for perfection in an imperfect world—their zeal to protect us from the perceived perils of daily existence.[3] Social regulation is flagrantly destructive of individual freedom. . . .

Large Government Promotes Dishonesty

The prominence of government in modern society has contributed in subtle ways to the breakdown of the basic principle of honesty, without which any social fabric will come unraveled. Many people who are honest with friends and family think nothing of cheating the government, either claiming more benefits from government programs than they deserve or paying less in taxes than the law requires. Examples of individuals' cheating the government abound: the university professor released from one job in the spring who accepts an offer from another college for the fall but does not sign the contract in order to qualify for unemployment compensation during the summer months; the professional society that organizes a meeting in a foreign country in order to allow members to count vacation expenses as tax deductions; and the government employee who fraudulently secures welfare payments from the programs his agency administers. Each cheater can reason that his individual actions have virtually no effect on government programs and the taxes imposed on others. One person simply does not count in the context of a large government budget. In addition, friends of cheaters are unlikely to object to (and may even support) the actions of those who cheat; they know that this cheating does not significantly affect their own welfare. In short, a level of cheating unacceptable in private relationships is quite rational when government is large and impersonal. . . .

Political Investment Rather than Market Investment

Firms are interested in making a profit. In private markets the competitive struggle for profits leads them to produce what consumers want and to restrict long-run profits. When government is small with little power to redistribute income or to determine people's welfare, businesses have little incentive to invest resources in lobbying, bribing, or in other ways trying to manipulate government. There is simply little that government can do to help them in securing profits. However, when government is large and has considerable power, as it does today, firms view huge public budgets as a source of profits. Their resources can be used in two ways: investment in capital goods that can be used to produce a product for sale in competitive markets, or investment in lobbying and bribing politicians and in trying to develop legislation that will protect firms from competition or provide them with a share of the public budget. Under a large government, "political investment" can become relatively more profitable than "market investment," and a shift in investment from the market to the political arena should be expected. In private competitive markets, a firm must appeal to buyers to enter mutually beneficial trades; in political markets it can enlist the power of the state to force people to give up part of their income for the firm's benefit.[4]

Businesses can also reason that if they do not enlist the power of the state in an effort to secure an income, then other firms and groups will. Those who refrain may be forced to pay for the political favors secured by others. Sadly, all groups—environmentalists, educators, union members, government employees, electricians, pacifists, farmers, students, welfare recipients, and consumers—can, when government is powerful, follow business groups into the political arena, a trend that threatens to destroy the democratic system by the sheer burden of political conflict and turn the productive society into the politicized society.

In government, "small is beautiful." The great need of today is for people to recognize that simple fact and to understand that the case for the free market is constructed largely on the premise that people should not be free to use the power of the state to protect themselves from the forces of competition in free exchanges between individuals. . . .

Conclusion

Now, better than ever, we can clearly see what it is like to have an unconstrained government. It is a state of affairs that appeals to virtually no one. Even the poor are beginning to see that the welfare state was probably never intended for their benefit and that there is a better way. Perhaps, just perhaps, we will observe in the 1980s a new approach to government, one that recognizes three important principles: (1) the power of any government to do good is limited; (2) the expansion of governmental decision making reduces individual freedom; and (3) without constitutional constraints on government, the free market system contains the seeds of its own demise.

1. Eugene McCarthy, *The Ultimate Tyranny: The Majority over the Majority* (New York: Harcourt Brace Jovanovich, 1980).
2. Walter B. Wriston, *Warning: The Law May Be Hazardous to Your Health* (New York: Citicorp, 1977), p. 3.
3. Researchers, for example, found that workers occasionally fall off wooden ladders that they make on construction sites. Hence, the Occupational Safety and Health Administration (OSHA) formulated very precise regulations on how these ladders must be built, specifying the minimum rung width and the angles of the side rails. For a review of other OSHA rules, see Robert Stewart Smith, *The Occupational Safety and Health Act: Its Goals and Its Achievements* (Washington, D.C.: American Enterprise Institute, 1976).
4. Research has found the obvious, that the efforts of people to influence government through campaign contributions rise exponentially with growth in government. Today, we have to be concerned with campaign contributions. One of the reasons campaign contributions are as high as they are is that government is as large as it is. See Mark Crain and Robert Tollison, "Some Monopoly Aspects of Politics" (Blacksburg: Virginia Polytechnic Institute and State University, Center for the Study of Public Choice, 1979).

"There has been a causal connection between the enlargement and the deepening of liberty in America and the growth of a strong national government."

Strong Government Has Promoted Liberty

Henry Steele Commager

Born in 1902, Henry Steele Commager is a history professor at Amherst College in Massachusetts and has authored dozens of books on American history. The recipient of numerous honors and awards, he is currently editing a fifty volume series, *The Rise of the American Nation.* An astute observer and chronicler of the American scene for decades, he argues that those who "declaim against Big Government as the enemy of liberty are ignorant of America's history."

As you read, consider the following questions:

1. What distinctions does the author make between a big government versus a strong government?
2. What evidence does he present to support his claim that national government, not state governments, has promoted the growth of liberty in the US?

Those who today declaim against Big Government as the enemy of liberty are ignorant of America's history. The most elementary and overshadowing fact of that history is that there has been a causal connection between the enlargement and the deepening of liberty in America and the growth of a strong national government.

America Has a Strong, Not Big Government

What is meant by "strong national government"? Perhaps the most astonishing feature of the current attack on centralization—an attack that President Reagan has turned into a crusade—is the argument that the United States today has not a strong national government but a Big Government. This notion has been so bolstered by repetition that it is unthinkingly accepted by most Americans. Yet what is most interesting to the foreign observers who have followed in Tocqueville's tracks is how meager, outside of what is involved in "national security," are the responsibilities and activities of the American national government compared with those assumed by most other national governments. In almost every country of Europe and Asia, the national government owns and controls all forms of transportation. It owns or controls the banks, the utilities, most radio and television stations, and most natural resources. All institutions of higher learning are government administered, as are opera companies and orchestras. The national government provides or finances medical services, a far broader range of social services than in our country, and much of the housing. This is not a phenomenon of communist nations; it is a matter of course in Britain, France, Holland, Denmark, Sweden, Australia, Italy, Japan, and scores of other nations. In short, Americans do not have a Big Government.

The Adversaries of Centralization

It is an interesting paradox that the passionate adversaries of centralization today are generally not ardent champions, as was Tocqueville, of the town meeting, the county court, the local militia. Most of those who are in public life appear to prefer life in Washington to life in their state capitals. Their devotion to states' rights has taken the form of devotion to white supremacy (Alabama) or to revenues from coal (Montana), oil (Texas), or tobacco (North Carolina). Many of them seem to be successors to those distinguished senators of the 1890s who were known as the senator from Standard Oil, the senator from the Sugar Trust, and the senator from the Pennsylvania Railroad. But today's "conservatives" have made some progress: popular hostility toward economic centralization has been deflected in the direction of political centralization.

Not that these "conservatives" are critical of all forms of centralization. They lend their support almost automatically to what

74

has been the most centralizing force in American history: the military. It was the veterans of the American Revolution who were the most ardent champions of a strong national government. It was the Civil War that dramatized the need for centralization and that led to the passage of legislation nationalizing transportation, finance, and industry.

Government Should Be an Active Force

It is not my purpose to defend all government programs, nor do I believe that government should be involved in all aspects of our lives. I do believe, however, that the government should be a creative force in the improvement of the quality of life. Government should be activist in nature, ready to step in to solve problems that individuals, private enterprise or local government cannot or will not solve.

Joseph Giordano, *Los Angeles Times*, May 1, 1985.

This experience, of course, was duplicated in World War I and World War II. President Eisenhower, who viewed the problem from both a military and a civilian vantage point, warned in his farewell address against the "military-industrial complex." It is almost superfluous to add that this "complex"is celebrated with unrestrained enthusiasm by precisely those whose energies are otherwise devoted to deploring centralization and celebrating states' rights and localism.

National Government Has Promoted Liberty

But let us turn again to the growth of liberty that has resulted from the growth of the national government. From the beginning, it has not been the states that have been the chief instruments of democracy but the central government in Washington. It was the states that maintained slavery, the national government that abolished it. It was the states that fought for slavery and tried to reinstate it, through "black codes," even after Appomattox. It was the national government that intervened with the Thirteenth, Fourteenth, and Fifteenth amendments and a succession of civil rights acts designed to emancipate and free. It would be asking a great deal to expect blacks to look to the states or to their communities for the protection of their rights.

It would also be asking a great deal to expect women, so long denied not only their political and property rights but even access to the professions and control over their children, to look to the states for their equality. From *Muller v. Oregon* in 1908 to *Roe v. Wade* in 1973, it was the federal not the state courts that vindicated the rights of women. Suffrage, too, though first granted by the federal territory of Wyoming in 1869, required in the end a federal amendment, which was bitterly fought by those states that, half a century later, defeated the Equal Rights Amendment.

Further, it would be asking a great deal to expect labor to take its chances with state rather than national legislation. It is Congress that, over more than half a century, has enacted various charters of freedom for labor. It should be sufficient to note here the Clayton Antitrust Act of 1914, the La Follette Seamen's Act of 1915, the Civilian Conservation Corps Act of 1933, the National Labor Relations Act of 1935, the revolutionary Social Security Act of 1935, and the Fair Labor Standards Act of 1938. These laws did more to establish social justice than the whole corpus of state labor legislation since the Civil War. Nor should we forget that it was Congress and the Supreme Court that, over the vociferous opposition of state economic interests, put an end to the disgrace of child labor.

National Government Has Promoted General Welfare

This record of the role of the national government in promoting justice and the general welfare is mirrored in federal efforts to encourage the conservation of natural resources. It was President Jefferson who launched the Lewis and Clark expedition and several others, whose mission it was to explore and chart the whole of America. . . . Theodore Roosevelt launched a conservation movement early in this century, and Franklin Roosevelt reinvigorated it. FDR did more to save and restore America's natural resources—through the Civilian Conservation Corps, the hundred-mile tree belt on the border of the Great Plains, and the Tennessee Valley Authority—than had been achieved in a hundred years. As every natural resource is continental, if not global, local governments cannot control any one of them. By neglect or exploitation, however, they can damage all of them.

In the arena of education the story is much the same. Ever since Massachusetts Bay enacted the first education laws in modern history, education has been the responsibility of local communities. But not all communities have fulfilled that responsibility. Our greatest educator, Thomas Jefferson, drafted ordinances making land grants to help support public schools and universities. That policy was expanded by the Morrill Act of 1862, which provided federal contributions to state universities throughout the nation, and by the Hatch Act of 1887, which set up scores of agricultural experiment stations. Those who now assert that education is a purely local matter are as wanting in logic as in a familiarity with history. The nation has an interest in the education of all children, each of whom, when an adult, can vote for congressmen and for president, and each of whom, therefore, can legislate for the whole of the nation, and for posterity.

"The natural progress of things is for government to gain ground and for liberty to yield."

Bureaucratic Government Has Reduced Liberty

Edward H. Crane

Edward H. Crane is president of the Cato Institute, which describes itself as "a public policy research foundation dedicated to the traditional American principles of limited government, individual liberty, and peace." In the following viewpoint, excerpted from a speech delivered in October 1986, Crane argues that American government is monolithic and makes "the abuses of King George—which precipitated the American revolution—pale by comparison." He argues that the reason for the problem is systemic and cites specific programs in American society that exemplify the bureaucratic growth and bungling that lessen the liberties of all Americans.

As you read, consider the following questions:

1. Why does the author claim that "the natural progress of things is for government to grow?
2. What governmental process does he refer to as the "tyranny of the status quo"? What does he identify as "policy myopia"?
3. Why does he claim the institutions of private property are grossly under-appreciated in America?

Edward H. Crane, "On the Problem of America's Policy Myopia," a speech given to the San Francisco Press Club on October 22, 1986.

About two hundred years ago a very bright fellow by the name of Thomas Jefferson had this observation: "The natural progress of things," he said, "is for government to gain ground and for liberty to yield." And, if Jefferson were around today, I think he'd probably hold by that statement. We do, after all, live in a society in which the average person pays more than 40 percent of his or her earnings to government at the local, state, or federal level. The government controls the value of our currency. It regulates our businesses down to the number and placement of restrooms in the workplace. Government forces us to participate in a universal retirement plan that now accounts for the majority of income for the majority of retired Americans. For most of us, the taxes we pay are such that we can only afford to send our children to government schools. The government tells us which drugs we may and may not take, even when we are terminally ill. If we want to start a business, it requires us to have a phalanx of lawyers on hand. It denies poor teenagers the experience of honest work by setting union-approved minimum wages, then offers the stultifying entrapment of the web of the welfare state.

Government does this and much, much more. It permeates our society. It taxes us and controls us in ways that make the abuses of King George—which precipitated the American revolution—pale by comparison. And government continues to grow. How did it happen? Why does it happen?

America's Government Is Too Large

Most Americans, I think, believe government is too large; that it's too intrusive. We elected Ronald Reagan in 1980 and again in 1984 in large part because of his unique ability to articulate our concerns over this ominous, persistent growth of the state. Americans have a heritage of liberty, of individualism, and a love of freedom. Yet during this century, and particularly during the past fifty years, we've witnessed this seemingly inexorable growth of government and felt helpless in the face of it.

Indeed, after six years of the most conservative president in half a century, government spending as a percentage of GNP is today higher than at any point in the nation's peacetime history—and that's not simply a function of the increase in military spending because spending for domestic programs is also at an all time high.

The overriding reason for this problem is systemic. . . .

The Public Choice school of economics, under the leadership of James Buchanan and Gordon Tullock, has developed the theoretical and empirical evidence to confirm what Thomas Jefferson knew intuitively. The natural progress of things *is* for government to grow. Why? Because bureaucrats are like the rest of us. They respond to incentives and for most of them the incentive is to increase funding, to increase the number of

"No, I'm not over-staffed. I do the work and the others keep the records for the government."

bureaucrats under them, to increase their power. Unlike the private sector, which has a bottom line and, therefore, incentives to reduce costs and please consumers, bureaucrats generally find themselves with no such market discipline and often in a monopoly situation.

Which is not to say that bureaucrats lack what might be termed a concern for the greater good of society. It's simply a case of them responding to incentives which motivate them to constantly generate rationalizations for increasing their budgets, expanding existing programs, and creating new programs. And one program begets another. . . .

Our Stupid Farm Program

This year's farm bill courageously attempts to deal with the nagging problem of surplus cheese, butter, and powdered milk. That there is an excess of these commodities is itself a direct result of federal price supports that artificially lift dairy products above the market clearing price. Congress, in response to a problem Congress created, located a scapegoat—or scapecow in this case—blaming America's Bossie population for flooding the nation with milk. So they put a bounty on cows, offering farmers cold cash for killing up to 600,000 of them. But, as is so often the case with the best laid plans of mice, a new problem was created. All those slaughtered moo-cows were going to depress the price of beef, so Congress magnanimously agree to use your money to buy up some 400 million pounds of beef.

Now, what Congress is going to do with all that beef stacked up around their desks is anybody's guess, but we do know that over half of the direct benefits of our truly, truly stupid farm program go to the largest 12 percent of U.S. farms.

Dispersed Cost and Concentrated Benefits

On top of these perverse incentives is the legislative phenomenon of dispersed costs and concentrated benefits. If, say, a military base means millions of dollars to a local community even though it is not needed militarily, it behooves civic and business leaders to lobby Congress hard (particularly the congressman in whose district the base is located) to get the funding for the base renewed. To you and I as taxpayers the base may cost a few cents—hardly worth our time and effort to fly to Washington to register our objection—so while a Pentagon study showed we need about 312 military bases throughout the world, we have, in fact, 3,868 in the United States alone, including one in Virginia dating back to the War of 1812, which is surrounded by a moat—designed, I presume, to protect it from angry taxpayers.

Tyranny of the Status Quo

And finally we have as part of this systemic problem what my friends Milton and Rose Friedman call the "tyranny of the status quo." A given program may be debated for years only to pass through Congress by a single vote and from that point forward, the only debate over the program concerns whether its budget should be increased 6 percent or 16 percent. Is the program achieving its goals? Did it cost more than its supporters had projected? To raise these and other seemingly germaine questions is considered in Washington to be, well, a bit naive. Each new program is protected by what the Friedmans call the Iron Triangle: The direct beneficiaries of the program, the bureaucracy implementing it, and the congressional oversight committee. As far as defense goes, the Chicago Bears should have it so good.

Policy Myopia

A corollary to the tyranny of the status quo is what I call policy myopia. Everyone pretty much accepts each major government program as a given, if not possessing a divine imprimatur. And so the focus is on the minutiae—tinkering with the status quo unconcerned with what disastrous consequences the status quo may be steering us toward. Shuffling deck chairs on the Titanic, as they say. President Reagan himself is a prime example of this phenomenon. One of the first things he did when he set out to cut the budget was to say that military spending and so-called entitlements were off limits. Well, when you add entitlements and military spending to interest on the national debt—over which the president has no control—you've got over 80 percent of the federal budget. So we shouldn't be too surprised when the president's budget balancing efforts fall a couple of hundred billion short of the target.

An article in the *Atlantic Monthly* earlier this year described the Cato Institute as being "in the vanguard of market thinking." I rather like that description and I'd like to discuss a few policy areas in which we have stood back from this myopic policy debate and come up with some proposals that would perhaps chart a new and more constructive course for America.

The Social Security Example

First, let's take up the subject of entitlements, by which we mean primarily Social Security. The tab for Social Security in fiscal '87 will be about $280 billion. For the majority of American workers the payroll tax takes more from their paycheck than the income tax does. It's worth noting that as recently as 1965 the maximum combined, employee-employer payroll tax was only $348. By the end of this decade—in just a few years—it will be nearly $8,000. As Cato Adjunct Scholar Peter Ferrara points out, for most young workers today, Social Security has become the largest investment they will make in their entire lives.

State Intervention Should Be Last Resort

The overriding principle to be revived in American political life is that which sets individual liberty as the highest political value— that value to which all other values are subordinate and that which, at all times, is to be given the highest "priority" in policy discussions.

By the same token, there must be a conscious philosophical prejudice against any intervention by the state into our lives, for by definition such intervention abridges liberty. Whatever form it may take, state intervention in the private and productive lives of the citizenry must be presumed to be a negative, uncreative, and dangerous act, to be adopted only when its proponents provide overwhelming and incontrovertible evidence that the benefits to society of such intervention far outweigh the costs.

William E. Simon, *A Time for Truth*, 1978.

And that's too bad on several counts. First, I think it's inconsistent with the principles on which this nation was founded that Americans, once they've reached some arbitrary age, should have to turn over responsibility for their lives to the federal

81

government. Yet today, the majority of Americans depend on the Social Security system for the majority of their retirement income. Second, Social Security is compulsory, which is patronizing, paternalistic, and again, inconsistent with the voluntary nature of most of our societal arrangements. And third, Social Security is increasingly a bad deal, particularly for today's younger workers.

In work he's done for both the Cato Institute and the National Chamber Foundation (of the U.S. Chamber of Commerce), Ferrara has calculated that for the great majority of workers in two-earner families entering the workforce today, the real rate of return offered by Social Security is one percent or less. For many, it's actually negative. And this is assuming that the eternally optimistic assumptions of the Social Security Administration prove accurate. I won't dwell on this here other than to point out that the SSA's so-called "realistic" actuarial assumptions include 70 years of uninterrupted 4 percent inflation and their annual hope that Americans stop living longer. The point is, even if these assumptions prove to be true, Social Security is an incredibly bad investment for today's younger workers. The payroll tax, being a tax on employment, causes unemployment and, by increasing the cost of labor, makes it more difficult to compete internationally. And it is only going to go up in the future.

A Super IRA

Rather than just accept the depressing state of the status quo with regard to retirement income, the Cato Institute and Peter Ferrara have come up with a plan—now endorsed by the National Chamber Foundation, the Heritage Foundation, and the Institute for Research on the Economics of Taxation, among others—that would allow younger workers to opt out of Social Security by investing a portion of the amount they pay in payroll taxes into a kind of Super IRA that would be privately owned by each individual participant. The money for the Super IRA would come from a dollar-for-dollar income tax credit, so the payroll tax would continue to be paid, ensuring that those workers now on Social Security or nearing retirement age would continue to be paid. The choice of participating in this plan or not would be entirely left up to the individual, so that if you wanted to remain in Social Security you'd be free to do so.

But, the advantages of a private system really are overwhelming, especially when compared to the rate of return now available from Social Security. To begin with, you have to turn over control of your life to the government when you retire. The corpus of the money you pay into the Super IRA is yours—*you* own it—unlike Social Security, which, since it's a pay-as-you-go system and has no funds set aside for you, doesn't allow you to spend the principal you've invested or leave it to your children. And it's remarkable what you could accumulate at a relatively low rate of interest in this Super IRA. Consider this: If a family with two full-time working spouses were allowed to invest what the law now requires them to pay in Social Security taxes instead into a Super IRA earning just 6 percent annually, and if they were entering the work force today, by the time they retired they would have a fund worth $1.3 million in 1986 dollars yielding a retirement income of $78,000 a year, or about two and a half times what Social Security offers. In addition, the entire $1.3 million would be available to leave to their children or loved ones.

Alternatively, if the couple chose to spend the capital along with the income when they retired, they would receive an annuity of $184,000, or about six times what Social Security now only promises. Interestingly enough, even two individuals earning a career minimum wage would accumulate a fund of $557,000 yielding $33,000, or about twice what Social Security would.

And, of course, the Super IRA plan would create a massive inflow of capital into the economy, creating jobs and increasing productivity. This radical restructuring of retirement income in America makes sense politically, economically, and especially from the standpoint of personal independence. The only, and I repeat *only*, argument against it is that it will reduce federal revenues and therefore, add to the national debt.

But, you know, this idea that any reduction of revenues can't be matched by spending cuts is just nonsense. Our congressmen are fibbing to us when they say we've got a "bare bones" budget. We've already looked at the waste of our farm program. If that's "bare bones" I say it's time to start cutting the bones. And interestingly enough, there's no better place to start than with the military budget.

The Military Budget

Now, as Dick Nixon used to say, let me make myself perfectly clear on this issue: There is no stronger anticommunist than I. I believe President Reagan was correct when he called the Soviet Union an "evil empire." And I believe we as a nation need to spend whatever is necessary to ensure our integrity as a nation—that the Soviets have no illusions about our ability to defend ourselves and/or inflict unacceptable damage on them should they initiate an attack against us.

Having said that—that we should spend whatever is necessary on our defense budget—let me say that there's a big difference between our defense budget and our military budget. The latter is nearly $300 billion and most of it goes to pay for the defense of nations other than the United States. I think what we need to recognize—and increasingly I think intelligent conservatives *are* beginning to recognize—is that Parkinson's Law is alive and well at the Pentagon, just as it is at Health and Human Services.

Take NATO as a prime example. After World War II, a strong case existed for a continued U.S. military presence in the European theatre. But for those who haven't been paying attention, our European allies have recovered from the devastation of that war. In fact, many of them are outcompeting us in world markets. So why are we paying for more than half of the cost of NATO? In a time of $200 billion deficits, how do we rationalize spending more than $130 billion a year on NATO? The plain reality of the situation is that our Western European allies have more than twice the GNP of the Warsaw Pact nations (including the Soviet Union). They have a larger population and they have superior technology. They are, in a word, fully capable of defending themselves. Yet most of them spend less than half what the United States does per capita on defense. Breaking out of the status quo with regard to our outmoded web of military alliances could pay for the privatization of Social Security by itself. Certainly there are tens of billions of dollars to be saved in the military budget—and I should say not from waste, fat, and fraud, but from a reassessment of the value of our military commitments. Waste, fat, and fraud is fun for politicians to talk about and it makes for good media, but it is not a budget line item and people who think they can remove it from government bureaucracies are, to put it charitably, engaging in wishful thinking. . . .

Too Much Government a Danger

The danger to our freedom comes from the growth of a government in which we, all of us here in this room and elsewhere in this country, see an opportunity to improve our lot. There's nothing wrong with that. The way in which the world is run, and should be run, is by people separately seeking to improve their lot by *voluntary means*.

The problem is that once a government that has power is set up, it offers the possibility to people of improving their lot, not by voluntary means, but by compulsory means. That danger to freedom has been made manifest in recent years. Public opinion polls ask people, ''Do you want government to be bigger or smaller?'' The reply is invariably that a large majority want government to be smaller.

Milton Friedman, undated pamphlet, Americanism Educational League.

That brings me to my final point. The institutions of private property are grossly under-appreciated in this nation. Not only in our policies toward the Third World, but in our own domestic policies. Property is a liberating force. It ensures that we will benefit from the efforts of our labor. It protects us and our families from big government and, for that matter, from big business, as well. Private property gives us independence and control over our own lives. Which is precisely why, in *The Communist Manifesto*, Mssrs. Marx and Engels wrote, "The theory of the communists may be summed up in the single sentence: abolition of private property." Yet, increasingly in this country we witness the courts and legislatures weakening the rights of property; the right to acquire, possess, use, and dispose of that which we have earned through honest effort. The courts, in particular, seem bent on undermining the sanctity of property rights. In the area of tort liability, judges are carrying on an egalitarian political agenda of income redistribution through such dubious doctrines as "joint and several liability" wherein if you're determined to have one percent responsibility for some alleged tort, you pay for all of it if your pockets are deep enough. Punitive damages, which under common law tradition were to be applied only in cases involving willful tortfeasors, are now generally employed where it is clear no such intent was involved, and for the sole apparent reason of taking from those who have and giving to those who want it.

But perhaps the worst example of this is at the Supreme Court level where, since the Court caved in to pressure from FDR, there no longer exists substantive due process for economic rights, which prior to the Thirties had been protected on a par with so-called personal liberties like freedom of speech and the right to privacy. Yet the Constitution clearly *does* protect economic liberties. The framers of the Constitution understood that civil liberties and economic liberties went hand-in-hand. The phrase, Life, Liberty, and Property was found everywhere in the writings of Eighteenth century American intellectuals. And, indeed, Article II, Section 10 of the Constitution specifically protects the obligations of contracts. The last sentence of that amendment reads, no person shall "be deprived of life, liberty, or property, without due process of law; nor shall private property be taken for public use, without just compensation."

Yet discriminatory taxation, double taxation, rent control laws, much business regulation, zoning laws, all are abridgements of property rights or examples of takings without just compensation. . . .

What I've discussed here—radical Social Security reform, a new approach to our military alliances . . . and the need for our court system to once again give proper deference to property rights— are all areas that involve the necessity to challenge the status quo. If we don't, then Jefferson's admonition that the natural progress of things is for government to grow and for liberty to lose ground, will continue to prove all too true.

4 VIEWPOINT

---

*"A sharp reduction of the social role of the
Federal government is clearly not in the
interests of the nation."*

Government Agencies
Promote Social Equality

Alan Pifer

The role of the federal government has been debated since the
early days of the republic when Thomas Jefferson's Democrats
and Alexander Hamilton's Federalists contested the issue. In the
following viewpoint, Alan Pifer, president of the Carnegie Corporation in New York, a foundation created by Andrew Carnegie
in 1911 to "promote the advancement and diffusion of
knowledge," argues that this debate has traditionally favored large
government. He contends that the American public has historically
endorsed the efforts of the federal government to improve the lives
of all Americans. For federal agencies to now withdraw from the
arena of promoting social equality, he believes, would be to in-
vite disaster.

As you read, consider the following questions:

1. Why does the author believe that arguments "to get
   government off our backs" are nonsensical?
2. Pifer argues that the election of President Reagan does not
   necessarily mean an endorsement of new government
   policies. Why?
3. What conclusions does the author make? Do you agree?

Alan Pifer, "The Social Role of Government in a Free-Enterprise System." Reprinted
from USA TODAY MAGAZINE, September 1982. Copyright 1982 by the Society for the
Advancement of Education.

It may seem quaintly anachronistic to be reexamining the legitimacy of social intervention by our national government as our complex, highly developed society moves on toward the end of the 20th century. Wasn't that issue settled once and for all back in the 1930s, or if not then, certainly in the 1960s and 1970s? We thought so, but new political currents, of which the present Administration is representative, has reopened the question and restored it to the national agenda.

The Reagan Administration has proposed as a broad goal for the nation a drastic reduction of the Federal social role, to be achieved through budget cuts, deregulation, and a transfer of responsibilities to the states and the private sector. Just what the prospects are for the passage of the full program is as yet unclear, but the first steps have certainly been taken. Let us examine the Federal social role in today's circumstances—an effort that, perhaps, can clear away some of the misleading rhetoric that has obscured understanding of why there came to be such a phenomenon in the first place and why there must continue to be, if we are to remain a strong, secure, and stable nation.

The Federal Social Role?

First of all, what do we mean by the Federal social role? Normally, we conceive of this as comprising only those programs that provide direct services or cash or in-kind benefits to designated beneficiaries—programs which have as their general purposes the promotion of human development, the alleviation of misfortune, or the easing of social tension. Such programs have developed over a long period of time and have been added to by nearly every administration in this century, although we tend to associate them particularly with the New Deal and Great Society eras. They cover such areas as health, welfare, education, equal opportunity, housing, income security, nutrition, job training, and aid to the handicapped. Some of them are aimed at the poor, while others are available for all who qualify, regardless of income. Some require matching funds at the state or local level; some do not. Within them, varying amounts of administrative responsibility are delegated to the states or localities. Taken together, they free the private enterprise system from having to assume responsibility for such major tasks as income redistribution, social insurance, and the provision of social services—tasks for which it is ill-suited and which would divert its energies from its classic economic function of producing goods and services for purchase.

Additional Federal Activities

There is, however, a wide range of additional activities of the Federal government that we do not ordinarily think of as being part of its social role and that have a far greater impact than the activities I have just mentioned. Here would fall such matters as protection of the environment; tax policy; fiscal and monetary policy; the construction of highways, dams, harbors, airports, and sewers; aid for public transportation; much of the regulatory function, such as enforcement of the pure food and drug laws; agricultural price supports; the provision of investment incentives; immigration policy; and energy policy. All of these activities have a great bearing, directly or indirectly, on fundamental social matters, such as where people live, how they support themselves, how large their income is, and what the quality of their lives is.

Keeping Americans Out of Poverty

According to a study done for the House Ways and Means Committee by the Congressional Research Service, one American in four would now fall below the poverty level without government support programs, compared with the actual portion of about one in seven in 1982, the latest year for which accurate data are available. Put another way, government cash benefits of one kind or another are keeping some 23 million Americans out of poverty who otherwise would be there.

Even more dramatic, 55 percent of the nation's elderly would be living in poverty today if there were no government programs at all.

Spencer Rich, *The Washington Post National Weekly Edition*, May 21, 1984.

The true social role of government, therefore, is very wide and penetrates into the remotest corners of our daily lives in ways that are so familiar to us we are scarcely conscious of them. In view of this, the currently popular call to "get government off our backs" seems rather ludicrous. Equally nonsensical to me is the assertion that the taxing power of the Federal government should never be used to promote social change. Willy-nilly, the Federal government is in the business of influencing social change every minute of every day. To eliminate its social role—its responsibility to promote constructive social change—would be to eliminate a vast part of its *general* role and would take us back to the earliest days of the Republic when we tried, unsuccessfully, to govern ourselves through a loose confederation of the states. It was not without reason that the Founding Fathers, in setting forth the prescription for the successor federation, wrote:

We the people of the United States, in order to form a more perfect union, establish justice, insure domestic tranquility, provide for the common defense, promote the general welfare, and secure the blessings of liberty to ourselves and our prosperity, do ordain and establish this Constitution for the United States of America.

In those words, they authorized—indeed mandated—a purposeful social role for the Federal government.

Origins and Growth of the Social Role

It is true to say, however, that, throughout the first century and more of our history as an independent nation, this mandate was largely ignored. Almost immediately after the Union was consummated, a deep split developed between those who wanted a relatively powerless central government (the Democrats, led by Thomas Jefferson) and those who wanted a strong one (the Federalists, led by Alexander Hamilton). In due course, the Jeffersonian view prevailed, with the result that we experienced a long succession of intentionally weak and often ineffectual national administrations. This had its moments of disaster, as when we got into a war in 1812 for which we failed to arm, but, on the whole, the rural, agrarian society of those days drifted along without much need for a strong government in Washington.

An exception, of course, was the gathering crisis over the issue of slavery. As this deepened and sectional strife became increasingly bitter, it became more and more obvious that the problem could no longer be left to the states, but would have to be dealt with by the national government. Fortunately, there came to the surface of our political life at the juncture a remarkable leader in the person of Abraham Lincoln, who understood that the power available to the Federal government had to be used forcefully to save the Union. A great war, costing half a million American lives, was then fought to achieve that purpose.

Despite the Civil War and its aftermath in the three notable postwar amendments to the Constitution—the Thirteenth, abolishing slavery; the Fourteenth, giving the former slaves citizenship; and the Fifteenth, giving them the right to vote—which collectively seemed to have set the stage for a massive Federal intervention in behalf of black people, such an undertaking did not materialize. Mounting resistance in the South and a loss of will in the North soon ended that possibility.

The Reign of Laissez-Faire

There followed, then, 30 to 40 more years during which the concept of negative government prevailed. In the economic realm, *laissez-faire* reigned supreme, and, in the social realm, Social Darwinism was the gospel of the day. Together, these two philosophies were sanctified into something close to a religion by the professional and propertied classes and invested with a range of allegedly moral and ethical qualities that could excuse even the most callous disregard of the rights of others or the suffering of the underprivileged.

Nonetheless, in the observance of this quasi-religion, there was considerable discrepancy between dogma and practice. The

89

Federal government, in fact, intervened on numerous occasions to promote the interests of businessmen and farmers and occasionally to regulate the excesses of unrestrained free enterprise, as with the passage of the Interstate Commerce Act of 1887 and the Sherman Anti-Trust Act of 1890. Other notable Federal social interventions in the Civil War and post-bellum years were the granting of 50,000,000 acres of public lands to the railroad companies; the Homestead Act of 1862, which helped to open up the West; the Morrill Act of 1862, which did so much to promote the growth of higher education; the Hatch Act of 1887, which established agricultural experiment stations; and, finally, the Reclamation Act of 1902, which made possible the development of a huge agricultural industry in the West based on irrigation.

Government Programs Reduce Misery

What we are buying with all these programs is a vast reduction in poverty, misery and sickness. Whatever the cost of these programs, it must be acknowledged that they have changed the American social landscape for the better. They have moved the country closer to its own lofty ideals of a society that is compassionate to the disadvantaged, as well as rewarding to the fortunate.

Spencer Rich, *The Washington Post National Weekly Edition*, May 21, 1984.

By the end of the 19th century, the doctrines of *laissez-faire* and Social Darwinism were under heavy attack, for several reasons. First, a public awareness had begun to develop of their extremely unethical character when measured against religious and humanitarian ideals. Second, a new school of theorists— economists, sociologists, political scientists, and philosophers— had arisen to question the scientific basis of these doctrines. Third, it had become apparent to thoughtful people that the doctrines were both harmful to the public welfare and ineffectual in addressing the new problems of a rapidly urbanizing and industrializing society, with its attendant problems of social unrest. Finally, people began to see that, in a democratic society, government should be not the master, but the agent of the people. The use of governmental power to promote the common good through social intervention was, therefore, a justifiable form of self-help and not a form of paternalism. Herbert Croly expressed this idea persuasively in his book, *The Promise of American Life*, which became widely influential after its publication in 1909.

The Birth of the Welfare State

In these new perceptions was born the notion of the general welfare state, a concept that, with the exception of the period of so-called normalcy from 1921 to 1932, would hold sway for the next 80 years—right down to the most recent presidential election. No longer, men and women began to see, did they need to accept passively the dictates of blind economic forces or the cruel tyranny of a social system which eulogized selection of the "fittest" for reward, even if this had to be at the expense of the weak. They could use democratic government as a deliberate instrument to reduce injustice and guarantee at least minimal social and economic security to every American.

This vision, which began to take legislative shape during the Progressive Era, in particular during the presidencies of Theodore Roosevelt and Woodrow Wilson, matured in Franklin Roosevelt's New Deal, Harry Truman's Fair Deal, John Kennedy's New Frontier, and Lyndon Johnson's Great Society. Expanded in each of those administrations, as well as in the Nixon presidency, in response to new social needs and expectations, the general welfare state was reformist, rather than revolutionary, in character. Its underlying purpose was to rescue our capitalist economic system from its own excesses and weaknesses through the institution of social controls and a program of social amelioration. Accused at various times of fostering "creeping socialism," it was, on the contrary, inherently antipathetic to a collectivist philosophy and steadfastly devoted to preservation of private ownership of the means of production.

One could, in fact, say of the general welfare state that its greatest triumph has been the safeguarding of private initiative over three-quarters of a century of worldwide turbulence, marked by two great wars, communist revolution in a number of countries, and the adoption of state ownership in many others. In 1937, after the worst of the Depression crisis was over, Franklin Roosevelt said, "Action was necessary to remove the sore spots which had crept into our economic system, if we were to keep the system of private property for the future. To preserve we had to reform." Indeed, reform and social amelioration as an alternative to revolution have been the hallmarks of the general welfare state from its inception to the present day—a fact that has always made the conservative distrust of the very idea of a Federal social role difficult for me to comprehend.

To sum up, we can see in our roughly two centuries as an independent nation certain broad trends. From the early years until about the end of the 19th century, except for the Lincoln period, a weak, negative concept of government triumphed. After that, in response to the needs created by changing conditions—such as the closing of the frontier, mass immigration, industrialization, and urbanization—there gradually developed the full-blown general welfare state. It should be noted, of course, that this happened not as the result of some sort of left-wing conspiracy, but with the enthusiastic concurrence of the vast majority of the American people.

A Reversal of Direction?

In view of this history, how are we to interpret the election of 1980 and all that has happened since? Does it signify a true reversal of direction—a fundamental rejection by the American people of the general welfare state? Or are the efforts of the present Administration no more than a brief aberration—a quixotic tilting at windmills that will look progressively more and more absurd as time goes by? Can we, indeed, even if we yearn nostalgically to do so, actually move back toward the "golden age" of Herbert Spencer and William Graham Sumner? Or will such an effort quickly fall victim to the same economic, social, and political realities that caused the development of the general welfare state in the first place? I don't believe any of us can tell yet exactly what the future is going to bring, but I do think we can note some straws in the wind.

First, no definitive evidence has emerged thus far to suggest that there really is a broad popular wish to see the general welfare state severely curtailed—especially as it benefits the great middle class, which it does to a remarkable extent. On the contrary, when the Administration tried to reduce Social Security benefits in 1981, the outcry was instantaneous and politically decisive, and it is having a similar problem now with student aid. There will be other outcries like these when middle class interests are affected. Budget cuts, therefore, have had to be made at the expense of those who can least well defend themselves; but even there, in the current round of budget negotiations, the Administration is encountering stiff opposition in the Congress.

Second, the present Administration, if one is to judge by its public statements, is the most ideological we have had in a very long time, and its policies reflect such an approach. The American people, on the other hand, historically have always been skeptical of ideology and more impressed by pragmatic approaches to issues of the day. Tempers rise, and voices become shrill at times. Demagogues and ideologues flit across the scene peddling their wares. However, decisions in our mixed economy as to what government will do and what private enterprise will do generally reflect political, economic, and social realities, rather than ideological purity. Our history shows this, and there is no reason to think that American attitudes have changed. I believe, therefore, that, as the impractical and ill-considered nature of much of the Administration's program gradually becomes clear to the public, the program will begin to fall of its own weight. Indeed, this is already happening.

Third, Americans are beginning to wake up to the inequitable consequences of the tax and budget cuts already enacted, to say nothing of the proposals for further cuts. . . .

Conclusion

I must state my unequivocal view that a sharp reduction of the social role of the Federal government is clearly not in the interests of the nation. Looking backward over the past two decades, we can see that it is myth, not fact, that Federal social programs for the most part failed. On the contrary, they greatly reduced poverty, hunger, malnutrition, infectious disease, and infant mortality— the last of these by 50%. They increased equality of opportunity for minorities and women. They made health care much more widely available. They gave dignity and opportunity to many of our fellow citizens. In these and other ways, they accomplished a great deal. Looking forward, we can see many pressing social problems, some new, some old, that demand the nation's attention. Why, we may ask, as we face these problems, should we abandon a public policy approach that achieved so much? Why not simply correct its evident faults and press ahead? . . .

The proper social role of our national government gets to the very heart of the controversy raised by the policies of the Reagan Administration. If one believes that the development of people—*all* people, whatever their economic status, physical or mental characteristics, sex, or color—is our highest priority, because it is fundamental to economic growth and to national security, and if one believes that equity among individual Americans on a national basis is the *sine qua non* of a workable society, then one must, as I do, favor strong participation by the Federal government in meeting the nation's social needs. The issues, in that case, will be how to make the Federal role efficient; how to make it operate in such a way that the states, the localities, the business community, and voluntary organizations will be encouraged to do their part; and how to keep the costs from getting out of control. These are scarcely small issues, but they are not insoluble.

If, on the other hand, one is not particularly concerned about the prospect of social unrest ahead, if one does not fear the consequences of reduced investment in people for economic growth and national security, if equity on a national basis is not high on the agenda, and if one believes that the workings of a free market economy can take care of most of the nation's social ills, with perhaps a residual role for state and local government, then there will be little desire to see the Federal social role maintained. This basically is the issue now before the nation, and on its outcome will depend the nature of American society for many years to come.

It is my clear faith that, once our present national state of confusion over what the Federal government should be doing in the social arena has passed, there will be much to look forward to. Through a wise and skillful exercise of Federal executive and legislative power, we have the ability to ensure that every American child has a chance to reach his or her true potential; that discrimination against any person on account of race, sex, or cultural background is eradicated; that the hungry are fed and the handicapped cared for; that every family has a decent place to live; that minimum standards of health care are available to all; and that the elderly are protected. All of this we can do, and we can do it with the resources that will be available to the nation, without sacrificing either our security or economic growth.

In the quest to reach these goals, the business community and voluntary sector and the states and localities will be essential partners of the Federal government. Indeed, the construction of that partnership—now in jeopardy—has been one of the great achievements of recent decades. Let us, then, not hold back from using our national government for broad social purposes in the mistaken notion that to do so is somehow wrong. Government at the national level is not an alien institution to be reviled or ridiculed. It belongs to us—all of us—to use as we will. We must use it intelligently and purposefully to realize at long last the great promise that has always been present in American life.

Ranking Lobbies

"It's a matter of principle with me. I vote on every issue
whether I need the money or not!"

Reprinted with special permission of King Features Syndicate, Inc.

The cartoon above, implying that lobbyists bribe legislators to
vote the way they want, may be an exaggeration of the way the
American political system works. It is true, however, that there
are currently several thousand registered lobbyists in Washington,
DC. Each of them attempts to influence legislation on its behalf.
What is good for a particular lobby, however, may not be good
for the country as a whole. For example, legislation providing sub-

sidies for tobacco growers may be good for the growers, but, since tobacco has been proven to be a health danger, one could argue that the country as a whole is ill served.

Below is a list of ten lobbies with a short description of each. Consider each carefully. Rank the ten in the order you think their successful efforts are most likely to help America or would be least harmful. Assign the number one to the group you think most helpful. Assign the number two to the second most helpful group, and so on, until all ten groups are ranked.

If you are doing this activity as a member of a group or class, work in small groups of four to six. Compare your group's results with those of the other groups.

American Civil Liberties Union Lawyers who initiate legislation on behalf of unpopular causes and groups to protect the constitutional rights of all Americans.

Center for Defense Information Although it supports a strong defense, CDI opposes excessive expenditures for weapons and policies that increase the danger of nuclear war. It is critical of the rise of militarism in the US.

Committee on the Constitutional System A group of 200 former legislators, governors, party officials, and others from both political parties who study the problems of government and propose reforms.

Committee on the Present Danger The Committee describes its function as directing attention to the unfavorable military balance between the US and the USSR.

National Council to Control Handguns A citizens' group that works to stop the spread of handguns in the US.

National Rifle Association Hunters and other gun owners who lobby to eliminate gun controls.

National Taxpayers Union Dedicated to controlling federal taxes and spending.

National Organization for Women An organization of women and men who work for full equality for women in truly equal partnership with men.

National Association for the Advancement of Colored People Organized to achieve equal rights and eliminate racial prejudice for all American citizens by removing racial discrimination in housing, employment, and other societal institutions.

Moral Re-Armament A program based on fundamental Christian values that aims to advance the Christian religion by bringing about a transformation of character in Americans.

Periodical Bibliography

The following periodical articles deal with the subject matter of this chapter.

Fred Block, et al.   "The Trouble With Full Employment," *The Nation*, May 17, 1986.

Daryl Borquist   "Empowering the Poor," *Eternity*, June 1984.

Scott Cooper   "The Next Public Works Program," *Social Policy*, Winter 1987.

John C. Davis   "Governmental Responsibility," *The Churchman*, March 1981.

Michael Fabricant and Michael Kelly   "No Haven for Homeless in a Heartless Country," *Radical America*, vol. 30, nos. 2 and 3.

Joseph Giordano   "Government *Can* Matter in Quality of Life," *Los Angeles Times*, May 4, 1985.

J. Peter Grace   "The Problem of Big Government," *Vital Speeches of the Day*, May 1, 1985.

Warren L. McFarren   "Big Government Is Unconstitutional," *The New American*, March 30, 1987.

Olof Palme   "In Praise of the Welfare State," *Harper's*, August 1984.

F. John Perna   "Attack of the Bureaucrats," *The New American*, March 30, 1987.

Spencer Rich   "Look Again, the Anti-Poverty Programs Do Work," *The Washington Post National Weekly Edition*, May 21, 1984.

Andre Ryerson   "Capitalism and Selfishness," *Commentary*, December 1986.

Barry Sussman   "Welfare Isn't a Life Sentence, and It Has Helped Many," *The Washington Post National Weekly Edition*, February 24, 1986.

Gus Tyler   "A Case for Economic Redistribution," *Dissent*, Spring 1985.

US Catholic Bishops   "Economic Justice for All: Catholic Social Teaching and the U.S. Economy," *Origins*, November 27, 1986.

Who Controls America?

American GOVERNMENT

Chapter Preface

Conspiratorial theories of history have always been present in American thought. Whether it is an ethnic group, an ideology, or in some minds, the devil, sinister controlling forces have often been described as determining American affairs. In the 1950s Senator Joseph McCarthy introduced a new level of hysteria with his charges of communism having infiltrated high levels of American government. To this day, three decades later, Americans still disagree on the nature and severity of a communist threat.

This chapter raises the issue of special interests, and it debates the extent of their control. It begins with C. Wright Mills' classic case for control by a power elite. Mills, a sociologist writing in the 1950s, claimed America was in the fifth epoch of centuries of control by successive elites. The chapter includes viewpoints by others who make claims similar to Mills, arguing America is currently unduly influenced by elites or special interest groups. It also contains the viewpoints of those who argue that a case for control by elites has never been proven. It concludes with a viewpoint by Steven Kelman, a professor of government, writing thirty-one years after Mills' influential book, claiming that important national public policy decisions are not controlled by elites or special interest groups. He claims important decisions are guided by an altruistic public spirit of doing what is right for the country.

"The power elite is composed of political, economic, and military men."

America Is Controlled by a Tripartite Elite

C. Wright Mills

In 1956 C. Wright Mills wrote a provocative and influential book, *The Power Elite*. A professor of sociology at Columbia University at the time, Mills claimed that a power elite comprised of politicians, corporate executives, and military men determine public policy in the United States, relegating the official governmental structure to a secondary role. United by a coincidence of background and outlook, the power elite, he argued, maintains the status quo, protecting the common interests of its members. He identified five epochs of structural change in the elite over the course of American history. The following viewpoint, excerpted from *The Power Elite*, describes the fifth or present epoch, the ascendance of the military to prominence.

As you read, consider the following questions:

1. According to Mills, what factor contributed to the ascendancy of the military?
2. In the author's opinion, in what ways are the current economic order and the military's ascendancy related?
3. Do you think that the author's claim of the existence of a power elite has merit?

We study history, it has been said, to rid ourselves of it, and the history of the power elite is a clear case for which this maxim is correct. Like the tempo of American life in general, the long-term trends of the power structure have been greatly speeded up since World War II, and certain newer trends within and between the dominant institutions have also set the shape of the power elite and given historically specific meaning to its fifth epoch:

I. In so far as the structural clue to the power elite today lies in the political order, that clue is the decline of politics as genuine and public debate of alternative decisions—with nationally responsible and policy-coherent parties and with autonomous organizations connecting the lower and middle levels of power with the top levels of decision. America is now in considerable part more a formal political democracy than a democratic social structure, and even the formal political mechanics are weak.

The long-time tendency of business and government to become more intricately and deeply involved with each other has, in the fifth epoch, reached a new point of explicitness. The two cannot now be seen clearly as two distinct worlds. It is in terms of the executive agencies of the state that the rapprochement has proceeded most decisively. The growth of the executive branch of the government, with its agencies that patrol the complex economy, does not mean merely the 'enlargement of government' as some sort of autonomous bureaucracy: it has meant the ascendancy of the corporation's man as a political eminence.

During the New Deal the corporate chieftains joined the political directorate; as of World War II they have come to dominate it. Long interlocked with government, now they have moved into quite full direction of the economy of the war effort and of the postwar era. This shift of the corporation executives into the political directorate has accelerated the long-term relegation of the professional politicians in the Congress to the middle levels of power.

The Ascendancy of the Military

II. In so far as the structural clue to the power elite today lies in the enlarged and military state, that clue becomes evident in the military ascendancy. The warlords have gained decisive political relevance, and the military structure of America is now in considerable part a political structure. The seemingly permanent military threat places a premium on the military and upon their control of men, material, money, and power; virtually all political and economic actions are now judged in terms of military definitions of reality: the higher warlords have ascended to a firm position within the power elite of the fifth epoch.

In part, at least, this has resulted from one simple historical fact, pivotal for the years since 1939: the focus of elite attention has been shifted from domestic problems, centered in the 'thirties around slump, to international problems, centered in the 'forties and 'fifties around war. Since the governing apparatus of the United States has by long historic usage been adapted to and shaped by domestic clash and balance, it has not, from any angle, had suitable agencies and traditions for the handling of international problems. Such formal democratic mechanics as had arisen in the century and a half of national development prior to

"Whadda ya mean who won the election? Both candidates was our guy!"

Ollie Harrington for the *Daily World*.

1941, had not been extended to the American handling of international affairs. It is, in considerable part, in this vacuum that the power elite has grown.

III. In so far as the structural clue to the power elite today lies in the economic order, that clue is the fact that the economy is at once a permanent-war economy and a private-corporation economy. American capitalism is now in considerable part a military capitalism, and the most important relation of the big corporation to the state rests on the coincidence of interests between military and corporate needs, as defined by warlords and corporate rich. Within the elite as a whole, this coincidence of interests between the high military and the corporate chieftains strengthens both of them and further subordinates the role of the merely political men. Not politicians, but corporate executives, sit with the military men and plan the organization of war effort.

The Shape of the Power Elite

The shape and meaning of the power elite today can be understood only when these three sets of structural trends are seen at their point of coincidence: the military capitalism of private corporations exists in a weakened and formal democratic system containing a military order already quite political in outlook and demeanor. Accordingly, at the top of this structure, the power elite has been shaped by the coincidence of interest between those who control the major means of production and those who control the newly-enlarged means of violence; from the decline of the professional politician and the rise to explicit political command of the corporate chieftains and the professional warlords; from the absence of any genuine civil service of skill and integrity, independent of vested interests.

The power elite is composed of political, economic, and military men, but this instituted elite is frequently in some tension: it comes together only on certain coinciding points and only on certain occasions of 'crisis.' In the long peace of the nineteenth century, the military were not in the high councils of state, not of the political directorate, and neither were the economic men—they made raids upon the state but they did not join its directorate. During the 'thirties, the political man was ascendant. Now the military and the corporate men are in top positions.

Of the three types of circles that compose the power elite today, it is the military that has benefited the most in its enhanced power, although the corporate circles have also become more explicitly entrenched in the more public decision-making circles. It is the professional politician that has lost the most, so much that in examining the events and decisions, one is tempted to speak of a political vacuum in which the corporate rich and the high warlord, in their coinciding interests, rule.

It should not be said that the three 'take turns' in carrying the initiative, for the mechanics of the power elite are not often as deliberate as that would imply. At times, of course, it is—as when political men, thinking they can borrow the prestige of generals, find that they must pay for it, or, as when during big slumps, economic men feel the need of a politician at once safe and possessing vote appeal. Today all three are involved in virtually all widely ramifying decisions. Which of the three types seems to lead depends upon 'the tasks of the period' as they, the elite, define them. Just now, these tasks center upon 'defense' and international affairs. Accordingly, as we have seen, the military are ascendant in two senses: as personnel and as justifying ideology. That is why, just now, we can most easily specify the unity and the shape of the power elite in terms of the military ascendancy.

Militarism Pervades America

Most Americans do not think of the United States as being particularly militaristic. We are not at war. Gun-toting soldiers do not patrol our streets. Young men are no longer drafted. In many ways, however, militarism pervades America.

Since 1945 the role of the military in American government and society has changed dramatically. Military issues have been given high priority in shaping American foreign and domestic political policies. The militarization of our domestic political economy and everyday American society is an increasingly dangerous phenomenon that demands careful examination if we are to keep it in check. . . .

The Pentagon greatly influences America's foreign policy, domestic priorities, economy, and the nature of our government. The long established tradition of civilian control over the military is eroding as an increasing number of military men fill government positions previously held by civilians and our civilian leaders permit the military to play a greater role in policy-making.

Center for Defense Information, *The Defense Monitor*, Vol. 15, #3, 1986.

But we must always be historically specific and open to complexities. The simple Marxian view makes the big economic man the *real* holder of power; the simple liberal view makes the big political man the chief of the power system; and there are some who would view the warlords as virtual dictators. Each of these is an oversimplified view. It is to avoid them that we use the term 'power elite' rather than, for example, 'ruling class.'

In so far as the power elite has come to wide public attention, it has done so in terms of the 'military clique.' The power elite does, in fact, take its current shape from the decisive entrance into it of the military. Their presence and their ideology are its major legitimations, whenever the power elite feels the need to provide any. But what is called the 'Washington military clique' is not composed merely of military men, and it does not prevail merely in Washington. Its members exist all over the country, and it is a coalition of generals in the roles of corporation executives, of politicians masquerading as admirals, of corporation executives acting like politicians, of civil servants who become majors, of vice-admirals who are also the assistants to a cabinet officer, who is himself, by the way, really a member of the managerial elite.

Neither the idea of a 'ruling class' nor of a simple monolithic rise of 'bureaucratic politicians' nor of a 'military clique' is adequate. The power elite today involves the often uneasy coincidence of economic, military, and political power.

"The evidence for a ruling elite, either in the United States or any specific community, has not yet been properly examined."

The Case for a Ruling Elite Has Never Been Proven

Robert A. Dahl

Robert A. Dahl is Sterling Professor Emeritus of Political Science at Yale University. A past president of the American Political Science Association, he was voted the most influential political scientist of the 1960s by his colleagues. Professor Dahl is an advocate of the pluralist view of dispersed power, which he describes as follows: "Instead of a single center of sovereign power there must be multiple centers of power, none of which is or can be wholly sovereign." Accordingly, he is critical of theories of governmental control by elites in American society. He claims the burden of proof is on those who promote theories of control by elites. To date, in his view, no such proof has been forthcoming.

As you read, consider the following questions:

1. What is the author's basic argument with theories of elite control of American society?
2. What does Dahl propose to test the hypothesis of a ruling elite?

Robert A. Dahl, "A Critique of the Ruling Elite Model," *The American Political Science Review*, June 1958. Reprinted by permission.

A great many people seem to believe that "they" run things: the old families, the bankers, the City Hall machine, or the party boss behind the scene. This kind of view evidently has a powerful and many-sided appeal. It is simple, compelling, dramatic, "realistic." It gives one standing as an inside-dopester. For individuals with a strong strain of frustrated idealism, it has just the right touch of hard-boiled cynicism. Finally, the hypothesis has one very great advantage over many alternative explanations: It can be cast in a form that makes it virtually impossible to disprove.

Consider the last point for a moment. There is a type of quasi-metaphysical theory made up of what might be called an infinite regress of explanations. The ruling elite model *can* be interpreted in this way. If the overt leaders of a community do not appear to constitute a ruling elite, then the theory can be saved by arguing that behind the overt leaders there is a set of covert leaders who do. If subsequent evidence shows that this covert group does not make a ruling elite, then the theory can be saved by arguing that behind the first covert group there is another, and so on.

Now whatever else it may be, a theory that cannot even in principle be controverted by empirical evidence is not a scientific theory. The least that we can demand of any ruling elite theory that purports to be more than a metaphysical or polemical doctrine is, first, that the burden of proof be on the proponents of the theory and not on its critics; and, second, that there be clear criteria according to which the theory could be disproved.

With these points in mind, I shall proceed in two stages. First, I shall try to clarify the meaning of the concept "ruling elite" by describing a very simple form of what I conceive to be a ruling elite system. Second, I shall indicate what would be required in principle as a simple but satisfactory test of any hypothesis asserting that a particular political system is, in fact, a ruling elite system. Finally, I shall deal with some objections.

I. A Simple Ruling Elite System

If a ruling elite hypothesis says anything, surely it asserts that within some specific political system there exists a group of people who to some degree exercise power or influence over other actors in the system. I shall make the following assumptions about power:[1]

1. In order to compare the relative influence of two actors (these may be individuals, groups, classes, parties, or what not), it is necessary to state the scope of the responses upon which the actors have an effect. The statement, "A has more power than B," is so ambiguous as to verge on the meaningless, since it does not specify the scope.

2. One cannot compare the relative influence of two actors who

107

always perform identical actions with respect to the group influenced. What this means as a practical matter is that ordinarily one can test for differences in influence only where there are cases of differences in initial preferences. At one extreme, the difference may mean that one group prefers alternative A and another group prefers B, A and B being mutually exclusive. At the other extreme, it may mean that one group prefers alternative A to other alternatives, and another group is indifferent. If a political system displayed complete consensus at all times, we should find it impossible to construct a satisfactory direct test of the hypothesis that it was a ruling elite system, although indirect and rather unsatisfactory tests might be devised.

No Single Group Dominates American Politics

If you were to pick at random any year in American history since the Constitutional Convention to illustrate the workings of the political system, you would stand a rather good chance of being able to describe American politics during that year as follows:

Important government policies would be arrived at through negotiation, bargaining, persuasion, and pressure at a considerable number of different sites in the political system—the White House, the bureaucracies, the labyrinth of committees in Congress, the federal and state courts, the state legislatures and executives, the local governments. No single organized political interest, party, class, region, or ethnic group would control all of these sites.

Robert A. Dahl, *Pluralist Democracy in the United States: Conflict and Consent*, 1967.

Consequently, to know whether or not we have a ruling elite, we must have a political system in which there is a difference in preferences, from time to time, among the individual human beings in the system. Suppose, now, that among these individuals there is a set whose preferences regularly prevail in all cases of disagreement, or at least in all cases of disagreement over key political issues (a term I propose to leave undefined here). Let me call such a set of individuals a "controlling group." In a full-fledged democracy operating strictly according to majority rule, the majority would constitute a controlling group, even though the individual members of the majority might change from one issue to the next. But since our model is to represent a ruling elite system, we require that the set be *less than a majority in size*.

However, in any representative system with single member voting districts where more than two candidates receive votes, a candidate *could* win with less than a majority of votes; and it is possible, therefore, to imagine a truly sovereign legislature elected under the strictest "democratic" rules that was nonetheless governed by a legislative majority representing the first preferences of a minority of voters. Yet I do not think we would want to call such a political system a ruling elite system. Because of this kind of difficulty, I propose that we exclude from our definition of a ruling elite any controlling group that is a product of rules that are actually followed (that is, "real" rules) under which a majority of individuals could dominate if they took certain actions permissible under the "real" rules. In short, to constitute a ruling elite a controlling group must not be *a pure artifact of democratic rules.*

A ruling elite, then, is a controlling group less than a majority in size that is not a pure artifact of democratic rules. It is a minority of individuals whose preferences regularly prevail in cases of differences in preference on key political issues. If we are to avoid an infinite regress of explanations, the composition of the ruling elite must be more or less definitely specified.

II. Some Bad Tests

The hypothesis we are dealing with would run along these lines: "Such and such a political system (the U.S., the U.S.S.R., New Haven, or the like) is a ruling elite system in which the ruling elite has the following membership." Membership would then be specified by name, position, socio-economic class, socio-economic roles, or what not.

Let me now turn to the problem of testing a hypothesis of this sort, and begin by indicating a few tests that are sometimes mistakenly taken as adequate.

The First Improper Test

The first improper test confuses a ruling elite with a group that has a high *potential for control.* Let me explain. Suppose a set of individuals in a political system has the following property: there is a very high probability that if they agree on a key political alternative, and if they all act in some specified way, then that alternative will be chosen. We may say of such a group that it has a *high potential for control.* In a large and complex society like ours, there may be many such groups. For example, the bureaucratic triumvirate of Professor Mills would appear to have a high potential for control.[2] In the City of New Haven, with which I have some acquaintance, I do not doubt that the leading business figures together with the leaders of both political parties have a high potential for control. But a potential for control is not, except in a peculiarly Hobbesian world, equivalent to actual control. If the military leaders of this country and their subordinates agreed that it was desirable, they could most assuredly establish a military dictatorship of the most overt sort; nor would they need the aid of leaders of business corporations or the executive branch of our government. But they have not set up such a dictatorship. For what is lacking are the premises I mentioned earlier, namely agreement on a key political alternative and some set of specific implementing actions. That is to say, a group may have a high potential for control and a *low potential for unity*. The actual *political effectiveness* of a group is a function of its potential for control *and* its potential for unity. Thus a group with a relatively low potential for control but a high potential for unity may be more politically effective than a group with a high potential for control but a low potential for unity.

The Second Improper Test

The second improper test confuses a ruling elite with a group of individuals who have more influence than any others in the system. I take it for granted that in every human organization some individuals have more influence over key decisions than do others. Political equality may well be among the most Utopian of all human goals. But it is fallacious to assume that the absence of political equality proves the existence of a ruling elite.

The Third Improper Test

The third improper test, which is closely related to the preceding one, is to generalize from a single scope of influence. Neither logically nor empirically does it follow that a group with a high degree of influence over one scope will necessarily have a high degree of influence over another scope within the same system. This is a matter to be determined empirically. Any investigation that does not take into account the possibility that different elite groups have different scopes is suspect. By means of sloppy questions one could easily seem to discover that there exists a unified ruling elite in New Haven; for there is no doubt that small groups of people make many key decisons. It appears to be the case, however, that the small group that runs urban redevelopment is not the same as the small group that runs public education, and neither is quite the same as the two small groups that run the two parties. Moreover the small group that runs urban redevelopment with a high degree of unity would almost certainly disintegrate if its activities were extended to either education or the two political parties.

III. A Proposed Test

If tests like these are not valid, what can we properly require?

Let us take the simplest possible situation. Assume that there have been some number—I will not say how many—of cases where there has been disagreement within the political system on key political choices. Assume further that the hypothetical ruling elite prefers one alternative and other actors in the system prefer other alternatives. Then unless it is true that in all or very nearly all of these cases the alternative preferred by the ruling elite is actually adopted, the hypothesis (that the system is dominated by the specified ruling elite) is clearly false.

I do not want to pretend either that the research necessary to such a test is at all easy to carry out or that community life lends itself conveniently to strict interpretation according to the requirements of the test. *But I do not see how anyone can suppose that he has established the dominance of a specific group in a community or a nation without basing his analysis on the careful examination of a series of concrete decisions.* And these decisions must either constitute the universe or a fair sample from the universe of key political decisions taken in the political system.

Now it is a remarkable and indeed astounding fact that neither Professor Mills nor Professor Hunter has seriously attempted to examine an array of specific cases to test his major hypothesis.[3] Yet I suppose these two works more than any others in the social sciences of the last few years have sought to interpret complex political systems essentially as instances of a ruling elite.

To sum up: The hypothesis of the existence of a ruling elite can be strictly tested only if:

1. The hypothetical ruling elite is a well-defined group.
2. There is a fair sample of cases involving key political decisions in which the preferences of the hypothetical ruling elite run counter to those of any other likely group that might be suggested.
3. In such cases, the preferences of the elite regularly prevail. . . .

Conclusion

The whole point of this paper is that the evidence for a ruling elite, either in the United States or in any specific community, has not yet been properly examined so far as I know. And the evidence has not been properly examined, I have tried to argue, because the examination has not employed satisfactory criteria to determine what constitutes a fair test of the basic hypothesis.

1. See Robert A. Dahl, "The Concept of Power," *Behavioral Sciences,* Vol. 2 (July 1957), pp. 201-215.
2. C. Wright Mills, *The Power Elite* (New York, 1956), *passim.*
3. Mills, *op. cit.:* Floyd Hunter, *Community Power Structure* (Chapel Hill, 1953).

"Almost all the social institutions existing in this society . . . are under plutocratic control ruled by non-elected, self-selected, self-perpetuating groups."

America Is Controlled by a Capitalist Plutocracy

Michael Parenti

Michael Parenti, an articulate advocate for democratic socialism in America, is currently a Visiting Fellow at the Institute for Policy Studies in Washington, DC. A former instructor of political and social science at various colleges and universities, his writings have appeared in numerous liberal publications, including the *Progressive, The Nation, Monthly Review,* and *In These Times.* The viewpoint that follows is taken from his provocative book, *Democracy for the Few,* which argues that America's politico-economic system, if not undemocratic, at best provides democracy for only a select few.

As you read, consider the following questions:

1. Why does the author think America is a plutocratic society?
2. In his opinion, how is this plutocracy justified by capitalism?
3. Why does Parenti claim American conservatives resist most reforms?
4. How does he think American conservatives, liberals, and socialists view capitalism differently?

It is said we live in a democratic society, but more accurately it should be described as a plutocracy, or rule by and for the rich, because our nation's industrial and cultural institutions serve the interests of the dominant owning class. American capitalism represents more than just an economic system; it is an entire cultural and social order. Most universities and colleges, publishing houses, mass circulation magazines, newspapers, television and radio stations, professional sports teams, foundations, churches, private museums, charity organizations, and hospitals are organized as corporations, ruled by self-appointed boards of trustees (or directors or regents) composed overwhelmingly of affluent business people. These boards exercise final judgment over all institutional matters.[1]

Consider the university: most institutions of higher education are public or private corporations (e.g., the Harvard Corporation, the Yale Corporation) run by boards of trustees with authority over all matters of capital funding and budget; curriculum, scholarships, and tuition; hiring, firing, and promotion of faculty and staff; degree awards; student fees; etc. Most of the tasks related to these activities have been delegated to administrators, but the power can be easily recalled by the trustees, and in times of controversy it usually is. These trustees are granted legal control of the property of the institution, not because they have claim to any academic experience but because as successful business people they supposedly have proven themselves to be the responsible leaders of the community.[2]

This, then, is a feature of real significance in any understanding of political power in America: *almost all the social institutions existing in this society, along with the immense material and vocational resources they possess, are under plutocratic control, ruled by non-elected, self-selected, self-perpetuating groups of affluent corporate representatives who are answerable to no one but themselves. . . .*

Many Americans believe as they were taught, that they are a free people, a belief held even by persons who refuse to voice controversial opinions for fear of jeopardizing their career opportunities. By controlling the wealth and economic life of the country, the corporate elites are able to control the major institutions that, in turn, enable them to control the flow of mainstream ideas and information and even the behavior and choices of otherwise recalcitrant persons. . . .

Criticism of Capitalism Is Equated with Un-Americanism

The power of business does not stand naked before the public; rather it is enshrouded in a mystique of its own making. The agencies of the plutocratic culture, namely the media, the schools, the politicians, and others, associate the capitalist system with the symbols of patriotism, democracy, prosperity, and progress.

Criticisms of the system are equated with un-Americanism. Capitalism is treated as a force that breeds democracy, although, in truth, capitalism also flourishes under the most brutally repressive regimes, and capitalist interests have supported the overthrow of democracies in Chile and other Third World countries and the installment of right-wing dictators who make their lands safe for corporate investments. Capitalism is presented as the sole alternative to "communist tyranny." The private enterprise system, it is taught, creates equality of opportunity, rewards those who show ability and initiative, relegates the parasitic and slothful to the bottom of the ladder, provides a national prosperity that is the envy of other lands, safeguards (through unspecified means) personal liberties and political freedom, promises continued progress in the endless proliferation of goods and services, and has made America the great and beautiful nation it is. . . .

American Capitalism Has Created an Individualist Treadmill

Living in a capitalist society, one is bombarded daily with inducements to maintain values and a life style that promote the plutocratic culture. Each year business spends billions to get people to consume as much as they can—and sometimes more than they can afford. Mass advertising offers not only commodities

© Taylor/Rothco

114

but a whole way of life, teaching us that the piling up of possessions is a worthwhile life goal, a measure of one's accomplishment and proof of one's worth.

In the plutocratic culture, one is admonished to "get ahead." Ahead of whom and what? Of others and of one's present material status. This kind of "individualism" is not to be mistaken for the freedom to choose deviant political and economic practices. Each person is expected to operate "individually" *but in more or less similar ways and similar directions.* Everyone competes against everyone else but for the same things. "Individualism" in the United States refers to *privatization* and the absence of social forms of ownership, consumption, and recreation. You are individualist in that you are expected to get what you can for yourself and not to be too troubled by the needs and problems faced by others. This attitude, considered inhuman in some societies, is labeled approvingly as "ambition" in our own and is treated as a quality of great social value. . . .

This competitive individualism spawns a good deal of loneliness and limits the opportunities for meaningful and joyful experiences with other people. The emphasis is on self-absorption: "do your own thing" and "look out for number one." We are taught to seek more possessions and more privacy: a private home, private car, private vacation place; and we "feel more and more alienated and lonely" when we get them.[3] Born of a market economy, the plutocratic culture is essentially a market culture, one that minimizes cooperative efforts and human interdependence and keeps us busily competing as workers and consumers.

Public man gives way to private competitor. One's peers are potentially one's enemies; their successes can cause us envy and anxiety, and their failures bring secret feelings of relief. The ability or desire to work collectively with others is much retarded. . . .

To be sure, Americans have their doubts about the rat race, and those who are able to, seek an alternative life style, consuming less and working in less demanding jobs. But the economy does not always allow such a choice. With wage cutbacks, inflation, and growing tax burdens, most people must keep running on the treadmill just to stay in the same place. . . .

America's Three Political Ideologies

Political ideologies in the United States might be roughly categorized as conservative, liberal, and socialist. Each of these terms carries certain ambiguities and within each category there are variations and differences. Here we will try to draw the broad outlines of the three tendencies.

American Conservatism

The *conservative* ideology, held most firmly by corporate and political elites and by many—but not all—persons of high income and substantial property, supports the system of capitalism and defends the interests of business as the primary mainstays of the good society. Conservative leaders believe that most reforms should be resisted. They may recognize that there are some inequities in society, but these will either take care of themselves or, as with poverty, will always be with us. Conservatives believe that people are poor usually because, as Richard Nixon once noted, they are given to a "welfare ethic rather than a work ethic."

Conservatives are for strong or weak government depending on what interests are being served. They denounce as government "meddling" those policies that appear to move toward an equalization of life chances, income, and class, or that attempt to make business more accountable to public authority. But they usually advocate a strong government that will enforce "law and order,"[4] restrict dissent, intervene militarily in other countries, and regulate our private lives and personal morals.[5]

America Is Controlled by a Small Economic Elite

America is still controlled by a small economic elite which owns most of the resources, capital, and property. The persons and corporations are American instead of British. In 210 years, Americans have gained independence from nothing. . . .

Nothing that benefits the majority of people in this nation has come through the House or Senate (and certainly not the White House) in years. Gramm-Rudman-Hollings was a bipartisan maneuver to justify further cuts in education, housing, and other programs which help most people. The exportation of capital (and jobs) to low-wage nations has been made easier by the massive military buildup (also financed by working people who will be paying for current weapons on the installment plan for the next thirty years). Future weapons purchases promise to be even more extravagant. The typical person is barely able to keep up with mortgage payments (another massive transfer of wealth from workers to major corporations) and is vulnerable to an economic downturn. The typical American is barely more than a feudal serf; he or she works hard but never gets ahead. The $410 billion in corporate profits went to less than one percent of the people in the U.S. Remember that, next time you wonder why your increased productivity doesn't translate into a higher standard of living for you.

Brian Lynch, *American Atheist*, August 1986.

Conservatives say they are for cutting government spending and bureaucracy, but the cuts they propose are selective, focusing on domestic services to the needy, while ever greater sums are given to the largest bureaucracy within the federal government—the Department of Defense. . . . Conservatives decry all government handouts except defense contracts, corporate subsidies, and tax breaks for business and the well-to-do. They believe taxes reduce the freedom of people to spend their own money, so they prefer to shift the tax burden onto those with less money, presumably thereby taking away less freedom.

"Supply-side" conservative theorists argue that recessions occur because corporations do not have enough money to invest, inflation occurs because people have too much money to spend, and unemployment occurs because people prefer to live off welfare. In other words, the rich must be given more money before they will work, while the poor must have money taken from them before they will work.

For conservatives, the keystone to individual rights is the enjoyment of property rights, especially the right to make a profit off other people's labor. Indeed, conservatives cherish private enterprise quite independently of the value placed on human beings, so when the two values conflict, private profit is often protected in preference to individual life and sometimes at a cost to individual life.[6] In sum, conservative leaders put their stock in individual acquisitiveness and other established values of the plutocratic culture such as institutional authority and hierarchy, support of big business, a strong police force, and a large and powerful military establishment.

Many people who are not members of the corporate elite, but who witnessed the failure of liberal programs to solve major social problems, oppose big government and high taxes and call themselves conservatives—for want of an alternative. Ultraconservative religious groups like Moral Majority, adhering to fundamentalist Christian doctrines—if not to Christian practices—have tried to direct this popular discontent toward moralistic life-style issues that have little to do with economic problems but that work against liberal and progressive candidates. While giving an appearance of offering something new, the "Christian" Right and the New Right in general, in their financing, leadership, and politics, are little more than a warmed-over version of right-wing Republicanism.[7]

There are, however, differences among conservatives (as among liberals and socialists). The true believers of the New Right dream of a mythic "free enterprise" in which business, once totally free of government restraints and taxes, will become so productive as to bring prosperity to all. In contrast, the more conventional corporate elites understand that government's true historic role is not to keep hands off business but to enhance business profits with subsidies, price supports, manipulated money supplies, market protections, and restrictions on labor. Differences also emerge in foreign policy as the corporate and financial elites, for profit's sake, show themselves willing to trade with, and lend

117

money to, existing socialist nations, while the New Rightist ideologues are more likely to call for embargoes and holy war confrontations with socialist countries.

American Liberalism

A *liberal*, like a conservative, accepts the basic structure and values of the capitalist system but believes that social problems should be rectified by a redirection of government spending and by better regulatory policies. Liberals do not usually see these problems as being interrelated and endemic to the present system. Since they assume that the ills of the politico-economic system are aberrations in the workings of capitalism, they believe that the fault must be with the particular policies of the personages who have gained power. If the right persons finally win office, and with the right combination of will, public awareness, and political push, the system will be able to take care of its major crises. Liberals generally support government intervention in the economy in the hope of curbing some of the worst abuses of the economic system and changing "our warped priorities" so that more money will be spent on needed public services and less on private privileges. Yet while liberals call for cuts in "excessive" military spending and advocate protection of individual rights against government suppression and surveillance, and assistance for the poor and needy, in the world of action many liberals vote for huge military budgets, support security and intelligence agencies, and make cuts in human services for the needy.

Some liberals are not overly fond of capitalism, but they like socialism even less. Socialism, in their minds, conjures up stereotyped images of "drabness" and "regimentation," of people waiting in line for shoddy goods wrapped in dull gray packages and of Stalinist purges and labor camps. The liberal's concern seems to be that freedom would be lost or diminished under socialism. (Many liberals believe they are free under the present politico-economic system.) They are also worried about the diminution of their own class and professional privileges and the loss of status they might suffer with the democratization of institutions advocated by American socialists. In this respect, they often resemble conservatives.

In matters of foreign policy, liberals generally have shown themselves as willing as conservatives to contain the spread of socialism in other lands and make the world safe for American corporate investments and markets. Since Vietnam, many liberals have come to think that we should not get involved in suppressing social revolutionary movements in other countries. But whatever their feelings about revolution abroad, most liberals have little tolerance for revolutionary struggle in the United States.

Only a small portion of Americans currently identify themselves as socialists—although many more adhere to views that are close to socialist principles, and socialist opinion has shown a modest but steady growth in recent years.[8] A *socialist* is someone who wants to replace the capitalist system with a system of public and communal ownership. Socialists are distinguished from liberal reformers in their belief that our social problems cannot be solved within the very system that is creating them. Socialists do not believe that *every* human problem at *every* level of existence is caused by capitalism but that many of the most important ones are and that capitalism propagates a kind of culture and social organization that destroys human potentials and guarantees the perpetuation of poverty, racism, sexism, and exploitative social relations at home and abroad. Socialists even argue that much of the unhappiness suffered in what are considered purely "interpersonal" experiences relates to the false values and insecurities of an acquisitive, competitive capitalist society.

Socialists believe that American corporate and military expansionism abroad is not the result of "wrong thinking" but the natural outgrowth of profit-oriented capitalism. To the socialist, American foreign policy is not beset by folly and irrationality but has been quite successful in maintaining the status quo and the interests of multinational corporations, crushing social change in many countries and establishing an American financial and military presence throughout much of the world.

1. My book *Power and the Powerless* (New York: St. Martin's Press, 1978) has a more detailed discussion of business power within social and cultural institutions.
2. *Ibid.*, pp. 156-63; also David N. Smith, *Who Rules the Universities?* (New York: Monthly Review Press, 1974); James Ridgeway, *The Closed Corporation* (New York: Random House, 1969). Even if it were true that trustees' guidance is needed on financial questions, should they have authority over all matters? In fact, on most financial and technical problems, the trustees rely on advisors and accountants. The argument is made that trustees take the financial risks for the university and therefore should have the authority. In fact, they seldom take on personal liabilities. Legal judgments made against their decisions are covered by insurance paid out of the university budget. If anything, trustees are likely to profit personally by awarding university contracts to their own firms or those of business associates. Another argument for trustee power is that students, faculty, and staff compose a transient population and therefore cannot be expected to run the university. But their stay at the university is longer than that of the average trustee, who serves for three years, often resides out of town, and visits the campus for board meetings once a month.
3. Philip Slater, *The Pursuit of Loneliness* (Boston: Beacon Press, 1970), p. 7.
4. The law-and-order issue focuses on street crimes. Corporate crimes and organized crimes are of less concern to conservatives.
5. Conservatives talk about "getting big government off the back of the American people" (President Reagan's words), yet in 1981 they pushed through a $30 million bill to create a new federal agency, the Office of Adolescent Pregnancy, which will oversee a network of storefront "chastity centers" to teach adolescents that celibacy is the one foolproof way of avoiding pregnancy and retaining one's virtue. The bill was sponsored by right-wing Senator Jeremiah Denton (R-Ala.), who once half-seriously advocated the death penalty for adultery. *Working Papers*, November/December 1981, p. 6. So much for keep-

ing government out of our lives.

6. See, for instance, the discussion on health, environment, and occupational safety in chapter 7, *Democracy for the Few,* by Michael Parenti, 1983.
7. Michael Lienesch, "Right-Wing Religion: A Study of Interest-Group Conservatism," (paper given at the annual meeting of the American Political Science Association, New York, September 1981). For an earlier statement of how irrational symbols are used for rational, dominant class interests, see Michael Rogin, *The Intellectuals and McCarthy* (Cambridge, Mass.: M.I.T. Press, 1967).
8. See, for instance, Paul W. Valentine, "The Coming Out of U.S. Socialists," *Washington Post,* March 25, 1979.

"Big business doesn't run the country . . . when it comes right down to it. We all maintain an intricate, delicate, and often painful balance among us."

Big Business Does Not Control America

Dwight Bohmbach

As the chief executive officer of a national ad agency, Dwight Bohmbach "never had time for college." At the age of 65 he received his BA, at 67 his MA, and now plans a Ph.D. before 70. The following viewpoint is taken from his third published book *What's Right with America*. He is currently working on two additional books aimed at "rediscovering America from different perspectives." Bohmbach argues that the claim that big business runs America is a myth that has persisted since the Constitutional Convention. He rebuts this myth, stating that it makes about as much sense as saying the Pope is Moslem.

As you read, consider the following questions:

1. What proof does Bohmbach present to support his claim that big business does not run America?
2. How does he think the myth of American business dominance may have started?
3. Do you agree or disagree with the author's argument?

This is a quotation from a Populist Party political manifesto, back in 1880:

> On the one side are the allied hosts of monopolies, the money power, great trusts and . . . corporations, who seek the enactment of law to benefit them and impoverish the people. On the other are the farmers, laborers, merchants, and all other people who produce wealth and bear the burdens of taxation. . . .[1]

The manifesto is long since forgotten. But its spirit—a deep-dyed suspicion of big money and big business—still is strong among American people. Perversely, we admire success—but we mistrust success translated into big business. A mid-1985 national poll asked Americans in every state if they had ever felt that "Big business runs the country." Better than eight out of 10 Americans said "Yes." Asked, "How do you feel right now?" slightly fewer (78%) blandly declared that yes, "Big business runs the country."[2]

Where Was Big Business?

Where have all these eight-in-10 Americans been looking lately? Did they see big business running the country when the Penn Central Railroad came to a shuddering halt and went broke? Railroad after railroad that once bestrode the continent like giants quietly disappeared in the face of competition from airlines and truckers. It turned out that big business couldn't even run its own railroads profitably, much less a country.

Was big business in charge of the country when Chrysler Corporation—one of the country's Big Three auto giants—teetered to the brink of bankruptcy? Not so you could notice. The other auto giants didn't turn a hand to help Chrysler. Seven out of 10 Americans were against giving Chrysler any help at all.[3] What put Chrysler back on its feet and led it back to join the leadership in its industry again was something even more powerful than government funding. It was what Chrysler's chairman, Lee Iacocca, has labeled "equality of sacrifice"—contributions by labor, management, the company's suppliers, car dealers, each giving something extra of themselves for the common good.

Was big business running the country when Continental Illinois National Bank & Trust Company of Chicago—one of the world's biggest big banks—began to run out of operating capital? Or when all those other once-formidable bankers across the nation got into financial hot water, and wise old Uncle Sam had to go and wring them out?

What about the day the courts broke AT&T up? The biggest communications monopoly in the world suddenly shrank. Seven scrambling individual companies, each with hundreds of hungry competitors, took over its territory. Was big business running the country that day?

Big Steel was a colossus of financial power in America not long ago. Look at it today: U.S. Steel, hoping to save itself by setting up a partnership with Koreans; Wheeling-Pittsburgh Steel, maneuvering to avoid bankruptcy; Bethlehem Steel, trying to diversify itself back to profitability. Is Big Steel running the country? (Is the Pope Moslem?)

How about all those grand old giant companies we see every day now, scurrying like little pigs to keep from being gobbled up by big, bad wolves who are much smaller than they are, or captured single-handedly by corporate pirates? Who's running whom?

And take Coca-Cola: the century-old reigning giant of the multibillion-dollar beverage industry decreed a change in the flavor of its own product. Who turned out to be calling the shots there? We did. Every little consumer with two bits for a soft drink had something to say about that. And what they said was, "Oh, no you *don't.*" Coca-Cola did what the populace ordered.

The Highest Standard of Living

In spite of all our two centuries of push-and-shove about whether or not big business is "taking us over," the American people generally enjoy the highest standard of living in the world. Fewer of us who are employed are working for "big companies" than in 1976 (32% worked for a company with over 250 employees in 1976; 30% in 1982, the latest years for which figures are available). And more new little businesses open their doors hopefully every day to compete with giants for our favor—and maybe grow up to be big companies themselves someday.

Dwight Bohmbach, *What's Right with America*, 1986.

It's enough to make me wonder, sometimes, "Where are the economic royalists of yesteryear?" And yet eight in 10 of my fellow Americans look around them and say, "I see big business is still running the country." How do they *get* that way?

A History of Mistrust

A couple of pages of capsulized American history may help answer that question. The deep-rooted conviction that big business is running everything goes back a long way in our country—as far back as the American Revolution and the first days of the infant American republic.

Bonds were issued by the new republic during the American Revolution to pay farmers, discharged soldiers, shopkeepers, and others. But during hard times after the war, the value of the bonds went down and down. When the farmers, soldiers, and small shopkeepers sold them, it was at a ruinous discount. By 1789 most of the public debt was held by monied interests in the big cities— Philadelphia, New York, Charleston, and Boston. Alexander

Hamilton pushed through Congress a scheme to pay the bonds (which had been selling for 25 cents on a dollar) off at *full value* using taxpayers' money. To make matters even more divisive, Hamilton proposed to raise the cash to do this by an excise tax on whiskey. This would wring the money right out of small farmers in the interior of the country—they turned much of their corn into this highly exportable and profitable commodity.[4] The direct result was an uproar that ended in the Whiskey Rebellion of 1794.

When furious Pennsylvania farmers mobbed tax collectors and started to march on Pittsburgh, President Washington called out the militia. That cooled the rebellion. But the suspicion that big money and the industrialists were out to take over government was firmly implanted. American political history from that time until 1865 was a constant battle for control of government between farming-planting interests and the mercantile-shipping-financial interests of the big cities. Even Thomas Jefferson suggested, in 1791, that Congress was being controlled by "stock-jobbers."[5]

In 1832 President Jackson vetoed a bill to recharter the Second Bank of the United States with these words to Congress:

> It is to be regretted that the rich and powerful too often bend the acts of government to their selfish purposes . . . to make the rich richer and the potent more powerful . . . [at the expense of] farmers, mechanics, and laborers—who have neither the time nor the means of securing like favors to themselves. . . .[6]

Actually, for all his rhetoric, once Jackson killed the bank by withdrawing its government deposits, he tucked them into selected state banks. Wildcat banks sprung up all over the West. Money in circulation grew threefold, and loans outstanding grew fourfold. An inflationary spiral began that came crashing down in financial panic—shortly after the president left office.

During the years before the Civil War, the myth that business is out to take over the government began to look like it could come true. Businessmen flocked to Washington to "put the arm" on Congress. One reputable economist of the time seriously suggested that "the friends of domestic industry should meet annually and prepare a schedule of legislation" that Congress could then turn into law!

Still, up to about 1870, there was no big business in the country in the sense that we know it today. In the 1840s there were not 20 millionaires in the whole country. The United States still enjoyed a comfortably widespread distribution of wealth and power. Local merchants, manufacturers, lawyers, editors, and preachers were the "powerbrokers" in a nation of small towns.

Later, in the post-Civil War era of rapid industrialization and growing urbanization, immense money and power began to accumulate. With it came growing public fear of concentration of wealth.

Between the end of the Civil War and the beginning of our century, business interests did very nearly take over in the seat of government. More businessmen than ever before entered Congress. Senate seats were bought outright by industrialists, and almost no legislation to control business even reached the floor of Congress for debate. One U.S. senator actually suggested that congressmen should be elected according to the industry they represented, rather than their geographic constituency.

The Balance Swings

The incredible expansion of America following the Civil War, opening up of vast natural resources, steadily automating industry, new communication means, a growing population hungry for goods, and the development of "pools" and "trusts" all worked together to raise the specter of "big-business monopoly." But, as often happens in America, when the pendulum swings too far in favor of one sector or another, the people themselves move in the other direction, as if on signal, counterbalancing overweening power.

The 1880s saw the formation of a great national labor federation, the American Federation of Labor. It drew together various national unions of skilled workers and would give organized labor a single voice and great political force in years ahead. Farmers also organized. There were dreams of uniting farmers and organized labor, and the Populist movement was born. As a unified political movement, the Populist party came to its fullest bloom in the national election of 1892. It withered in the same election as both Republicans and Democrats won far more votes. Even so, the Populist *idea*, the notion of social dualism—big money and big business vs. the people—was in our national bloodstream and remains there today.

In our own century, there's been a fairly steady side-by-side growth of business and government. The dynamic expansion of American business has been matched by creation and strengthening of governmental agencies to balance and control it. This intensified during the 50 years between the stock-market crash of 1929 and the beginning of the 1980s. Herbert Hoover began it by approving the Reconstruction Finance Corporation. This was created to bail out with direct federal loans large corporations that got into financial trouble. Franklin Roosevelt enlarged it with a whole series of innovations. The monetary system was reformed and management put into the hands of government. Citizens' bank deposits were guaranteed by the government for the first time. The Farm Credit Administration was established, along with the HOLC [Home Owners Loan Corporation], to provide federal credit for farm and home mortgages. Social Security was initiated.

Government created jobs for the unemployed at a time during the Depression when industry could not. The whole Keynesian notion of government spending to stimulate demand and employment was put into practice. The Securities and Exchange Commission laid a restraining hand on investments. And TVA [Tennessee Valley Authority] and REA [Rural Electrification Association] brought light, power, and new industry to parts of the country that had been neglected before.

The Influence of the Economic Elite

The belief that an "economic elite" controls governmental and community affairs, by means kept hidden from the public, is one that can be traced at least as far back in American history as the political attacks of some Jeffersonians on some Hamiltonians at the end of the eighteenth century. Scarcely any lower-class political movement in the United States has failed to express the theme that the upper classes successfully used nondemocratic means to thwart democratic processes. Perhaps the widest popular use of the theme was achieved by the Populist movement in the decades following 1890. . . .

The belief is not entirely wrong. But it presents only a portion of relevant reality and creates a significant misimpression that in itself has political repercussions. A more balanced analysis of the historical facts would probably arrive at something like the following conclusion: segments of the economic elite have violated democratic political and legal processes, with differing degrees of effort and success in the various periods of American history, but in no recent period could they correctly be said to have controlled the elected and appointed political authorities in large measure. The relationship between the economic elite and the political authorities has been a constantly varying one of strong influence, cooperation, division of labor, and conflict, with each influencing the other in changing proportion to some extent and each operating independently of the other to a large extent.

Arnold M. Rose, *The Power Structure: Political Process in American Society*, 1967.

By the time America entered World War II, government and business were working together rather than in an adversarial mode. Since that war the relationship has continued, and it has intensified more than many people might wish. In recent years, with "unbundling" of industry controls, government has sought to stimulate enterprise and step away, in effect, from such close relationship but without letting business "run wild." The result has appeared to be a growth of entrepreneurship. New-business starts in 1984 were at the highest level since 1978—102,329 new firms in a year.[7]

So when we look back over two centuries of give-and-take in our country, during which we've become the most powerful and dynamic economic force in the world, the theme of a threatening big business trying to dominate democracy weaves back and forth all through our history. Not only the people but also our leaders have kept it going from generation to generation. Hamilton may have started it in the federal convention of 1789 when he remarked, "All communities divide themselves into the few and the many. The first are the rich and well-born; the other the mass of the people . . . turbulent and changing, they seldom judge or determine right. Give therefore to the first class a distinct, permanent share in the government."[8] But Jefferson worried about "the rage of getting rich in a day"[9] that he saw in the speculative scramble for stock in the Bank of the United States. In our century, Theodore Roosevelt complained of "the dull, purblind folly of the very rich men; their greed and arrogance . . . and the corruption in business and politics"; he berated the "malefactors of great wealth."[10]

Woodrow Wilson (who also believed "Every great man of business has got somewhere . . . a touch of the idealist in him . . . love of integrity for its own sake")[11] nevertheless complained of the development of trusts, that it gave "to a few men a control over the economy of the country which they might abuse to the undoing of millions of men, it might even be to the permanent demoralization of society itself and of the government."[12]

Franklin Roosevelt told the Commonwealth Club in San Francisco (1932) that "Just as freedom to farm has ceased, so also the opportunity in business has narrowed . . . area after area has been preempted altogether by the great corporations . . . " and warned that "Put plainly, we are steering a steady course toward economic oligarchy, if we are not there already."[13] Even Herbert Hoover used Populist terminology in a backward swipe at Franklin Roosevelt during the 1936 presidential campaign: "I rejected the nation of great trade monopolies and price fixing through codes. That could only stifle the little business man by regimenting him under the big brother. That idea was born of certain American Big Business and grew up to be the NRA[National Rifle Association]."[14] And Harry Truman berated McKinley as "one of those who was good for the rich and bad for the poor"[15]; Cleveland's second term in office as "more interested in the big-money people than he was in the common people . . . "[16]; and Truman, himself, believed "people have to keep their eyes and ears open at all times or they'll be robbed blind by the Mugwumps in politics and by the big-business interests." When Merle Miller, author of an oral biography of President Truman, remarked to him, "You sound like a Populist," Mr. Truman said, "Maybe I do."[17]

Philosopher of business Peter Drucker has written that he considers "the claims on business by American populism," which he believes require that "business subordinate economic performance to non-economic performance and non-economic goals . . . are even less compatible with business performance than the European 'Socialist' hostility toward 'private enterprise.'" In fact, he considers it "basically hostile to economic performance altogether."[18]

Conclusion

In spite of all our two centuries of push-and-shove about whether or not big business is "taking us over," the American people generally enjoy the highest standard of living in the world. Fewer of us who are employed are working for "big companies" than in 1976 (32% worked for a company with over 250 employees in 1976; 30% in 1982, the latest year for which figures are available).[19] And more new little businesses open their doors hopefully every day to compete with giants for our favor—and maybe grow up to be big companies themselves someday.

Big business doesn't run the country. The unions don't run the country. Even the government doesn't run the country, when it comes right down to it. We all maintain an intricate, delicate, and often painful balance among us. In the midst of this endless dance of the giants, the American citizen goes about his or her daily life in an environment of personal freedom and opportunity that's unique in the world today.

1. Ray Allen Billington, *Westward Expansion* (New York: MacMillan Publishing Company, Inc., 1949).
2. Leo J. Shapiro & Associates special national survey done for this book (August 1985).
3. Leo J. Shapiro & Associates national consumer survey, "What should be done to help Chrysler Motors?" (August 1979).
4. As a farmer himself, President Washington owned a "particularly profitable" still on his home plantation, from which he "carried over" 755 quarter gallons of whiskey, after selling most of his rye-and-Indian-corn liquid dynamite, in a single year, according to Paul Leicester Ford's *The True George Washington* (Philadelphia: J.B. Lippincott Company, 1902), p. 123.
5. Letter to George Mason (February 7, 1791).
6. Message to Congress (July 10, 1832).
7. Dun & Bradstreet figures (1985).
8. Samuel Eliot Morison, *The Oxford History of the American People* (New York: Oxford University Press, 1965), p. 324.
9. Merrill D. Peterson, *Thomas Jefferson and the New Nation* (New York: Oxford University Press, 1970), p. 436.
10. Richard Hofstadter, *The American Political Tradition* (New York: Random House, 1948), p. 224.
11. Speech to Chicago Commercial Club (1902).
12. Woodrow Wilson, *History of the American People*, quoted in Hofstadter, op. cit., p. 244.
13. Richard Hofstadter, ed., *Great Issues in American History* (New York: Random House, 1969), pp. 348-49.
14. "Challenge to Liberty" speech (1936).
15. Merle Miller, *Plain Speaking* (New York: Berkley Publishing Corporation, 1974), p. 120.
16. Ibid., p. 118.
17. Ibid., p. 153.
18. Peter Drucker, *Managing in Turbulent Times* (New York: Harper & Row, 1980), p. 209.
19. *Statistical Abstract of the United States 1985* (Washington, D.C.: U.S. Department of Commerce, Bureau of the Census, 1984), table 873.

"There is a social upper class in the United States that is a ruling class by virtue of its dominant role in the economy and government."

America Is Controlled by a Ruling Social Class

G. William Domhoff

G. William Domhoff is a professor of psychology and sociology at the University of California, Santa Cruz. He has written numerous books and articles on the subject of political and social power. In 1967 he published a book titled *Who Rules America?*, that presented a case for the domination of American society by a ruling class. The following viewpoint is taken from *Who Rules America Now?*, a sequel to the earlier book. In his books he presents evidence that a fixed group of privileged people dominates the American economy and government. In his new book Domhoff argues that an upper class comprising only one-half of one percent of the population occupies key positions within the corporate community. He claims leaders within this "power elite" reach government and dominate it through processes of special-interest lobbying, policy planning and candidate selection.

As you read, consider the following questions:

1. Why does the author claim interacting and intermarrying are important to the upper class?
2. What impact do the extravagances of the upper class have on American society according to the author?

If the question is asked, Who rules in the United States? the answer is likely to be in terms of interest groups, elected officials, and the people in general. Contrary to this pluralistic view of power, [I wish] to present systematic evidence that suggests there is a social upper class in the United States that is a ruling class by virtue of its dominant role in the economy and government. It will be shown that this ruling class is socially cohesive, has its basis in the large corporations and banks, plays a major role in shaping the social and political climate, and dominates the federal government through a variety of organizations and methods.

The Ruling Class and the Power Elite

The upper class as a whole does not do this ruling. Instead, class rule is manifested through the activities of a wide variety of organizations and institutions. These organizations and institutions are financed and directed by those members of the upper class who have the interest and ability to involve themselves in protecting and enhancing the privileged social position of their class. Leaders within the upper class join with high-level employees in the organizations they control to make up what will be called the *power elite*. This power elite is the leadership group of the upper class as a whole, but it is not the same thing as the upper class, for not all members of the upper class are members of the power elite and not all members of the power elite are part of the upper class. It is members of the power elite who take part in the processes that maintain the class structure. . . .

Other Levels of Society Are Not Powerless

To claim that there is an upper class with enough power to be considered a ruling class does not imply that other levels of society are totally powerless. Domination does not mean total control, but the ability to set the terms under which other groups and classes must operate. Highly trained professionals with an interest in environmental and consumer issues have been able to couple their technical information and their understanding of the legislative process with well-timed publicity to win governmental restrictions on some corporation practices. Wage and salary workers, when they are organized into unions, have been able to gain concessions on wages, hours, and working conditions. Even the most powerless of people, the very poor and those discriminated against, sometimes develop the capacity to disrupt the system through strikes, riots, or other forms of coercion, and there is evidence that such activities do bring about some redress of grievances, at least for a short time.[1]

Most of all, there is also the fact that people can vote. Although one basic theme of the book is a critique of the pluralist notion that voting necessarily makes government responsive to the will

Money Has Corrupted the Legislative Process

Power of wealth has (with honorable exceptions) achieved dominion over the legislative process and, hence, the conduct of democratic government. Indeed, it has cast a cloud on the right of a legislature to be called democratic when its principal function, as expressed in its actions, has become to protect and enhance the fortunes of the large and powerful at the expense of working Americans.

The principal instrument of this dominion is the political-action committee, or PAC, which collects money from its members and gives it to the constitutional guardians of the public trust—members of Congress and aspirants to Congress.

Most of these committees belong to economic interests that have an important stake in the actions of government—insurance companies, real-estate developers, chemical and drug companies, for example. In less than a decade they have become the single most important force in the contest for federal office. . . .

PAC money is neither a "gift" nor a "contribution." It is an investment. The PACs expect recipients to give careful, and usually favorable, consideration to legislation that affects their economic well-being. Being experienced investors, they generally get what they expect. . . .

The meaning of the PACs is clear. Congress is not *influenced* by special interests. Congress does not *represent* special interests. Congress is *owned* by special interests. Morally the system is bribery. It is not criminal only because those who make the laws are themselves accomplices. Government is for sale. But the bids are sealed, and the prices are very high.

There is an easy way out: Eliminate PACs. We should place a rigorous ceiling on all congressional campaigns, allocate public funds to finance campaigns and require television stations—the most costly component of modern political campaigns—to give a specified amount of air time to candidates.

Our national legislative process has become corrupt. The money power is becoming the congressional power. This fact is readily acknowledged, in private, even by those who are struggling to restore integrity and principle to democratic government. It has been a losing battle. And we, the governed, whose consent is no longer asked or needed, are the losers.

Richard N. Goodwin, *Los Angeles Times*, December 12, 1985.

of the majority, it does not deny that under certain circumstances the electorate has been able to place restraints on the actions of the power elite as a whole, or to determine which leaders within the power elite will have the greatest influence on policy. . . .

Interaction in the Upper Class

There is an interacting and intermarrying upper social stratum or social elite in America that is distinctive enough in its institutions, source and amount of income, and life-style to be called an "upper class." This upper class makes up about 0.5 percent of the population, a rough estimate that is based upon the number of students attending independent private schools, the number of listings in past *Social Registers* for several cities, and detailed interview studies in Kansas City and Boston.[2]

Not everyone in this nationwide upper class knows everyone else, but everybody knows somebody who knows someone in other areas of the country thanks to a common school experience, a summer at the same resort, or membership in the same social club. With the social institutions described in this chapter as the undergirding, the upper class at any given historical moment consists of a complex network of overlapping social circles that are knit together by the members they have in common and by the numerous signs of equal social status that emerge from a similar life-style. Viewed from the standpoint of social psychology, the upper class is made up of innumerable face-to-face small groups that are constantly changing in their composition as people move from one social setting to another.

Research work in both sociology and social psychology demonstrates that constant interaction in small-group settings leads to the social cohesion that is considered to be an important dimension of a social class.[3] This social cohesion does not in and of itself demonstrate that members of the upper class are able to agree among themselves on general issues of economic and government policy. But it is important to stress that social cohesion is one of the factors that makes it possible for policy coordination to develop. Indeed, research in social psychology demonstrates that members of socially cohesive groups are eager to reach agreement on issues of common concern to them. They are more receptive to what other members are saying, more likely to trust each other, and more willing to compromise, which are no small matters in any collection of human beings trying to get something accomplished.[4]

The more extravagant social activities of the upper class—the debutante balls, the expensive parties, the jet-setting to spas and vacation spots all over the world, the involvement with exotic entertainers—are often viewed by pluralists and Marxists alike as superfluous trivialities best left to society page writers. However,

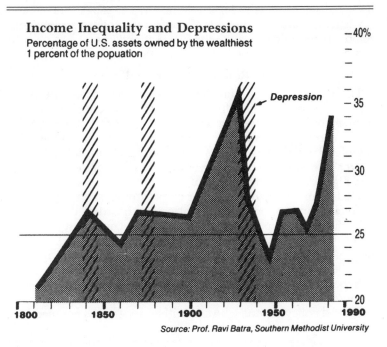

Income Inequality and Depressions
Percentage of U.S. assets owned by the wealthiest
1 percent of the popuation

Depression

−40%

− 35

−30

25

−20

1800   1850   1900   1950   1990

Source: Prof. Ravi Batra, Southern Methodist University

there is reason to believe that these activities play a role both in solidifying the upper class and in maintaining the class structure. Within the class, these occasions provide an opportunity for members to show each other that they are similar to each other and superior to the average citizen. As political scientist Gabriel Almond suggested in his 1941 study of the New York upper class and its involvement in city politics: "The elaborate private life of the plutocracy serves in considerable measure to separate them out in their own consciousness as a superior, more refined element."[5] Then, too, the values upon which the class system is based are conveyed to the rest of the population in this conspicuous consumption. Such activities make clear that there is a gulf between members of the upper class and ordinary citizens, reminding everyone of the hierarchical nature of the society. Social extravaganzas bring home to everyone that there are great rewards for success, helping to stir up the personal envy that can be a goad to competitive striving. . . .

Exhibiting high social status, in other words, is a way of exercising power. It is a form of power rooted in fascination and enchantment. It operates by creating respect, envy, and deference in others. Considered less important than force or economic power by social scientists who regard themselves as tough-minded and realistic, its role as a method of control in modern society goes relatively unnoticed despite the fact that power was originally in the domain of the sacred and the magical. . . .[6]

The Role of the Power Elite

This chapter has introduced the concept of a power elite as the leadership group of the upper class. This power elite is composed of members of the upper class who have taken on leadership roles in the corporate community and the policy network, along with high-level employees in these institutions. More formally, the power elite consists of active, working members of the upper class and high-level employees in profit and nonprofit institutions controlled by members of the upper class through stock ownership, financial support, or involvement on the board of directors.

In theory, the upper class, the corporate community, and the policy-planning network from which this power elite is drawn can be imagined as three intersecting circles. A person can be a member of one of the three, or two of the three, or all three. There can be upper class people who are only socialites, corporate leaders who are neither upper class nor involved in policy planning, and policy experts who are neither upper class nor members of the corporate community.

As a practical matter, however, the interrelations among these three sectors are even closer than the image of three intersecting circles would indicate. Most male members of the upper class between 45 and 65 are, in fact, part of the corporate community as owners, active investors, or titled executives even if they are not directors in top corporations. Then, too, a great many members of the policy network become involved in the corporate community as consultants and advisers even if they do not rise to the level of corporate directors. Thus, the corporate community becomes the common sector that encompasses most older males within the three overlapping circles. . . .

The Expertise of the Power Elite

The upper class and corporate community have created a complex and only partially coordinated set of institutions and organizations that often disagree among themselves about what policies are most compatible with the primary objectives of the corporate community, and that are only partially successful in convincing wage and salary earners that these policies are in everyone's interest.

Nonetheless, the weight of the emphasis has to be on the considerable similarity in viewpoint among institutions that range from moderately conservative to highly conservative in their policy suggestions and that have in their two contending camps a near monopoly for nongovernmental expertise and research support. Even if they are not able to agree completely among themselves, they have been able to discourage development of a large body of experts with a more liberal point of view. They also have been successful in keeping the few liberal programs that do exist at the fringe of serious discussion. . . .

Expert power is an important complement to the subtle status power and naked economic power. Since government officials with only small policy-planning staffs must often turn to foundations, policy groups, think tanks, and university institutes if they are to have new ideas for dealing with emerging problems, it is once again a form of power that can be exercised without any necessary direct involvement in government.

US Becoming a Class Society

We are accelerating toward the very kind of society against which we revolted—a society of economic classes, divided by formidable barriers. . . .

In 1947 we began to collect statistics on the distribution of income. Today the gap between upper- and lower-income families is wider than at any time since that date. In 1984, the latest numbers we have, 40% of all American families received only 15.7% of the national income; the middle 20% received only 17%. These are all-time records, accompanied by still another all-time first—the top 40% accumulated more than 67% of the national income.

And the movement toward inequality is accelerating. From 1980 to 1984, $25 billion of income was transferred from poor and middle-income families to those in the richest fifth of the population.

Richard N. Goodwin, *Los Angeles Times*, July 10, 1986.

Indeed, status power, economic power, and expertise are formidable quite independent of any involvement in government. But they are not enough to sustain the upper class as a ruling class without the ability to influence government directly. This is because the governmental system is the primary coordinating center within the society. . . .

Involvement in Government

Members of the power elite directly involve themselves in the federal government through three basic processes, each of which plays a slightly different role in ensuring access to the White House, Congress, and specific agencies, departments, and committees in the executive branch. Although some of the same people are involved in all three processes, most people specialize in one or two of the three processes. This is because each process requires slightly different knowledge, skills, and contacts. The three processes are:

1. The candidate selection process, through which members of the power elite attempt to influence electoral campaigns by means of campaign finances and favors to political candidates.
2. The special-interest process, through which specific individuals, corporations, and industrial sectors realize their narrow and short-run interests on taxes, subsidies, and regulation in dealing with congressional committees, regulatory bodies, and executive departments.
3. The policy-making process, through which the general policies of the policy-planning network are brought to the White House and Congress. . . .

The Power Elite's Domination of Government

[I have] demonstrated the power elite's wide-ranging access to government through the special interest and policy-planning processes, as well as the ability of its members to influence the kind of people elected and appointed to government through their financial involvement in the candidate-selection process. When coupled with the several different kinds of power, this access and involvement add up to power elite domination of the federal government.

By *domination* social scientists mean the ability of a class or group to set the terms under which other classes or groups within a social system must operate. By this definition, domination does not mean control on each and every issue, and it does not rest upon government involvement alone. Involvement in government is only the final and most visible aspect of power elite domination, which has its roots in the class structure, the nature of the economy, and the functioning of the policy-planning and opinion-shaping networks. If government officials did not have to wait on corporate leaders to decide where and when they will invest, and if government officials were not further limited by the acquiescence of the large majority to the present economic arrangements, then power elite involvement in elections and government would count for a lot less than it does under present conditions.

1. Robert R. Alford and Roger Friedland, "Political Participation and Public Policy." *Annual Review of Sociology,* 1, (1975); William A. Gamson, *The Strategy of Social Protest,* (Homewood, Ill: Dorsey Press, 1975); Frances Piven and Richard Cloward, *Regulating the Poor* (New York: Pantheon, 1971); Frances Piven and Richard Cloward, *Poor People's Movements* (New York: Random House, 1977).
2. Domhoff, *Who Rules America?* pp. 7n-8n; "Private Schools Search for a New Social Role," *National Observer,* August 26, 1968, p. 5; Coleman and Rainwater, *Social Standing in America,* p. 148. For a summary of many studies that concludes that "Capital S Society" in the United States includes "probably no more than four-tenths of one percent in large cities, and even a smaller proportion in smaller communities," see Coleman and Neugarten, *Social Status in the City,* p. 270.

3. Domhoff, *Bohemian Grove,* pp. 89-90, for a summary of this research.
4. Dorwin Cartwright and Alvin Zander, *Group Dynamics* (New York: Harper & Row, 1960), p. 89; Albert J. Lott and Bernice E. Lott, "Group Cohesiveness as Interpersonal Attraction," *Psychological Bulletin* 64 (1965): pp. 291-296; Michael Argyle, *Social Interaction* (Chicago: Aldine, 1969), pp. 220-223.
5. Gabriel Almond, "Plutocracy and Politics in New York City:" (Ph.D. diss., University of Chicago, 1941), p. 108.
6. See Norman O. Brown, *Life Against Death* (London: Routledge & Kegan Paul, 1959), pp. 242, 249-252, for a breathtaking argument on the roots of power in the sacred and the psychological. For one attempt to apply the argument to the class structure, *see* G. William Domhoff, "Historical Materialism, Cultural Determinism, and the Origin of the Ruling Classes,"*Psychoanalytical Review,* no. 2 (1969). For a discussion that rightly announces itself as "the first extensive treaties on prestige as a social control system," see William J. Goode, *The Celebration of Heroes: Prestige as a Social Control System* (Berkeley, Calif.: University of California Press, 1978).

"Government by and for special interests must give way to government in the public interest."

America Is Controlled by Special Interests and Ideologues

Peter Navarro

Peter Navarro is an economic researcher at Harvard University. His articles have appeared in academic journals and his op-ed pieces have been printed in many of the nation's major newspapers, including *The Wall Street Journal* and *The New York Times*. In the following viewpoint, excerpted from his book, *The Policy Game: How Special Interests and Ideologues Are Stealing America*, he presents a citizen's guide to understanding why American government isn't working. Very detailed and focusing on specific issues, his book presents a persuasive argument that special interests and ideologues have mastered the techniques needed to manipulate public policy. To counter this negative impact and to better serve the public interest, he suggests all Americans become more informed, involved, and adept at influencing public policy.

As you read, consider the following questions:

1. Why does the author claim the term "public policy," as used in America, is often a misnomer?
2. Whom does he identify as the main protagonists in America's "ideology wars"?

industries prospering under the protective shelter of
[...]e largess. At the same time, our ideological society must
[...] to the pragmatic society. We must eschew blind faith
[...]of the more precise compass of sound economics, the
[...]that will guide us fastest and farthest on our journey
[...]ational growth and prosperity.
[...]mplish these changes, we as citizens, taxpayers, and
[...]st learn to play the policy game better. To achieve this
[...]rst must become aware of the broad scope of America's
[...] political, and social problems. We then must be both
[...]d able to participate as a responsible electorate in find-
[...]rging solutions that will make us all better off.
[...]ingness to participate must stem from the realization
[...]fects of the policy game are never confined simply to
[...] interests or ideologues who appear to be its major
[...]e policy game spills over into all our lives by interfer-
[...]the nation's growth, prosperity, and health; any
[...]mean there is less abundance for all of us to share.
[...]y to participate must stem from an understanding of
[...]layers are, what they seek, and how the game
[...]he ultimate goal is to better understand and control
[...]political forces that affect our lives so that we can
[...]current economic austerity with a new prosperity.

Every time our government plays the policy game, some of us
win and some of us lose: The federal government slaps a quota
on Japanese car imports, and the auto industry gains at the expense of consumers, who pay higher prices for a more limited
selection of cars. State legislators in the Southwest vote to raise
severance taxes on coal, and their states gain revenues while
Midwest and Northeast consumers spend more for electricity. A
city council imposes rent controls, and tenants rejoice at frozen
rents while landlords watch their property values plunge.

Special Interests Harm the Public Interest

Who gains and who loses in these federal, state, and local policy
arenas is rarely an accident. More often than not, the distribu-
tional consequences of "public policies" are the intended result
of the private interests which have been instrumental in their
design, passage, and implementation. Thus, the term *public policy*,
which suggests government action designed to promote the
general welfare, is often a misnomer. This lofty but misleading
term imbues American democracy with much of its aura of
goodness while it disguises the real nature of the policy game.

Unfortunately, the private use of public policy does more than
merely benefit some interest groups at the expense of others. In
most cases, there is also a net loss to our nation so that the public
interest is almost always harmed. The litany of counterproduc-
tive public policies promoted by special interests is a long and
familiar one.

For example, the systematic suppression of free trade through
tariffs, quotas, trigger prices, and other import restrictions has protected the profits of a small core of domestic industries, but at
the same time has made the shoes on our feet more expensive,
the autos we drive less fuel efficient, and the color televisions we
buy less reliable. This protectionist umbrella has also weakened
the nation's productive capacity by deterring the investment in
new factories and advanced technology that is necessary to compete in world markets.

Similarly, a plethora of agricultural price supports has enriched
a small group of primarily large corporate farmers at the expense
of taxpayers, consumers, and small farmers. But these supports
have also institutionalized inflationary pressures—pressures that
are packaged with every loaf of bread, every bag of sugar, every
quart of milk, every pack of cigarettes, and every jar of peanut
butter we buy.

The Role of Ideology

Despite the obvious role of special interests, the policy game
is more than just a struggle among them to capture the powers
of government for their own gain. To a large extent, the outcome

of the policy game also represents the resolution of a battle of beliefs in which the spoils of victory go to the standard bearers of a particular ideology. In this country, the "ideology wars" are typically waged between liberals and conservatives, with each camp having a diverse set of competing principles at stake.

For example, conservatives see the road to economic prosperity as one paved with free market efficiency, but liberals often prefer to regulate markets on the grounds that the economic system will operate more fairly with the helping hand of government. Likewise, the liberal commitment to the "welfare state" rests on a conception that the responsibility of good government is to provide people with the basic human needs of food, clothing, and shelter, while the conservative's preference for a "minimal state" rests on the competing belief that the best government is that which intrudes least.

ONE OF THESE IS AN ILLEGAL, CONGRESSIONAL BRIBE TO INFLUENCE LEGISLATION—THE OTHER IS A PRIVATE CAMPAIGN CONTRIBUTION... CAN YOU TELL THE DIFFERENCE?

NEITHER CAN ANYONE ELSE...

Mike Peters. Reprinted by permission of United Feature Syndicate, Inc.

Despite the undeniably good intentions of both liberals and conservatives, the effects of ideological struggle on the public interest can be every bit as damaging as special interest politics. There is, for example, increasing evidence suggesting that many welfare policies, which have been designed and implemented by liberals since the beginnings of the New Deal, have actually created a permanent "welfare caste." Its hard-core "beneficiaries" are now trapped in a far-from-gilded welfare cage that has destroyed individual self-respect, the incentive to work, and the ability to raise

a family with true economic security
fect relegated large masses of the "de
ban ghettos and rural backwaters ar
on the economic ladder.

At the same time, while the conser
in such industries as the airlines ar
benefited the economy, their equall
tion in industries like the railroads
for free markets is much less cogen
to establish, bastions of monopoly
railroads wielding such power ha
the expense of energy consume
development of western coal res
the transition from foreign oil to
dependence on foreign energy

Similarly, while subsidies lik
havoc with the economy, ther
national security arguments th
subsidizing such activities as
sit, and public education. Yet
of their own faith, perenniall
an overly full bag of "bad"

America Cannot Tolerate

America has reached a poi
and prosper while buffet
devastating consequences
longer afford the increasin
use of the public interest.
misguided ideologues have
the dark corridors of a n
primary fact of America
product—our economic p
did. The slack, the fat,
hallmarks of American s
battles over the share
intensified.

Fortunately, this n
unalterable; contrary t
we do not live in a "
wins another must
economic pie is, in f
growth if we as a nat
game better.

Government by
government in the
cumbered by wast

prodiga
legislati
give wa
in favor
lodestar
toward

To acc
voters m
goal, we f
economic
willing an
ing and fo

The will
that the ef
the specia
players. Th
ing with
"miscues"

The abilit
who the p
works. . . .
the myriad
replace our

140

"The more important a policy is, the less important is the role of self-interest in determining that policy."

A Positive Public Spirit Guides American Government

Steven Kelman

This viewpoint challenges the Madisonian argument of the US political system being driven by competing factions and groups seeking primarily their own self-interests. Steven Kelman, professor of public policy and government at the John F. Kennedy School of Government at Harvard University, claims the main force behind national public policy decisions is a concern for the common good. He argues that a desire to do what is right is a better explanation than is self-interest for the public policy making process. The book from which this viewpoint is excerpted is appropriately subtitled, *A Hopeful View of American Government.*

As you read, consider the following questions:

1. How does the author define the term "public spirit"?
2. What evidence does he present to support his claim that self-interest does not dominate important public policy decisions?

I undertake to evaluate how well the policy-making process works in the United States. Like any evaluation, mine is based both on normative standards for judgment and empirical observations about how well the system performs according to those standards.

I evaluate the policy-making process against two standards—the ability to produce good public policy and the less tangible effects of the process itself on promoting our dignity as people and molding our character. I argue that for the policy-making process to work well, high levels of public spirit on the part of participants in the process are necessary. By "public spirit," I mean an inclination to make an honest effort to achieve good public policy. This contrasts with the behavior of self-interested participants in the process, who do not ask what policy would be right overall but, rather, simply what policy would be best for themselves. I realize the expression "public spirit" sounds somewhat archaic, and I am using it on purpose to recapture an approach to thinking about the policy-making process that has tragically suffered a precipitous decline in recent decades. (Indeed I toyed with using the expression "civic virtue" for the same reason.)

My conclusion is unfashionable: the public spirit is widespread enough so that the role the government plays in our lives is more worthy of admiration and faith than of dislike and cynicism. . . .

The Presence of Public Spirit

[I] argue for the unconventional proposition that the political process in the United States works reasonably well and hence merits the participation of people seeking a good society. The key issue I examine is the prevalence of public spirit. Public spirit, of course, is a state of mind, and states of mind are notoriously difficult to pin down. I "test" for the presence of public spirit in three ways. First, the best operational test of the importance of public spirit in the political process, I think, is the ability of ideas to overcome interests in determining the content of political choices. If self-interested behavior, whether of popular majorities or of interest groups, would have dictated one kind of outcome, and general ideas about good public policy another, then the extent to which political choices reflect the ideas rather than the interests constitutes a strong test of the importance of public spirit. Second, I look at individual political behavior, to see the extent to which the stands that citizens take in the political process are explained by their self-interest or by general ideas they have about right and wrong. Finally, I spend some effort examining directly the question of public spirit in the motivations of professional participants in the political process such as politicians and government officials.

Twenty years ago the conclusion that the political process

144

worked reasonably well was under attack in the scholarly community most insistently from the embittered Left. Critics of pluralism painted a dark portrait of a power elite and of domination over the system by the wealthy. Today, it is under attack most insistently from the crusading Right. Theorists of "public choice" find politics wanting compared with the market. This constitutes a defense from the impassioned center.

American Society Works Pretty Well

Although my argument is unfashionable, is it really when one stops and thinks so surprising? Seen over the broad span of historic time and place, American society works pretty well. We have been spared secret police knocking at our doors; we have enjoyed extended economic prosperity; there has been no widespread starvation. We have absorbed multitudes of the wretched of the earth, succeeded in assuring most people a decent old age, and saved a surprising amount of the natural beauty on the American continent. Compared with our achievements, our problems and shortcomings seem trivial. Although we should not give government all the credit for this, we should not deny it *any* credit either.

Steven Kelman, *Making Public Policy*, 1987.

My argument is not only unfashionable in conclusion but . . . untypical in form. In general, those who have evaluated the American political process against a standard of the presence of public spirit have found it wanting, while those who have been sanguine about the process have not evaluated it against a public spirit standard. By contrast, I evaluate it against a standard of the presence of public spirit, and I am still rather sanguine about it. . . .

Self-Interest Does Not Dominate Political Choices

Does self-interest in fact turn out to dominate the results of the political process? It is no trick to come up with countless specific examples of situations where political choices have been crucially determined by participants furthering quite narrow selfish interests. Everyone has a favorite story of the highway that got built because a powerful member of Congress wanted it in his district or of a tax loophole an interest group sneaked through with few in Congress knowing about it. Certainly there is no lack of straightforwardly self-interested behavior in the political process.

As a general rule, however, the more important a policy is, the less important is the role of self-interest in determining that policy. Self-interest does a great job explaining the location of a new federal building in Missoula. When all is said and done, it falls down with regard to the major policy upheavals of the past decades.

Self-interest cannot account, except through the grossest of contortions, for the vast increases in spending for the poor that occurred in the 1960s and early 1970s. The poor were not an electoral majority, nor were they well organized into interest groups. (Public choice theorists sometimes point to the power of interest groups representing providers of services to the poor. The hypothesis that an invincible lobby of social workers overwhelmed a defenseless political system is, to put it diplomatically, idiosyncratic.) What about the growth of health, safety, and environmental regulations during the late 1960s and early 1970s? These programs were adopted against the wishes of well-organized producers. They were intended for the benefit of poorly organized consumers and environmentalists. (Much of the organization of environmentalists into interest groups *followed* environmental legislation, rather than preceding it.)

In addition, biases in the political process that public choice advocates believe produce a government that is too big can hardly explain the *growth* of government in the 1960s and 1970s unless one can successfully argue that the size of any bias increased during the period when the growth took place. Otherwise, the bias should have already produced larger government in the earlier period.[1] Furthermore, the big increases in government spending since the 1950s have not been in grants to localities, which provide particularistic constituency benefits, but in various general transfer programs that do not allow members to demonstrate they have gotten something special for the district.[2]

The self-interest model of politics does equally poorly in accounting for rollbacks in government programs during the late 1970s and 1980s. In the late 1970s, the greatest victories for industry deregulation were won in exactly those industries, such as trucking and airlines, where well-organized producers benefited from regulation and the consumers who would benefit from deregulation were largely unorganized. By contrast, little occurred in areas such as environmental policy where well-organized producers supported deregulation.[3] In other words, the pattern of deregulation was exactly the *opposite* of that predicted by the self-interest model. . . .

The self-interest theories not only have a difficult time explaining most of what has been important in American politics over the past twenty years. They also give, at best, an incomplete feel for the process itself. . . .

The Media and Public Spirit

The view that self-interest is key to understanding how the political process works is also belied by the influence of the media. On superficial examination, the influence of the media might be seen as consistent with the view that people in government are out only for adulation or reelection, because the way officials are treated in the media certainly has an impact on their attaining either goal. It is necessary to remember, however, that what generates good (or bad) attention in the media is generally whether people have sought to do the right thing or whether instead they acted selfishly. If neither people in government themselves, nor the voters who select elected officials, thought that it was important to try to do the right thing in politics, media brickbats would be a matter of indifference to their intended victims. Sticks and stones could break their bones, but names would never hurt them. The great influence of the media suggests that failure to show public spirit *can* indeed hurt these people, in their own eyes and in the eyes of others. Alternately, media influence can be treated as a constant and the way the media cover politics as a variable. Seen this way, the choice of topics for muckraking and exposé reflects the role that public spirit plays in the system. In a political system where self-interest were the acceptable norm, what is presented as scandal would not be so. . . .

The Political Behavior of Citizens

What best explains the voting behavior of individual citizens? The classic view in the early empirical voting studies, such as *The American Voter*, was that voting behavior is guided mostly by self-interest. This view was developed in works appearing during the 1970s on the link between economic conditions and election results. With modern techniques of social science, these studies confirmed something politicians knew intuitively, namely, that incumbents do well in times of economic prosperity and badly during economic distress.[4]

In what has probably been the most interesting body of empirical political science research of the last decade, extensive evidence has now been developed questioning this view.[5] The connection between economic conditions and overall electoral results is indeed very clear. What researchers have now done is to move from the aggregate level of overall economic conditions and overall electoral results to the level of individual economic conditions and individual voting decisions. When they do so, the results are surprising. If voters vote their personal pocketbooks, we would expect those who have themselves become better off because of improved economic circumstances to favor the incumbents. Those not personally sharing in the prosperity would not be expected to display such a tendency. Likewise, in times of economic distress we would expect the individual victims of bad times to punish the incumbents. However, series of tests by Donald Kinder and Roderick Kiewiet using individual-level survey data have devastatingly shattered this hypothesis. Respondents' answers to a question about whether their personal financial situation has

147

improved, worsened, or stayed the same over the previous year show essentially *no* connection to changes in voting behavior. By contrast, though, there are substantial correlations between a voter's views of economic conditions in society *as a whole* and the individual's voting behavior. This relationship holds even when the possible effects of personal economic situation on judgments of overall economic conditions are controlled for. The observed connection at the aggregate level between the economy and the electoral success of incumbents results not from self-interested rewards or punishments from voters who have personally done well or badly. The connection comes instead from judgments by voters about whether the economy *as a whole* is doing well, independent of how the voter is doing *personally*.[6]

Concern for Others

My argument . . . begins . . . with an alternate view of human nature—that not just personal self-interest but also concern for others can motivate behavior.

Steven Kelman, *Making Public Policy*, 1987.

A conceptually similar body of research has been conducted by social psychologist David Sears and his colleagues, who have investigated how well personal self-interest in a political issue accounts for attitudes on the issues. Thus, for example, these scholars have examined the extent to which attitudes on busing among whites can be explained by whether one's own family has been affected by a busing plan, or the extent to which attitudes toward the war in Vietnam were influenced by whether one had family or close friends fighting there.[7] The findings are dramatic. Regarding attitudes on Vietnam, having a relative or close friend actually fighting in Vietnam had far less effect on views of what American policy should be than the respondent's self-anchoring on a liberal-conservative scale or his or her attitudes toward communism. In multiple regression equations where various possible sources of political attitudes appeared as independent variables, liberal or conservative ideology better predicted a respondent's views on government national health insurance or guaranteed jobs programs than whether the respondent himself was covered by health insurance or had recently been unemployed. In other words, conservatives who themselves had no health insurance protection were less likely to favor national health insurance than liberals who had coverage of their own. As part of a study on business and American foreign policy, Bruce Russett and Elizabeth Hanson did a survey of the attitudes of corporate executives on foreign policy issues. They found that respondents' views on domestic liberal-conservative issues such as civil rights were better predictors of their foreign policy views than whether their company had defense contracts or investments overseas. In fact, the connection between the self-interest economic variables and foreign policy views was quite small.[8]

These data taken as a whole suggest quite strongly that general ideas about what kinds of policies are right play an important role in influencing the attitudes of individual citizens on many political issues. . . .

Conclusion

The evidence is overwhelming that most people are not keenly interested in politics. Significant numbers of citizens have weakly held opinions, or no opinions at all, on many political issues. The point is not that people are saints, willing to sacrifice all for the sake of others. Having political opinions based on general views about what public policies would be right may indeed often be a low-cost form of altruism, although the cost in taxes may not be insignificant, at least in the case of those whose views lead them to support government programs that cost money. Nor are most people philosophers or professional policy analysts. Views can be based on general conceptions of right and wrong without being particularly sophisticated. Nonetheless, in a world of many political issues and of an overall modest level of interest in politics, we can expect to find a strong reservoir of political input based on general ideas of what policy would be right. Such input is likely to be an important factor in the process. . . .

My own judgment is that the level of public spirit remains high enough in our political system so that it both encourages the choice of good public policy and produces positive effects on us as people. This is a matter of feel and judgment, I concede. I certainly believe that the call is close enough so that we need to be vigilant about the level of civic virtue in our society. The norms that sustain public spirit need to be defended from assault.

1. Richard A. Musgrave, "Leviathan Cometh: or Does He?" in *Tax and Expenditure Limitations*, ed. Helen F. Ladd and T. Nicholaus Tideman (Washington: The Urban Institute Press, 1981), pp. 77-81. (The argument is similar to the one economists make against the notion that oligopoly pricing or large corporate profits explain inflation: inflation is an increase of prices, and unless one can demonstrate that oligopolization has increased during the period of inflation, any effect of oligopolies on the price level will have already occurred previously.)
2. See R. Douglas Arnold, "The Local Roots of Domestic Policy," in *The New Congress*, ed. Thomas E. Mann and Norman Ornstein (Washington: American Enterprise Institute, 1981), pp. 281-83.
3. See Martha Derthick and Paul J. Quirk, *The Politics of Deregulation* (Washington: The Brookings Institution, 1985).
4. Gerald H. Kramer, "Short-Term Fluctuations in U.S. Voting Behavior, 1896-1964," *American Political Science Review* 65 (March 1971): 131-43, and Samuel I. Popkin et al., "What Have You Done For Me Lately? Toward An Investment Theory of Voting," *American Political Science Review* 70 (September 1976): 779-805.

5. A prescient early discussion of this issue, which emphasized ethnic variations in voting behavior driven by public spirit, is James Q. Wilson, "Public-Regardingness as a Value Premise in Voting Behavior," *American Political Science Review* 58 (December 1964): 876-87.

6. Donald R. Kinder and D. Roderick Kiewiet, "Economic Discontent and Political Behavior: The Role of Personal Grievances and Collective Economic Judgments in Congressional Voting," *American Journal of Political Science* 23 (August 1979); 495-527. See also Donald R. Kinder, "Presidents, Prosperity and Public Opinion," *Public Opinion Quarterly* 45 (Spring 1981): 1-21.

7. David O. Sears et al., "Whites' Opposition of Busing: Self-Interest or Symbolic Politics?" *American Political Science Review* 73 (June 1979): 369-84; Richard R. Lau et al., "Self-Interest and Civilians' Attitudes Toward the Vietnam War," *Public Opinion Quarterly* 42 (Winter 1978): 464-83; and David O. Sears et al., "Self-Interest vs. Symbolic Politics in Policy Attitudes and Presidential Voting," *American Political Science Review* 74 (September 1980); 670-84.

8. Bruce M. Russett and Elizabeth C. Hanson, *Interest and Ideology: The Foreign Policy Beliefs of American Business* (San Francisco: W.H. Freeman, 1975), pp. 123-24.

150

a critical thinking activity

Distinguishing Between Fact and Opinion

This activity is designed to help develop the basic reading and thinking skill of distinguishing between fact and opinion. Consider the following statement as an example: If a conservative religious leader is elected president of the United States at some future date, that would be a fact. However, whether or not the United States would be better off socially, economically, politically, and even religiously with a conservative religious president is a matter of opinion. Future historians would agree that the individual in question was a president of the United States. But their interpretations of the impact of his or her presidency probably would vary greatly.

When investigating controversial issues it is important that one be able to distinguish between statements of fact and statements of opinion.

All of the following statements are taken from the viewpoints in this chapter. Consider each statement carefully. *Mark O for any statement you believe is an opinion or interpretation of facts. Mark F for any statement you believe is a fact.*

If you are doing this activity as a member of a class or group, compare your answers with those of other class or group members. Be able to defend your answers. You may discover that others will come to different conclusions than you. Listening to the reasons others present for their answers may give you valuable insights in distinguishing between fact and opinion.

O = *opinion*
F = *fact*

151

1. The long-established tradition of civilian control over the military is eroding.

2. No single organized political interest, party, class, religion, or ethnic group controls American society or government.

3. America is controlled by a small economic elite which owns most of the resources, capital, and property.

4. Congress is owned by special interests.

5. Seen over the broad span of historic time, American society works pretty well.

6. American capitalism is now in considerable part a military capitalism.

7. For conservatives, the keystone to individual rights is the enjoyment of property rights.

8. A socialist is someone who wants to replace the capitalist system with a system of public and communal ownership.

9. Big business doesn't run the country.

10. The American people generally enjoy the highest standard of living in the world.

11. There is a social upper class in the United States that is a ruling class by virtue of its dominant role in the economy and government.

12. There is an interacting and intermarrying upper social stratum or social elite in America.

13. There is increasing evidence suggesting that many welfare policies, which have been designed and implemented by liberals since the beginnings of the New Deal, have actually created a permanent "welfare caste."

14. The primary fact of American life is that the nation's gross national product—our economic pie—is no longer growing as fast as it once did.

15. Public spirit is widespread enough so that the role the government plays in our lives is more worthy of admiration and faith than of dislike and cynicism.

16. As a general rule, however, the more important a policy is, the less important is the role of self-interest in determining that policy.

Periodical Bibliography

The following periodical articles deal with the subject matter of this chapter.

James Fallows — "The Gridlocked Society," *The Washington Monthly*, March 1983.

Thomas Foley — "When Interest Groups Grade Lawmakers," *U.S. News & World Report*, June 10, 1985.

Andrew Hacker — "What Rules America?" *New York Review*, May 1, 1975.

Jim Leach — "PAC's Americana: The Threat of Political Action Committees," *USA Today*, May 1983.

Phillip Longman — "From Calhoun to Sister Boom-Boom: The Dubious Legacy of Interest Group Politics," *The Washington Monthly*, June 1983.

Brian Lynch — "Independence Day," *American Atheist*, August 1986.

National Forum — "The Citizen and the Government," Spring 1981.

Robert E. Norton — "Citizen Lobbyists," *Fortune*, October 14, 1985.

Madalyn O'Hair — "The Original Intent of the Founding Fathers," *American Atheist*, July 1986.

Irwin Ross — "Why PACs Spell Trouble," *Reader's Digest*, July 1983.

Larry Sabato — "PACs, Parties and Presidents," *Society*, May/June 1985.

Time — "Peddling Influence: Lobbyists Swarm Over Capitol Hill," March 1, 1986.

USA Today — "Special Interests in Control," December 1984.

James Wall — "Who Speaks for the Common Good?" *The Christian Century*, February 15, 1984.

4 CHAPTER

Should the Constitution
Be Revised?

**American
GOVERNMENT**

Chapter Preface

The United States has a constitution that is revered like scripture by many. Its framers are often venerated like prophets of a new political order. It has been amended infrequently—sixteen times since the Bill of Rights was added. The Constitution was formulated to be interpreted, not changed. The task of interpreting the Constitution lies with the Supreme Court. Rarely does the President or Congress challenge or defy the Court. Thus, the Court plays the role of high priest, protector and interpreter.

Because the Constitution is so revered, it is seldom criticized or called to task. In 1974, The Center for Democratic Institutions proposed a model constitution for what it called The New States of America. This heretical document was largely ignored. From 1987 to 1989 attention will be focused on the Constitution as the bicentennial is celebrated across the country (it was written in 1787, ratified in 1788, and became effective in the spring of 1789). In addition to simply celebrating these historic birthdays, we should also examine what we celebrate. Is the Constitution a near-perfect document, the most wonderful work ever struck by human hand, as the eminent 19th-century British Prime Minister William Gladstone claimed? Or is it a tool devised by elites to solidify their power, as claimed by some authors in this chapter? Should a new constitutional convention be called to correct imperfections, or should the Constitution simply be amended? The viewpoints in the following chapter address these pivotal questions.

"The Constitution of the United States was originated . . . by four groups . . . money, public securities, manufactures, and trade and shipping."

The Constitution Is the Result of Economic Self-Interest

Charles A. Beard

When Charles A. Beard's book, *An Economic Interpretation of the Constitution*, was first published in 1913, it created a sensation in academic circles and ignited a controversy that simmers yet today. Beard, a Columbia University historian, scrutinized the Constitution from the viewpoints of the economic interests and conflicts of the late eighteenth century, and of the individual makers and signers. He challenged the prevailing belief that the Constitution was the result of men intending to further the cause of democracy. Instead, he claimed, the Constitution was fashioned by men of property and wealth, working to protect their interests from a growing population and the demands for greater democracy.

As you read, consider the following questions:

1. What economic profile of the members of the Constitutional Convention does the author construct?
2. How does he use the ratification process in South Carolina to support his thesis?

Reprinted with permission of Macmillan Publishing Company from *An Economic Interpretation of the Constitution of the U.S.* by Charles A. Beard. Copyright 1913, 1935 by Macmillan Publishing Company renewed 1941 by Charles A. Beard, renewed 1963 by William Beard and Miriam Beard Vagts.

Suppose it could be shown from the classification of the men who supported and opposed the Constitution that there was no line of property division at all; that is, that men owning substantially the same amounts of the same kinds of property were equally divided on the matter of adoption or rejection—it would then become apparent that the Constitution had no ascertainable relation to economic groups or classes, but was the product of some abstract causes remote from the chief business of life—gaining a livelihood.

Suppose, on the other hand, that substantially all of the merchants, money lenders, security holders, manufacturers, shippers, capitalists, and financiers and their professional associates are to be found on one side in support of the Constitution and that substantially all or the major portion of the opposition came from the non-slaveholding farmers and the debtors—would it not be pretty conclusively demonstrated that our fundamental law was not the product of an abstraction known as "the whole people," but of a group of economic interests which must have expected beneficial results from its adoption? Obviously all the facts here desired cannot be discovered, but the data presented bear out the latter hypothesis, and thus a reasonable presumption in favor of the theory is created.

The Impelling Motive Was Economic Advantage

Of course, it may be shown (and perhaps can be shown) that the farmers and debtors who opposed the Constitution were, in fact, benefited by the general improvement which resulted from its adoption. It may likewise be shown, to take an extreme case, that the English nation derived immense advantages from the Norman Conquest and the orderly administrative processes which were introduced, as it undoubtedly did; nevertheless, it does not follow that the vague thing known as "the advancement of general welfare" or some abstraction known as "justice" was the immediate, guiding purpose of the leaders in either of these great historic changes. The point is, that the direct, impelling motive in both cases was the economic advantages which the beneficiaries expected would accrue to themselves first, from their action. Further than this, economic interpretation cannot go. It may be that some larger world-process is working through each series of historical events; but ultimate causes lie beyond our horizon.

A Survey of Economic Interests in 1787

The whole theory of the economic interpretation of history rests upon the concept that social progress in general is the result of contending interests in society—some favorable, others opposed, to change. On this hypothesis, we are required to discover at the very outset of the present study what classes and social groups existed in the United States just previous to the adoption of the Constitution and which of them, from the nature of their property, might have expected to benefit immediately and definitely by the overthrow of the old system and the establishment of the new. . . .

The Constitution Was Fashioned for Aristocrats

Our revolution was carried out by the landed aristocracy, which simply wanted to cut free from the domination of a foreign nation. They wanted a change of hands, not a change of system. . . .

What was had in America in 1776 was simply a ruling class revolution where the local good-old-boys wanted to break loose of foreign domination. One aspect of that revolution alone is sufficiently revealing to have you get the picture: *Our Constitution was never submitted to popular vote.*

The Constitution, in fact, was fashioned to save the aristocrats (the govern-ors) from any populace (the govern-ees) intervention into the governing process. Therefore, that process was compartmentalized:

(1) separation of powers into the executive, legislative, and judicial;
(2) a system of checks and balances;
(3) staggered elections;
(4) executive veto of legislation;
(5) Senate confirmation of appointees to specific federal offices;
(6) Senate ratification of treaties;
(7) a bicameral legislature.

Madalyn O'Hair, *American Atheist*, July 1986.

A survey of the economic interests of the members of the Convention presents certain conclusions:

A majority of the members were lawyers by profession.

Most of the members came from towns, on or near the coast, that is, from the regions in which personalty was largely concentrated.

Not one member represented in his immediate personal economic interests the small farming or mechanic classes.

The overwhelming majority of members, at least five-sixths, were immediately, directly, and personally interested in the outcome of their labors at Philadelphia, and were to a greater or less extent economic beneficiaries from the adoption of the Constitution.

1. Public security interests were extensively represented in the Convention. Of the fifty-five members who attended no less than forty appear on the Records of the Treasury Department for sums

varying from a few dollars up to more than one hundred thousand dollars. . . .

It is interesting to note that, with the exception of New York, and possibly Delaware, each state had one or more prominent representatives in the Convention who held more than a negligible amount of securities, and who could therefore speak with feeling and authority on the question of providing in the new Constitution for the full discharge of the public debt. . . .

2. Personalty invested in lands for speculation was represented by at least fourteen members. . . .

3. Personalty in the form of money loaned at interest was represented by at least twenty-four members. . . .

4. Personalty in mercantile, manufacturing, and shipping lines was represented by at least eleven members. . . .

5. Personalty in slaves was represented by at least fifteen members. . . .

It cannot be said, therefore, that the members of the Convention were "disinterested." On the contrary, we are forced to accept the profoundly significant conclusion that they knew through their personal experiences in economic affairs the precise results which the new government that they were setting up was designed to attain. As a group of doctrinaires, like the Frankfort assembly of 1848, they would have failed miserably; but as practical men they were able to build the new government upon the only foundations which could be stable: fundamental economic interests.[1] . . .

Ratification in South Carolina

South Carolina presents the economic elements in the ratification with the utmost simplicity. There we find two rather sharply marked districts in antagonism over the Constitution. "The rival sections," says Libby, "were the coast or lower district and the upper, or more properly, the middle and upper country. The coast region was the first settled and contained a larger portion of the wealth of the state; its mercantile and commercial interests were important; its church was the Episcopal, supported by the state." This region, it is scarcely necessary to remark, was overwhelmingly in favor of the Constitution. The upper area, against the Constitution, "was a frontier section, the last to receive settlement; its lands were fertile and its mixed population were largely small farmers. . . . There was no established church, each community supported its own church and there was a great variety in the district."[2]

A contemporary writer, R.G. Harper, calls attention to the fact that the lower country, Charleston, Beaufort, and Georgetown, which had 28,694 white inhabitants, and about seven-twelfths of the representation in the state convention, paid £28,081 : 5 : 10 taxes in 1794, while the upper country, with 120,902 inhabitants, and five-twelfths of the representation in the convention, paid only

£8390 : 13 : 3 taxes. The lower districts in favor of the Constitution therefore possessed the wealth of the state and a disproportionate share in the convention—on the basis of the popular distribution of representation.

These divisions of economic interest are indicated by the abstracts of the tax returns for the state in 1794 which show that of £127,337 worth of stock in trade, faculties, etc. listed for taxation in the state, £109,800 worth was in Charleston, city and county—the stronghold of Federalism. Of the valuation of lots in towns and villages to the amount of 656,272 in the state, £549,909 was located in that city and county.[3]

The records of the South Carolina loan office preserved in the Treasury Department at Washington show that the public securities of that state were more largely in the hands of inhabitants than was the case in North Carolina. They also show a heavy concentration in the Charleston district.

At least fourteen of the thirty-one members of the state-ratifying convention from the parishes of St. Philip and Saint Michael, Charleston (all of whom favored ratification) held over $75,000 worth of public securities. . . .

Of course we have a government of the RICH. You don't expect us to waste government on the poor, do you?

Conclusions

At the close of this long and arid survey—partaking of the nature of catalogue—it seems worthwhile to bring together the important conclusions for political science which the data presented appear to warrant.

The movement for the Constitution of the United States was originated and carried through principally by four groups of personalty interests which had been adversely affected under the Articles of Confederation: money, public securities, manufactures, and trade and shipping.

The first firm steps toward the formation of the Constitution were taken by a small and active group of men immediately interested through their personal possessions in the outcome of their labors.

No popular vote was taken directly or indirectly on the proposition to call the Convention which drafted the Constitution.

A large propertyless mass was, under the prevailing suffrage qualifications, excluded at the outset from participation (through representatives) in the work of framing the Constitution.

The members of the Philadelphia Convention which drafted the Constitution were, with a few exceptions, immediately, directly, and personally interested in, and derived economic advantages from, the establishment of the new system.

The Constitution was essentially an economic document based upon the concept that the fundamental private rights of property are anterior to government and morally beyond the reach of popular majorities.

The major portion of the members of the Convention are on record as recognizing the claim of property to a special and defensive position in the Constitution.

In the ratification of the Constitution, about three-fourths of the adult males failed to vote on the question, having abstained from the elections at which delegates to the state conventions were chosen, either on account of their indifference or their disfranchisement by property qualifications.

The Constitution was ratified by a vote of probably not more than one-sixth of the adult males.

It is questionable whether a majority of the voters participating in the elections for the state conventions in New York, Massachusetts, New Hampshire, Virginia, and South Carolina, actually approved the ratification of the Constitution.

The leaders who supported the Constitution in the ratifying conventions represented the same economic groups as the members of the Philadelphia Convention; and in a large number of instances they were also directly and personally interested in the outcome of their efforts.

In the ratification, it became manifest that the line of cleavage for and against the Constitution was between substantial personalty interests on the one hand and the small farming and debtor interests on the other.

The Constitution was not created by "the whole people" as the jurists have said; neither was it created by "the states" as Southern nullifiers long contended; but it was the work of a consolidated group whose interests knew no state boundaries and were truly national in their scope.

1. The fact that a few members of the Convention, who had considerable economic interests at stake, refused to support the Constitution does not invalidate the general conclusions here presented.
2. O.G. Libby, *Geographical Distribution of the Vote of the Thirteen States on the Federal Constitution*, pp. 42-43.
3. *State Papers:Finance*, vol. 1, p. 462. In 1783 an attempt to establish a bank with $100,000 capital was made in Charleston, S.C., but it failed. "Soon after the adoption of the funding system, three banks were established in Charleston whose capitals in the whole amounted to twenty times the sum proposed in 1783." D. Ramsey, *History of South Carolina* (1858 ed.), vol. 2, p. 106.

"The evidence does not justify the thesis."

The Economic Self-Interest Thesis Is Invalid

Robert E. Brown

In 1956, Robert E. Brown, an associate professor of history at Michigan State University, published a detailed rebuttal of Beard's economic self-interest theory. Brown was critical of Beard's use of evidence. He claimed that Beard used selective evidence, citing only those facts that supported his case while ignoring other pertinent facts. He found Beard guilty of not using the historical method required by historians who wish to construct an accurate record of the past. Brown concluded his book by stating, "After this critical analysis, we should not begin future research on this period of American history with the illusion that the Beard thesis of the Constitution is valid."

As you read, consider the following questions:

1. How does the author respond to Beard's (the author of the previous viewpoint) criticism that no popular vote was taken on the proposition to call the Constitutional Convention?
2. What role does the author suggest the protection of property and wealth played in drafting and ratifying the Constitution?
3. What point does the author make in claiming, "The men at Philadelphia were practical politicians, not political theorists"?

[In his book] Beard summarized his findings in fourteen paragraphs under the heading of "Conclusions" (pp. 324-25). Actually, these fourteen conclusions merely add up to the two halves of the Beard thesis. One half, that the Constitution originated with and was carried through by personalty interests—money, public securities, manufactures, and commerce—is to be found in paragraphs two, three, six, seven, eight, twelve, thirteen, and fourteen. The other half—that the Constitution was put over undemocratically in an undemocratic society—is expressed in paragraphs four, five, nine, ten, eleven, and fourteen. The lumping of these conclusions under two general headings makes it easier for the reader to see the broad outlines of the Beard thesis.

Before we examine these two major divisions of the thesis, however, some comment is relevant on the implications contained in the first paragraph. In it Beard characterized his book as a long and arid survey, something in the nature of a catalogue. Whether this characterization was designed to give his book the appearance of a coldly objective study based on the facts we do not know. If so, nothing could be further from reality. As reviewers pointed out in 1913, and as subsequent developments have demonstrated, the book is anything but an arid catalogue of facts. Its pages are replete with interpretation, sometimes stated, sometimes implied. Our task has been to examine Beard's evidence to see whether it justifies the interpretation which Beard gave it. We have tried to discover whether he used the historical method properly in arriving at his thesis.

Beard's Lack of Historical Method

If historical method means the gathering of data from primary sources, the critical evaluation of the evidence thus gathered, and the drawing of conclusions consistent with this evidence, then we must conclude that Beard has done great violation to such method in this book. He admitted that the evidence had not been collected which, given the proper use of historical method, should have precluded the writing of the book. Yet he nevertheless proceeded on the assumption that a valid interpretation could be built on secondary writings whose authors had likewise failed to collect the evidence. If we accept Beard's own maxim, "no evidence, no history," and his own admission that the data had never been collected, the answer to whether he used historical method properly is self-evident.

Neither was Beard critical of the evidence which he did use. He was accused in 1913, and one might still suspect him, of using only that evidence which appeared to support his thesis. The amount of realty in the country compared with the personalty, the vote in New York, and the omission of the part of *The Federalist* No. 10 which did not fit his thesis are only a few examples of the uncritical use of evidence to be found in the book. Sometimes he accepted secondary accounts at face value without checking them with the sources; at other times he allowed unfounded rumors and traditions to color his work.

The Philadelphia Convention

From his analysis of the Philadelphia Convention, Beard concluded that the Constitution was essentially "an economic document drawn with superb skill" by a "consolidated economic group . . . whose property interests were immediately at stake"; that these interests "knew no state boundaries but were truly national in their scope."

From a thorough reconsideration of the Philadelphia Convention, however, the following facts emerge. Fully a fourth of the delegates in the convention had voted in their state legislatures for paper-money and/or debtor-relief laws. These were the very kinds of laws which, according to Beard's thesis, the delegates had convened to prevent. Another fourth of the delegates had important economic interests that were adversely affected, directly and immediately, by the Constitution they helped write. The most common and by far the most important property holdings of the delegates were not, as Beard has asserted, mercantile, manufacturing, and public security investments, but agricultural property. Finally, it is abundantly evident that the delegates, once inside the Convention, behaved as anything but a consolidated economic group.

In the light of these and other facts it is impossible to justify Beard's interpretation of the Constitution as "an economic document" drawn by a "consolidated economic group whose property interests were immediately at stake."

Forrest McDonald, *We the People: The Economic Origins of the Constitution*, 1958.

Finally, the conclusions which he drew were not justified even by the kind of evidence which he used. If we accepted his evidence strictly at face value, it would still not add up to the fact that the Constitution was put over undemocratically in an undemocratic society by personalty. The citing of property qualifications does not prove that a mass of men were disfranchised. And if we accept his figures on property holdings, either we not know what most of the delegates had in realty and personalty, or we know that realty out numbered personalty three to one (eighteen to six). Simply showing that a man held public securities is not sufficient to prove that he acted only in terms of his public securities. If we ignore Beard's own generalizations and accept only his evidence, we would have to conclude that most of the property in the country in 1787 was real estate, that real property was widely distributed in rural areas, which included most of the country, and that even the men who were directly concerned with the Constitution, and especially Washington, were large holders of realty.

Perhaps we can never be completely objective in history, but certainly we can be more objective than Beard was in this book. Naturally the historian must always be aware of the biases, the subjectivity, the pitfalls that confront him, but this does not mean that he should not make an effort to overcome these obstacles. Whether Beard had his thesis before he had his evidence, as some have said, is a question that each reader must answer for himself. Certain it is that the evidence does not justify the thesis.

A Response to Beard's Fourteen Conclusions

So instead of the Beard interpretation that the Constitution was put over undemocratically in an undemocratic society by personal property, the following fourteen paragraphs are offered as a possible interpretation of the Constitution and as suggestions for future research on that document.

1. The movement for the Constitution was originated and carried through by men who had long been important in both economic and political affairs in their respective states. Some of them owned personalty, more of them owned realty, and if their property was adversely affected by conditions under the Articles of Confederation, so also was the property of the bulk of the people in the country, middle-class farmers as well as town artisans.

2. The movement for the Constitution, like most important movements, was undoubtedly started by a small group of men. They were probably interested personally in the outcome of their labors, but the benefits which they expected were not confined to personal property or, for that matter, strictly to things economic. And if their own interests would be enhanced by a new government, similar interests of other men, whether agricultural or commercial, would also be enhanced.

3. Naturally there was no popular vote on the calling of the convention which drafted the Constitution. Election of delegates by state legislatures was the constitutional method under the Articles of Confederation, and had been the method long established in this country. Delegates to the Albany Congress, the Stamp Act Congress, the First Continental Congress, the Second Continental Congress, and subsequent congresses under the Articles were all elected by state legislatures, not by the people. Even the Articles of Confederation had been sanctioned by state legislatures, not by popular vote. This is not to say that the Constitutional Convention should not have been elected directly by the people, but only that such a procedure would have been unusual at the time. Some of the opponents of the Constitution later stressed, without avail, the fact that the Convention had not been directly elected. But at the time the Convention met, the people in general seemed to be about as much concerned over the fact that they had not elected the delegates as the people of this country are now con-

cerned over the fact that they do not elect our delegates to the United Nations.

4. Present evidence seems to indicate that there were no "propertyless masses" who were excluded from the suffrage at the time. Most men were middle-class farmers who owned realty and were qualified voters, and, as the men in the Convention said, mechanics had always voted in the cities. Until credible evidence proves otherwise, we can assume that state legislatures were fairly representative at the time. We cannot condone the fact that a few men were probably disfranchised by prevailing property qualifications, but it makes a great deal of difference to an interpretation of the Constitution whether the disfranchised comprised ninety-five per cent of the adult men or only five per cent. Figures which give percentages of voters in terms of the entire population are misleading, since less than twenty per cent of the people were adult men. And finally, the voting qualifications favored realty, not personalty.

5. If the members of the Convention were directly interested in the outcome of their work and expected to derive benefits from the establishment of the new system, so also did most of the people of the country. We have many statements to the effect that the people in general expected substantial benefits from the labors of the Convention.

6. The Constitution was not just an economic document, although economic factors were undoubtedly important. Since most of the people were middle-class and had private property, practically everybody was interested in the protection of property. A constitution which did not protect property would have been rejected without any question, for the American people had fought the Revolution for the preservation of life, liberty, and property. Many people believed that the Constitution did not go far enough to protect property, and they wrote these views into the amendments to the Constitution. But property was not the only concern of those who wrote and ratified the Constitution, and we would be doing a grave injustice to the political sagacity of the Founding Fathers if we assumed that property or personal gain was their only motive.

7. Naturally the delegates recognized that the protection of property was important under government, but they also recognized that personal rights were equally important. In fact, persons and property were usually bracketed together as the chief objects of government protection.

8. If three-fourths of the adult males failed to vote on the election of delegates to ratifying conventions, this fact signified indifference, not disfranchisement. We must not confuse those who could *not* vote with those who *could* vote but failed to exercise their right. Many men at the time bewailed the fact that only a

small portion of the voters ever exercised their prerogative. But this in itself should stand as evidence that the conflict over the Constitution was not very bitter, for if these people had felt strongly one way or the other, more of them would have voted.

Even if we deny the evidence which I have presented and insist that American society was undemocratic in 1787, we must still accept the fact that the men who wrote the Constitution believed that they were writing it for a democratic society. They did not hide behind an iron curtain of secrecy and devise the kind of conservative government that they wanted without regard to the views and interests of "the people." More than anything else, they were aware that "the people" would have to ratify what they proposed, and that therefore any government which would be acceptable to the people must of necessity incorporate much of what was customary at the time. The men at Philadelphia were practical politicians, not political theorists. They recognized the multitude of different ideas and interests that had to be reconciled and compromised before a constitution would be acceptable. They were far too practical, and represented far too many clashing interests themselves, to fashion a government weighted in favor of personalty or to believe that the people would adopt such a government.

9. If the Constitution was ratified by a vote of only one-sixth of the adult men, that again demonstrates indifference and not disfranchisement. Of the one-fourth of the adult males who voted, nearly two-thirds favored the Constitution. Present evidence does not permit us to say what the popular vote was except as it was measured by the votes of the ratifying conventions.

10. Until we know what the popular vote was, we cannot say that it is questionable whether a majority of the voters in several states favored the Constitution. Too many delegates were sent uninstructed. Neither can we count the towns which did not send delegates on the side of those opposed to the Constitution. Both items would signify indifference rather than sharp conflict over ratification.

11. The ratifying conventions were elected for the specific purpose of adopting or rejecting the Constitution. The people in general had anywhere from several weeks to several months to decide the question. If they did not like the new government, or if they did not know whether they liked it, they could have voted *no* and there would have been no Constitution. Naturally the leaders in the ratifying conventions represented the same interests as the members of the Constitutional Convention—mainly realty and some personalty. But they also represented their constituents in these same interests, especially realty.

12. If the conflict over ratification had been between substantial personalty interests on the one hand and small farmers and

debtors on the other, there would not have been a constitution. The small farmers comprised such an overwhelming percentage of the voters that they could have rejected the new government without any trouble. Farmers and debtors are not synonymous terms and should not be confused as such. A town-by-town or county-by-county record of the vote would show clearly how the farmers voted.

The Beard Thesis Is Invalid

Professor Charles A. Beard put forward, a century and a quarter after the event, the most famous theory of the convention in his *Economic Interpretation of the Constitution*. This was that the dominant motive of the men who constructed the new instrument of government was that of rescuing their own property interests. . . . Beard's proposition was hasty and, in the sweeping fashion in which he presented it, invalid. . . .

An attentive reading of the records of the convention, plus some knowledge of the earlier and subsequent careers of influential members, was always sufficient to discredit suspicion of their motives. Generally men's personal interests cannot help but form an ingredient in their public advocacies. But we are warranted in believing that at a time of social crisis, when men offer themselves as saviors of the community, their selfish concerns are a tincture, but subordinated to their obligation to their fellows. One is not being sentimental or credulous in ascribing sincerity to those in the convention anxious to redeem America from imbecile government. They had invested more than money in the independence and prosperity of their country. They were men of integrity, incapable of playing a solemn farce in which they mouthed solicitude for the public while they were consciously animated by private purpose. From our ample knowledge of the architects of the new nation we are impelled to judge them men of good will, in fact of noble impulse. Of course they differed in commitment. Some sought places in the convention from ambition, but these were in the minority. More came from a conviction of duty, which may be measured against the refusal of others, in some cases, to be bothered.

Broadus Mitchell & Louise Pearson Mitchell, *A Biography of the Constitution of the United States*, 1964.

13. The Constitution was created about as much by the whole people as any government could be which embraced a large area and depended on representation rather than on direct participation. It was also created in part by the states, for as the *Records* show, there was strong state sentiment at the time which had to be appeased by compromise. And it was created by compromising a whole host of interests throughout the country, without

which compromises it could never have been adopted.

14. If the intellectual historians are correct, we cannot explain the Constitution without considering the psychological factors also. Men are motivated by what they believe as well as by what they have. Sometimes their actions can be explained on the basis of what they hope to have or hope that their children will have. Madison understood this fact when he said that the universal hope of acquiring property tended to dispose people to look favorably upon property. It is even possible that some men support a given economic system when they themselves have nothing to gain by it. So we would want to know what the people in 1787 thought of their class status. Did workers and small farmers believe that they were lower-class, or did they, as many workers do now, consider themselves middle-class? Were the common people trying to eliminate the Washingtons, Adamses, Hamiltons, and Pinckneys, or were they trying to join them?

Two Major Propositions

As did Beard's fourteen conclusions, these fourteen suggestions really add up to two major propositions: the Constitution was adopted in a society which was fundamentally democratic, not undemocratic; and it was adopted by a people who were primarily middle-class property owners, especially farmers who owned realty, not just by the owners of personalty. At present these points seem to be justified by the evidence, but if better evidence in the future disproves or modifies them, we must accept that evidence and change our interpretation accordingly.

After this critical analysis, we should at least not begin future research on this period of American history with the illusion that the Beard thesis of the Constitution is valid. If historians insist on accepting the Beard thesis in spite of this analysis, however, they must do so with the full knowledge that their acceptance is founded on "an act of faith," not an analysis of historical method, and that they are indulging in a "noble dream," not history.

"The Constitution continues to function as intended, serving as a legitimating cloak and workable system for the propertied interests at the expense of the ordinary populace."

The Constitution Is an Elitist Document

Michael Parenti

Michael Parenti is a Visiting Fellow at the Institute for Policy Studies in Washington, DC. In the viewpoint that follows, Parenti argues that the intent of the framers of the Constitution was to contain democracy rather than expand it. He claims the founders were motivated by personal financial interests and not national concerns. The impetus for their deliberations was protection from popular uprisings and pressure, and not a desire to create a democratic utopia.

As you read, consider the following questions:

1. Who does the author claim were the Constitution's framers, and what was their primary purpose?
2. How does Parenti answer the question of whether the framers were motivated by personal or national interests?
3. What proof does he offer to support his claim that the Constitution is an elitist document? Do you agree?

Michael Parenti, "The Constitution as an Elitist Document" in *How Democratic Is the Constitution?* Washington, DC: The American Enterprise Institute, 1980. Reprinted with permission.

How democratic is the Constitution? Not as democratic as we have been taught to believe. I will argue that the intent of the framers of the Constitution was to *contain* democracy, rather than give it free rein, and dilute the democratic will, rather than mobilize it. In addition, their goal was to construct a centralized power to serve the expanding interests of the manufacturing, commercial, land-owning, and financial classes, rather than the needs of the populace. Evidence for this, it will be shown, can be found in the framers' opinions and actions and in the Constitution they fashioned. Finally, I will argue that the elitist design of the Constitution continues to function as intended, serving as a legitimating cloak and workable system for the propertied interests at the expense of the ordinary populace. . . .

Dealing with Insurgency

The Constitution was framed by financially successful planters, merchants, lawyers, and creditors, many linked by kinship and marriage and by years of service in Congress, the military, or diplomatic service. They congregated in Philadelphia in 1787 for the professed purpose of revising the Articles of Confederation and strengthening the powers of the central government. They were impelled by a desire to do something about the increasingly insurgent spirit evidenced among poorer people. Fearful of losing control of their state governments, the framers looked to a national government as a means of protecting their interests. Even in a state like South Carolina, where the propertied class was distinguished by the intensity of its desire to avoid any strong federation, the rich and the well-born, once faced with the possibility of rule by the common people "and realizing that a political alliance with conservatives from other states would be a safeguard if the radicals should capture the state government . . . gave up 'state rights' for 'nationalism' without hesitation," according to Merril Jenson in *The Articles of Confederation.* It swiftly became their view that a central government would be less accessible to the populace and would be better able to provide the protections and services that their class so needed.

The landed, manufacturing, and merchant interests needed a central government that would provide a stable currency; impose uniform standards for trade; tax directly; regulate commerce; improve roads, canals, and harbors; provide protection against foreign imports and against the discrimination suffered by American shipping; and provide a national force to subjugate the Indians and secure the value of western lands. They needed a government that would honor at face value the huge sums of public securities they held and would protect them from paper-money schemes and from the large debtor class, the land-hungry agrarians, and the growing numbers of urban poor. . . .

The specter of Shays' Rebellion hovered over the delegates who gathered in Philadelphia three months later, confirming their worst fears about the populace. They were determined that persons of birth and fortune should control the affairs of the nation and check the "leveling impulses" of that propertyless multitude which composed "the majority faction." "To secure the public good and private rights against the danger of such a faction," wrote James Madison in *Federalist* No. 10, "and at the same time preserve the spirit and form of popular government is then the great object to which our inquiries are directed." Here Madison touched the heart of the matter: how to keep the *spirit* and *form* of popular government with only a minimum of the *substance*, how to provide the appearance of republicanism without suffering its leveling effects, how to construct a government that would win mass acquiescence but would not tamper with the existing class structure, a government strong enough both to service the growing needs of an entrepreneurial class while withstanding the egalitarian demands of the poor and propertyless.

The Founding Fathers Were Men of Wealth and Privilege

Today, 200 years later, we try to forget that the Founding Fathers displayed a distrust of the common man and a fear of democratic rule. With no more than a half-dozen exceptions, the men of the Philadelphia Convention were scions of wealth and privilege, disdaining the people as little more than a dirty mob. As for the inclination toward serious thought by the populace, it was something only to be discouraged. In the words of the young Governeur Morris: "The mob begin to think and reason, Poor reptiles! . . . They bask in the sun, and ere noon they will bite, depend upon it."

Louis Rene Beres, *Washington Post*, May 24, 1987.

The framers of the Constitution could agree with Madison when he wrote in the same *Federalist* No. 10 that "the most common and durable source of factions has been the various and unequal distribution of property. Those who hold and those who are without property have ever formed distinct interests in society." They were of the opinion that democracy was "the worst of all political evils," as Elbridge Gerry put it. Both he and Madison warned of "the danger of the leveling spirit." "The people," said Roger Sherman, "should have as little to do as may be about the Government." And according to Alexander Hamilton, "All communities divide themselves into the few and the many. The first are the rich and the well-born, the other the mass of the people. . . . The people are turbulent and changing; they seldom judge or determine right." . . .

The propertyless majority, as Madison pointed out in *Federalist*

No. 10 must not be allowed to concert in common cause against the established economic order. First, it was necessary to prevent unity of public sentiment by enlarging the polity and then compartmentalizing it into geographically insulated political communities. The larger the nation, the greater the "variety of parties and interests" and the more difficult it would be for a majority to find itself and act in unison. As Madison argued, "A rage for paper money, for an abolition of debts, for an equal division of property, or for any other wicked project will be less apt to pervade the whole body of the Union than a particular member of it. . . ." An uprising of impoverished farmers could threaten Massachusetts at one time and Rhode Island at another, but a national government would be large and varied enough to contain each of these and insulate the rest of the nation from the contamination of rebellion. . . .

Plotters or Patriots?

The question of whether the founders were motivated by financial or national interest has been debated since Charles Beard published *An Economic Interpretation of the Constitution* in 1913. It was Beard's view that the delegates were guided by their class interests. Arguing against Beard's thesis are those who believe that the framers were concerned with higher things than lining their purses and protecting their property. True, they were moneyed men who profited directly from policies initiated under the new Constitution, but they were motivated by a concern for nation building that went beyond their particular class interests, the argument goes. To paraphrase Justice Holmes, these men invested their belief to make a nation; they did not make a nation because they had invested. "High-mindedness is not impossible to man," Holmes reminded us.

That is exactly the point: High-mindedness is one of man's most common attributes even when, or especially when, he is pursuing his personal and class interest. The fallacy is to presume that there is a dichotomy between the desire to build a strong nation and the desire to protect property and that the delegates could not have been motivated by both. In fact, like most other people, they believed that what was good for themselves was ultimately good for the entire society. Their universal values and their class interests went hand in hand; to discover the existence of the "higher" sentiment does not eliminate the self-interested one.

Most persons believe in their own virtue. The founders never doubted the nobility of their effort and its importance for the generations to come. Just as many of them could feel dedicated to the principle of "liberty for all" and at the same time own slaves, so could they serve both their nation and their estates. The point is not that they were devoid of the grander sentiments of nation building but that *there was nothing in the concept of nation which*

174

worked against their class interest and a great deal that worked for it. . . .

The small farmers, tradesmen, and debtors who opposed a central government have been described as motivated by self-serving parochial interests—as opposed to the supposedly higher-minded statesmen who journeyed to Philadelphia and others of their class who supported ratification. How or why the propertied rich became visionary nation builders is never explained. In truth, it was not their minds that were so much broader but their economic interests. Their motives were neither higher nor lower than those of any other social group struggling for place and power in the United States of 1787-1789. They pursued their material interests as single-mindedly as any small freeholder—if not more so. Possessing more time, money, information, and organization, they enjoyed superior results. How could they have acted otherwise? For them to have ignored the conditions of governance necessary for the maintenance of their enterprises would have amounted to committing class suicide—and they were not about to do that. . . .

The Ultimate Objective of Government

Those who argue that the founders were motivated primarily by high-minded objectives consistently overlook the fact that the delegates repeatedly stated their intention to erect a government strong enough to protect the haves from the have-nots. They gave voice to the crassest class prejudices and never found it necessary to disguise the fact—as have latter-day apologists—that their uppermost concern was to diminish popular control and resist all tendencies toward class equalization (or "leveling," as it was called). Their opposition to democracy and their dedication to the propertied and moneyed interests were unabashedly and openly avowed. Their preoccupation was so pronounced that one delegate did finally complain of hearing too much about how the purpose of government was to protect property. He wanted it noted that the ultimate objective of government was the ennoblement of mankind—a fine sentiment that evoked no opposition from his colleagues as they continued about their business.

Michael Parenti, *How Democratic Is the Constitution?*, 1980.

More important than conjecturing about the framers' motives is to look at the Constitution they fashioned, for it tells a good deal about their objectives. It was, and still is, largely an elitist document, more concerned with securing property interests than personal liberties. Bills of attainder and ex post facto laws are expressly prohibited, and Article I, Section 9, assures us that "the Privilege of the Writ of Habeas Corpus shall not be suspended, unless when in Cases of Rebellion or Invasion the public Safety may require it," a restriction that leaves authorities with a wide measure of discretion. Other than these few provisions, the Constitution that emerged from the Philadelphia Convention gave no attention to civil liberties.

When Colonel Mason suggested to the Convention that a committee be formed to draft "a Bill of Rights"—a task that could be accomplished "in a few hours"—the representatives of the various states offered little discussion on the motion and voted almost unanimously against it. The Bill of Rights, of course, was ratified only after the first Congress and president had been elected.

For the founders, liberty meant something different from democracy; it meant liberty to invest and trade and carry out the matters of business and enjoy the security of property without encroachment by king or populace. The civil liberties designed to give all individuals the right to engage actively in public affairs were of no central concern to the delegates and, as noted, were summarily voted down. . . .

Support for Constitution Was Not Overwhelming

If the Constitution is so blatantly elitist, how did it manage to win enough popular support for ratification? First, it should be noted that it did not have a wide measure of support, initially being opposed in most of the states. But the same superiority of wealth, leadership, organization, control of the press, and control of political office that allowed the rich to monopolize the Philadelphia Convention worked with similar effect in the ratification campaign. Superior wealth also enabled the Federalists to bribe, intimidate, and, in other ways, pressure and discourage opponents of the Constitution. At the same time, there were some elements in the laboring class, especially those who hoped to profit from employment in shipping and export trades, who supported ratification.

Above all, it should be pointed out that the Constitution never was submitted to popular ratification. There was no national referendum and none in the states. Ratification was by state convention composed of elected delegates, the majority of whom were drawn from the more affluent strata. The voters who took part in the selection of delegates were subjected to a variety of property restrictions. In addition, the poor, even if enfranchised, carried all the liabilities that have caused them to be underrepresented in elections before and since: a lack of information and organization, illiteracy, a sense of being unable to have any effect on events, and a feeling that none of the candidates represented their interests. There were also the problems of relatively inaccessible polls and the absence of a secret ballot. Even if two-thirds or more of the adult white males could vote for delegates, as might have been the case in most states, probably not more than 20 percent actually did.

In sum, the framers laid the foundation for a national government, but it was one that fit the specifications of the propertied class. They wanted protection from popular uprisings, from fiscal uncertainty and irregularities in trade and currency, from trade barriers between states, from economic competition by more powerful foreign governments, and from attacks by the poor on property and on creditors. The Constitution was consciously designed as a conservative document, elaborately equipped with a system of minority checks and vetoes, making it hard to enact sweeping popular reforms or profound structural changes, and easy for entrenched interests to endure. It provided ample power to build the services and protections of state needed by a growing capitalist class but not the power for a transition of rule to a different class or to the public as a whole. . . .

Conclusion

The endeavor the framers began in Philadelphia, for a stronger central government to serve the commercial and industrial class, has continued and accelerated. As industrial capitalism has expanded at home and abroad, the burden of subsidizing its endeavors and providing the military force needed to protect its markets, resources, and client states has fallen disproportionately on that level of government which is national and international in scope—the federal—and on that branch which is best suited to carry out the necessary technical, organizational, and military tasks—the executive. The important decisions increasingly are being made in federal departments and corporate boardrooms and in the advisory committees that are linked to the upper echelons of the executive branch, staffed by public policy makers and private representatives of the major industries. . . . By offering well-protected havens for powerful special interests, by ignoring substantive rights and outcomes, by mobilizing the wealth and force of the state in a centralizing and property-serving way, by making democratic change difficult, the Constitution has served well an undemocratic military-industrial corporate structure. The rule of the "minority faction," the "persons of substance," the "propertied interest," the "rich and the well-born"—to mention a few of the ways the founders described their class—has prevailed. The delegates would have every reason to be satisfied with the enduring nature of their work.

"We can have nothing but high praise for what they then produced and handed down to succeeding generations."

The Constitution Was a Magnificent Accomplishment

Mortimer J. Adler

Mortimer J. Adler is chairman of the Board of Editors of the Encyclopaedia Britannica and Director of the Institute for Philosophical Research in Chicago. The author of thirty-eight books, he has spent a lifetime studying and explaining even the most difficult philosophical concepts to the average reader. His most recent book, *We Hold These Truths*, from which this viewpoint is taken, explores the ideas and ideals on which the Constitution is founded. Although he believes the Constitution needs amending, he argues that it remains a magnificent accomplishment for its time.

As you read, consider the following questions:

1. How successfully does the author think the Constitution deals with the six objectives stated in the Preamble?
2. In his opinion, how did the Constitution's drafters relate property holding to suffrage?

Did the Constitution as drafted in 1787, ratified in 1788, and extended by the first ten amendments before the close of the eighteenth century fully realize the ideals set forth in its Preamble and give full effect to the ideas it inherited from the Declaration of Independence? If not, how far did it go in that direction?

To answer the first question negatively and the second by saying not nearly far enough is not to detract from the magnificence of the achievement that we see fit to celebrate in the current years. Perfection is not achieved on earth. It can never be closely approximated in one attempt.

What was achieved in the eighteenth century by American statesmen—a group of brilliant men unequaled since in this country's history—must be measured against the conditions and circumstances of the time in which they were living. Judged in that way, we can have nothing but high praise for what they then produced and handed down to succeeding generations as a basis for carrying their work forward.

There is only one way in which we can soberly assess how to give life to their ideas and how to realize the ideals they had in mind. To accomplish that we must recognize the defects in the Constitution they delivered to us who are alive many generations later.

To Form a More Perfect Union

Of the six objectives stated in the Preamble, the first—to form a more perfect union—was the one most completely realized by the adoption of the federal Constitution, which transformed a plurality of states into one: *E Pluribus Unum.* Let us consider the degree to which the Union was firm and solid before the Civil War and after it. Let us remember that Abraham Lincoln's controlling motive throughout those dire years was to preserve the Union. Thus we cannot fail to see that even the first objective was far from being consummated in the eighteenth century.

To Insure Domestic Tranquility

For largely the same reasons, domestic tranquility was more threatened in the early years of the Republic than in later periods. The seeds of strife between the states, and even within the states, which undermined civil peace were removed—some completely, some partly—by the resolution of the conflict between the states and by the amendments that followed thereupon.

In addition, the indispensable instrument for law enforcement in a republic—a civil police force, not the paramilitary force of a despotic regime—was a mid-nineteenth-century innovation. It is only in the twentieth century that we have recognized the necessity for perfecting its operations as well as the means that must be employed to do so.

To Establish Justice

When we come to the establishment of justice, which certainly involves the equal treatment of equals, we are confronted with one of the two great defects of the eighteenth-century Constitution. Liberty, not equality, was foremost in the minds of our Founding Fathers. They may not have forgotten that the one clearly self-evident truth proclaimed in the Declaration was the equality of all human beings by virtue of their common humanity, but the self-evidence of that truth did not overcome the strong prejudices against equality rampant at the time.

To Promote the General Welfare

We encounter the other of the two great defects when we come to the Preamble's aim to promote the general welfare. The general welfare, as a distinct component in the public common good, must be conceived as the economic welfare of the country as a whole and of its individuals. When the statesmen of the eighteenth century thought about inalienable human rights, they had only political rights in mind.

Not only those thinkers and leaders but also their nineteenth-century descendants were blind to the existence of economic rights in the inventory of inalienable human rights. They did not see that economic goods were needed by all to facilitate the pursuit of happiness, quite as much as were civil peace and political liberty. The recognition of economic rights as natural human rights did not occur until the twentieth century, and that recognition was not even partially implemented by legislation until the midpoint of this century. . . .

To Provide for the Common Defense

Of the Preamble's objectives, two remain to be considered. It is certainly more difficult today to provide for the common defense than it was in the eighteenth century. It is also much more costly. That fact, together with the investment of our resources to promote economic welfare, has resulted in the financial crisis the country now faces. Does this call for a remedy that would involve changes in our Constitution?

To Secure the Blessings of Liberty

Last, but not least, is the Preamble's dedication to securing the blessings—and the inalienable right—to liberty. Inalienable rights can be secured only by safeguarding them through the enforcement of civil rights, either through the provisions of the Constitution itself or through legislative enactments.

Certain provisions in the Constitution, taken together with the first ten amendments—the Bill of Rights—took some of the steps necessary to protect individual freedom. Suspension of the writ of habeas corpus was forbidden except in cases of rebellion or in-

AMERICAN CONSTITUTION

...most wonderful work ever struck off at a given time by the brain and purpose of man.
— Gladstone, 1878

CONSTITUTIONAL CONVENTION RESOLUTIONS

GRAHAM
ROTHCO

vasion; bills of attainder and ex post facto laws were prohibited; trial by jury was required; unreasonable searches and seizures were not allowed.

So far so good, but not nearly far enough to protect individual freedom from unjustifiable governmental interference or constraint. Even more inadequate was the constitutional recognition in the eighteenth century of the inalienable right of all human beings to political liberty—all with the sole exception of those justly excluded from suffrage because of infancy, insanity, or felony. We began to remedy this inadequacy with the post-Civil War amendments, and we have continued in the same direction with amendments adopted in the twentieth century, but we still have not gone the whole distance required to complete the job.

Of all the great ideas, and especially ones that project ideals to be realized, those that fall in the sphere of politics are most subject to change in relation to differing circumstances in successive periods of time. To be deeply sensitive to the limitations of time and circumstance under which our Founding Fathers worked, one need only think of the subsequent developments in this country's life, and of the new institutions and the new problems that they did not contemplate and could not even imagine.

In the eighteenth century, there were few private corporations chartered by government; there were no labor unions having a status politically recognized; there was no public school system; there was no energy shortage; there was no threat to the healthfulness of the environment; there was no need for the Federal Reserve System.

In the eighteenth century, no one would have been able to imagine travel by any means other than by horse or foot on land or by boat on water; to imagine communication by any means other than by direct oral discourse or by the conveyance of handwriting or print on paper; to imagine the spread of industrialization from factories to farms; to imagine the economic interdependence of all the nations of the world; to imagine a national debt of staggering proportions; to imagine world wars and one that might result in nuclear holocaust; to imagine the role that science and its technological applications might play in the operations of government, not only in providing for the common defense but also in promoting the general economic welfare. . . .

The Founding Fathers' Concept of Property and Suffrage

Before we go any further, it is necessary to give some thought to income-producing property, for which another name is capital: the ownership of land or other instruments for the production of wealth.

John Locke, who influenced the thought of many of our Founding Fathers, in formulating the triad of basic natural rights, had said that they were either "life, liberty, and property" or "life, liberty, and estates." In the agricultural preindustrial economy of his day, the possession of landed estates was equivalent to the possession of income-producing property.

When, a little less than a hundred years later, George Mason drafted a Declaration of Rights for adoption by the Virginia Constitutional Convention in 1776, he proclaimed that "all men are by nature equally free . . . and have certain inherent rights," among which are "the enjoyment of life and liberty, with the means of acquiring and possessing property, and pursuing and obtaining happiness and safety."

Thomas Jefferson, as we know, in writing the Declaration of

Independence, altered Mason's phrasing of our inherent human rights, substituting "the pursuit of happiness" for "the means of acquiring and possessing property" and eliminating the words "obtaining" and "safety."

These alterations were more than merely rhetorical. We must attribute to Jefferson a profound understanding of the fact that the possession of income-producing property implemented the right to life and to the pursuit of happiness. For a decent human life and for the pursuit of happiness, a sufficient supply of economic goods is needed. It is also needed for the exercise of political liberty.

America's Spiritual Lodestar

Everything since 1787 has changed except the Constitution and the Bill of Rights. In other lands scores of constitutions have been written and thrown on the junk pile of history. Yet the Constitution of the United States still provides not only a practical outline of the structure, powers and limits of government but also a spiritual lodestar to which Americans turn.

What explains this miracle?

Surely a large part of the explanation lies in the framers' strong sense of the importance of institutional arrangements coupled with their determination that ours be a government of laws and not of men. They were practical politicians responding to the urgent pressures of inflation, commercial warfare and instability. But they were also men of learning who had reflected long and hard on the lessons of history beginning in the Hellenic world. They were keenly aware of human weakness, of the temptations of power, self-interest and ambition; but they also knew noble dedication to the public good. The key—they thought—was to organize the institutions of government for the long run, so as to control the one and channel the other.

Archibald Cox, *Common Cause Magazine*, March/April 1987.

This last point explains why our ancestors thought they were justified in limiting suffrage to men of sufficient property. Only those with landed estates or other income-producing property in the form of industrial capital had enough free time and other advantages, including schooling, to devote to public affairs and to engage in them intelligently.

This was not the case for individuals whose only income derived from the miserable pittances they received for their labors. For them, toil consumed the greater part of their waking lives from early childhood until the grave. They had neither the free time nor the other advantages required for a good use of the political liberty enjoyed by enfranchised citizens. To have conferred suffrage upon them under these circumstances would have jeopardized the conduct of public affairs.

Our ancestors failed to realize that those whom they felt justified in disfranchising by imposing a property qualification for suffrage were not unfit to be citizens by any natural inferiority to men of property, but rather by the economic deprivations they suffered as wage-earners, and by the way in which they were nurtured under the conditions of life that resulted from their being economic have-nots.

Conclusion

It never occurred to our ancestors that if, as human beings, the poor and unpropertied had an equal right to political liberty along with the propertied rich, then they also had a right to the economic conditions that would have made it expedient as well as just to enfranchise them as citizens with suffrage.

As we have already observed, the way in which historic developments actually occurred involved extending the franchise to the laboring poor before it was prudent to do so because they had not yet been surrounded by conditions of life that enabled them to become good citizens and exercise their political liberty for the public good. For the sake of expediency as well as justice, it remained necessary to recognize the existence of economic rights and to secure them for the establishment of the economic as well as political equality that justice requires. Some progress in that direction has been made in this century and especially in recent years. But we must do much more, either by constitutional amendments or by legislative enactments, to establish economic equality and to secure economic rights.

"*Most impartial experts see nothing to fear from a convention.*"

A Call for a Constitutional Convention

National Taxpayers Union

Article V of the Constitution requires Congress to call a constitutional convention at the request of two-thirds (34) of the state legislatures. As this book goes to press, 32 states have called for a limited convention to consider a balanced federal budget amendment. The National Taxpayers Union, a Washington-based lobby dedicated to controlling federal taxes and spending, has been in the forefront of the drive for a convention. In the following viewpoint, the NTU presents its arguments for calling a limited Constitutional Convention.

As you read, consider the following questions:

1. What evidence does the NTU present to back up its claim that the pressure of a successful drive to call a constitutional convention will force Congress to act?
2. The NTU describes eight checks that limit the danger of a runaway convention. Which do you think is the most compelling?

The National Taxpayers Union, "The Hoax of a 'Runaway' Constitutional Convention." Reprinted with permission.

The founding fathers had no way of predicting the current irresponsible spending policies of Congress. Yet although they could not foretell the future, they were men of great wisdom. They did foresee the possibility that Congress might fail the people. It is for that reason that Article V of the U.S. Constitution enables states to amend the Constitution—if Congress fails to act—by calling a limited convention. When 34 state legislatures call for a limited constitutional convention, Congress must propose an amendment or call a limited convention.

Today, through the efforts of the National Taxpayers Union, 32 states have officially called for a limited constitutional convention to consider a balanced federal budget amendment.

As the drive for a convention nears success, Congress will probably propose the amendment on its own, and no convention will be necessary. This has happened before. Congress proposed an amendment to provide for the direct election of U.S. senators only after enough states had called for a convention. Today it's clear that Congress will not propose a balanced budget amendment unless the states again call for a limited convention.

When two more states act, and if Congress still has not acted, a limited convention will be called to write an amendment to restore order to federal finances.

The delegates to a convention would be elected for one purpose only—to draft a balanced budget amendment. They would not have any other powers which Congress has. This convention can only propose a balanced budget amendment.

This amendment would become law only after it is ratified by 38 states.

Many who oppose a constitutional amendment for a balanced federal budget fear a "runaway" constitutional convention.

What the opponents seldom say, however, is that most impartial experts see nothing to fear from a convention. A two-year commission of the American Bar Association, which included the Dean of the Harvard Law School and other leading experts, unanimously concluded that a convention could be limited.

There Are Eight Checks on a Constitutional Convention

The eight checks on a limited constitutional convention would ensure that it stays on the balanced budget amendment topic.

1. Congress could avoid the convention by acting itself.

If 34 states called for a constitutional convention on the balanced budget amendment, the Congress would have the option of proposing such an amendment itself. The odds are overwhelming that the Congress would prefer to do so. Why? Because the Congress would rather live with an amendment which its members drew up themselves than one which was drafted by others. Furthermore, if a convention were successfully held, it would weaken the powers of the Congress. This is something which few of the members of the Congress want. They also do not want to see convention delegates elected from their home districts—delegates who might later decide to challenge the congressmen for reelection.

The Zero Danger of a Runaway Convention

The specter of a "runaway" convention is a disingenuous argument. . . .

To begin with, a convention would not be a gathering of thousands. The entire Constitution (some 8,500 words) was drafted by fewer than 100 people. The proper size of a modern convention would be about 100 people, similar in scope to the platform-writing committees of the major political parties.

Let each state send two delegates to the convention. This could be done by statewide election. Or, in a system that would be easier and faster, the governors could appoint two delegates, with the stipulation that there must be one man and one woman and one Democrat and one Republican in each state delegation. The intense publicity focused on the selection process by the media would go a long way toward ensuring that only responsible, outstanding citizens are chosen. . . .

The zero danger of a "runaway" constitutional convention is doubly confirmed by the fact that neither Congress nor a convention has the power to change the Constitution. Both can only propose that something be changed. Then that proposed amendment must be submitted to the states for their approval. And three-fourths of the states—38 of them—must ratify the amendment before it becomes part of the Constitution. The Founding Fathers created a political gantlet for any amendment to run that is so thorough and tough that only the most important, sensible amendments can ever make it.

Martin Anderson, *The Wall Street Journal*, March 11, 1987.

2. Congress establishes the convention procedures.

Any confusion about how a convention would operate would be the fault of Congress. Congress has the power to determine exactly under what conditions the delegates would be chosen, when the election of delegates would be held, where they would meet, and how they would be paid. Congress can and will limit the agenda of the convention. All 32 state convention calls on the balanced budget issue are limited to that topic and no other.

3. The delegates would have both a moral and a legal obligation to stay on the topic.

There is a long history in the United States of individuals limiting their actions to the job for which they were chosen. Members of the Electoral College could, if they wished, elect anyone to be the President of the United States, even someone who was not a candidate and had received no popular votes. Yet this has never happened. There have been 19,180 electors since 1798 and only seven have voted for a candidate other than the one for whom they were elected. The odds against delegates to a convention behaving differently would be astronomical.

Also, legislation unanimously approved by the Senate Judiciary Committee in 1984 would enforce this limit by requiring that each delegate swear to an oath to limit the convention to the topic for which it was called. Similar legislation has been passed by the Senate twice on unanimous votes.

4. *Voters themselves would demand that a convention be limited.*

Many groups say they oppose an unlimited constitutional convention. So do advocates of the balanced budget amendment. If this is the majority opinion, as it seems to be, it is reasonable to expect that delegates elected to a convention would reflect that view. Certainly if a convention were to be held, every candidate would be asked whether he favored limiting the convention to the subject of the call. Even if the voters in some areas did favor an open convention, or some candidates lied and were elected, it it still improbable that a majority of delegates would be elected who favored opening the convention to another issue when the majority of voters do not.

5. *Even if delegates did favor opening the convention to another issue, it is unlikely that they would all favor opening it to the same issue.*

Opponents of the constitutional convention call on the balanced budget amendment have listed dozens of issues which they allege might be brought up at a constitutional convention. There have been allegations that the Bill of Rights would be tampered with, that amendments would be inserted banning abortion, or doing other things which polls show a majority of the citizens oppose. Yet those who raise these fears have never offered any analysis of where support for such propositions would come from. Consequently, even if it were true that some delegates to a convention would favor reviving the ERA, and others might favor banning abortion, that does not mean that either group would be likely to control a convention. The odds are against it.

6. *Congress would have the power to refuse to send a nonconforming amendment to ratification.*

As the American Bar Association indicated in its study of the amendment by the convention mode, the Congress has yet another way of preventing a runaway amendment. It could simply refuse to send such an amendment to the states for ratification.

7. *Proposals which stray beyond the convention call would be subject to court challenge.*

Leaders in legislatures which have petitioned for a constitutional convention on the balanced budget issue have indicated that they would institute court challenges to any proposal which went beyond their original call. According to the American Bar Association, such challenges are possible to convention-proposed amendments, but not to those which originate in the Congress. There is an excellent chance that the Supreme Court would prohibit a stray amendment from being sent to the states for ratification.

8. *Thirty-eight states must ratify.*

The final and greatest check against a "runaway" convention is the fact that nothing a convention would propose could become part of the Constitution until it was ratified by 38 states. It is by no means easy to obtain 38 states to ratify any controversial proposition. The fate of the ERA and the proposed amendment granting voting representation in Congress for the District of Columbia proves this point. If there are even 13 state legislatures in the country that are not convinced that any amendment proposed by a convention represents an improvement in our Constitution, that amendment would not be ratified. It would mean nothing.

One Hundred Million to One

The odds against many of these events are remote. Even if you assume the odds of all eight of these possibilities are 50-50, the chance that all eight could happen and produce a runaway convention are only four in a thousand. But the odds against many of these events are remote. Even if you assume average odds of just 10-1, the chance of a runaway convention would fall to one in one hundred million.

However you calculate the odds, the danger of a convention "running away" is slight. Much less remote is the danger to our country of continued, runaway deficit spending. Staggering deficits stretch out on the horizon as far as the eye can see. Deficits which mean high interest rates. More high inflation. Or both. We would be fools if we attempted to prove that America would be the exception to the rule that protracted financial turmoil weakens and eventually destroys free institutions. The best way to preserve our constitutional order which we all cherish is a constitutional amendment to bring runaway federal deficits under control.

"The unintended consequences of holding any constitutional convention now are too unknown and may well be too severe to risk."

A Call Against a Constitutional Convention

American Civil Liberties Union

The American Civil Liberties Union (ACLU) is a non-profit organization formed to defend the Bill of Rights. It often initiates litigation on the behalf of unpopular causes and groups, not because it agrees with their views or politics, but because of its goal to protect the constitutional rights of all Americans. The ACLU's annual caseload makes it the largest private law firm in the country. Litigation is only one of its methods of defending civil liberties. Lobbying of legislatures and negotiation with officials are some others. In the viewpoint that follows, the ACLU presents its case against the call for a constitutional convention. Although it is not against changing the Constitution, it claims that a convention would be undemocratic and its results could endanger the rights of Americans.

As you read, consider the following questions:

1. Why does the ACLU oppose the call for a constitutional convention on the balanced budget issue?
2. Why does it claim the convening of a constitutional convention would be undemocratic?
3. How does the ACLU suggest the Constitution be changed?

American Civil Liberties Union, "The Call Against a Constitutional Convention." Reprinted with permission.

The Constitution is the basic law of our land. How can it be changed?

Under Article V of the United States Constitution, there are two ways to change, or amend, the Constitution.

1. Congress, by a vote of two-thirds of both houses, can propose particular amendments.

2. A constitutional convention for the purpose of proposing amendments can be convened by Congress, if two-thirds of the state legislatures ask Congress to do so.

In either case, any amendments proposed become part of the Constitution if ratified by three-quarters of the states.

Has the convention method ever been used to propose amendments?

No. The only constitutional convention in our history was the one that wrote the Constitution in the first place, nearly two hundred years ago. Every amendment to the Constitution since has been proposed by a two-thirds vote of both houses of Congress, and then ratified by three-quarters of the states.

Is there an attempt being made now to have a constitutional convention?

Yes. Although not many people are aware of it, we are very close to the calling of a constitutional convention.

Proponents of a constitutional amendment requiring the federal government to have a balanced budget have succeeded in getting thirty states to call for a convention for that purpose. Only four more states are needed.

In addition, anti-abortion forces have succeeded in getting fifteen states to call for a convention to press for a so-called "human life" amendment that would outlaw abortion.

Does the ACLU oppose the convening of such constitutional conventions?

Yes. The ACLU opposes both convention calls, but for different reasons.

We oppose the call for a convention to propose a "human life" amendment, because such an amendment if passed would prohibit a woman's right to choose to have an abortion.

By declaring the fertilized egg—from the moment of conception—to be equal to a person under the law, the "human life" amendment would impose on all Americans the religious beliefs of some, and would invest the state with more control over women's bodies and lives than has ever before been contemplated. Some experts believe that, under this proposed amendment, women could be tried for murder if they obtained an illegal abortion, or even perhaps for self-aborting.

We oppose any law that abridges civil liberties. We therefore oppose any legislation or amendment that would deny a woman's

"First thing to do is toss out a lot of this
stuff adopted by the previous Convention."

right to choose, and we oppose the call for a constitutional convention whose only purpose is to pass such an amendment.

The Constitution safeguards individual rights. Amendments should be instruments for protecting and expanding these rights, not restricting them. Any constitutional convention designed specifically to eliminate or narrow existing civil rights should be opposed.

But the economic question of whether or not we should have a balanced budget is not a civil liberties issue. Why then does the ACLU oppose the call for a constitutional convention on the balanced budget?

If we were certain that a constitutional convention called for the sole purpose of proposing a balanced budget amendment would limit itself to that purpose, we would probably not oppose it. For example, if the Congress proposed a balanced budget amendment, the ACLU would not take a position on it one way or the other, unless we believed that the specific language of the amendment was discriminatory or otherwise threatened civil liberties.

But no one knows whether a constitutional convention called for one purpose could propose other amendments as well.

Some scholars believe that a constitutional convention can be called *only* for the purpose of proposing general amendments, and not for any single purpose. No one knows for sure, and Article V of the Constitution doesn't say. It is also not clear whether Congress or even the U.S. Supreme Court would have the power to limit a constitutional convention to the purpose for which it was called.

Once a constitutional convention is called for any one purpose, therefore, it could decide to propose other amendments as well. For example, a constitutional convention called for the purpose of proposing a balanced budget amendment could decide to propose an amendment outlawing a woman's right to choose an abortion. For that matter, it could decide to propose amendments to repeal the First Amendment, or other parts of the Bill of Rights.

So what? Isn't it democratic to allow the people to change the Constitution?

No, it isn't democratic as long as the rules governing such conventions are so unclear. For example, some of the thirty states that have called for a constitutional convention for the single purpose of proposing a balanced budget amendment have specified that they would oppose any convention called for any other purpose.

Those states therefore would not have voted to call for a constitutional convention if they believed such a convention would have the power to propose other amendments, such as the "human life" amendment. They assume that a convention called for one purpose would be limited to that purpose.

But no one knows if a convention can be so limited. If some legislatures were aware of that problem, they might well have voted differently.

Is it possible that state legislatures would vote for a constitutional convention that could radically alter our system of government without being aware of it?

It's not only possible, it's what has happened. According to Citizens for the Constitution, a group opposing the current call for a constitutional convention, the resolution calling for a constitutional convention for the purpose of proposing a balanced budget amendment was passed in many state legislatures with hardly any debate or study at all.

- In sixteen states where the resolution has passed, there were no full committee hearings and public witnesses weren't even allowed to testify.
- In fifteen states there were no committee reports.
- In six states there was no recorded vote.

"In many statehouses resolutions to change the Constitution of the United States are introduced at noon and adopted before dinner," U.S. Senator Edmund Muskie has said. "Without a single hearing, without as much debate as a new state song might engender, they endorse a substantial revision of the fundamental law of the land."

It is fairly certain that, at least in these states, there was an assumption that a constitutional convention called for one purpose could be limited to that purpose.

The ACLU believes that if the people and their state legislatures had known of the dangers, the vote to call for a constitutional convention would have been different, and certainly would have not been taken so cavalierly or with so little democratic debate.

Are there other unresolved problems with having a constitutional convention?

Yes. The confusion over whether or not a convention called for one purpose can be limited to that purpose is only one of many unresolved problems. There are others:

- When a state calls for a constitutional convention, does it require votes in both state legislative houses? Must the vote be by two-thirds or is a simple majority sufficient? Can a state governor veto the legislature's call?
- Who would be eligible to serve as a delegate to a constitutional convention? How would such delegates be elected? Could Congress appoint its own members as delegates?
- Must the states be equally represented, as they were at the original constitutional convention in 1787, or must the one-person one-vote rule apply, as it does now in elections for all legislative bodies other than the U.S. Senate?
- May Congress prescribe rules for the convention, or limit its amending power?
- How is the convention to be funded? Could Congress withhold appropriations?

A Second Constitutional Convention Would Be Unwise

I wish I could unhesitantly recommend a second constitutional convention in light of novel conditions and innovations that exist today but did not exist in the preceding centuries and were not even imaginable or conceivable then.

I cannot do so for three reasons. The first is the prevalence in our day of single-issue politics that would prevent a constitutional convention from concentrating on the public common good instead of trying to serve the interests or prejudices of special groups in the population.

My second reason also has to do with the adverse effect on a constitutional convention of certain aspects of contemporary society. The first constitutional convention was conducted in secrecy. No word of the proceedings reached the public until the work was done and the document drafted was ready for submission to the states for ratification. If there were to be a second constitutional convention, it probably could not be conducted in the same way. Its daily sessions would be exposed to the disturbing glare of nationwide publicity, including television broadcasts of the proceedings. Considering the kind of response that this would probably elicit from the general public, and the level of citizenship we now have in this country, it is highly doubtful that a second convention could do its work in an atmosphere conducive to rational deliberation, cool reasoning, and farsighted as well as prudent judgment.

My third and final reason is the absence in our society today of statesmen or persons in public life of a caliber comparable to those who assembled in Philadelphia in 1787. . . .

Even if a second constitutional convention were to assemble statesmen of a character comparable to those who met in Philadelphia in 1787, and even if that second convention could be conducted under circumstances favorable to a good result, the resulting constitution would not find a receptive and sympathetic audience among our present citizenry, to whom it would have to be submitted for adoption.

They would not have the kind of schooling that enabled them to understand its provisions and to appraise their worth. The vast majority would not even be able to read intelligently and critically the kind of arguments in favor of adopting the new constitution that were written by Alexander Hamilton, James Madison, and John Jay, and published in current periodicals in the years 1787 and 1788.

A radical reform of basic schooling in the United States would have to precede any attempt by whatever means to improve our system of government through improving its Constitution.

Mortimer Adler, *We Hold These Truths*, 1987.

- How long could the convention remain in session?
- Could Congress refuse to submit to the states for ratification an amendment proposed by the convention? Could Congress set a short time limit for ratification? Who would decide such disputes between Congress and the convention?

No one knows the answers to these questions. Constitutional scholars disagree. And no one knows if even the U.S. Supreme Court would have the authority to resolve such disputes.

Until these questions are answered, says Harvard law professor Laurence H. Tribe, a leading constitutional scholar, attempts to convene a constitutional convention, for whatever purpose, are "irresponsible, profoundly misguided, and likely to precipitate a constitutional crisis."

The ACLU agrees, and for that reason opposes all current calls for a constitutional convention, regardless of the purpose.

Under current conditions, no legislature that votes for such a convention can possibly know what it is voting for. No citizen who otherwise might want to have a constitutional convention can possibly know what the consequences of a convention would be.

Until the rules governing such conventions are made clear, consistent with principles of fairness and equality of representation, calls for a constitutional convention represent the opposite of democracy. Those who support such calls are asking the American people to buy a pig in a poke.

How can these questions be resolved? Can Congress pass a law that establishes rules governing constitutional conventions?

Yes, Congress can pass such a law. However, it would be much better if the rules governing constitutional conventions were themselves enacted as part of the Constitution. A law passed by Congress might be inadequate because the authority of Congress over a constitutional convention is one of the unanswered questions.

If a constitutional convention, once convened, decided to ignore Congress' authority, it could also ignore any statute Congress passed, and decide to proceed by its own rules. The disputes that would arise would create precisely the kind of constitutional crisis we want to avoid. For that reason, rules governing constitutional conventions would be better established by a constitutional amendment.

That sounds good, but is likely to take a long time. In the meantime, how can people who want to amend the Constitution proceed?

There is the other method of amending the Constitution. As described above, this method allows Congress to propose amendments which, if ratified by three-fourths of the states, become part of the Constitution. Such amendments are proposed one at a time, and this method contains none of the dangers, or unresolved problems, of the convention method.

In any event, the convention method was intended as a drastic alternative, and should probably be reserved for major revisions of the U.S. Constitution, if such revisions are perceived to be necessary by two-thirds of the states.

At the first and only constitutional convention in 1787, the delegates added the calling of a new convention by the states as a safeguard against the power of Congress. Leaving amendments exclusively to the initiative of Congress, George Mason argued, could prove insufficient if Congress itself "should become oppressive." The provision for calling a constitutional convention was written into Article V along with the statement that "no state without its consent shall be deprived of its equal suffrage in the Senate."

"The framers of the Constitution," says Professor Tribe, "thus included the drastic possibility of a new convention, called by the states, as part of an effort to curb the power of Congress in the event of extreme threats to state sovereignty."

The United States was in its infancy when the constitutional convention of 1787 met. No state representative knew for sure how well the new union would work, so it seemed prudent to have a way for the states to force a reconsideration of the master plan.

But the new government did work. For almost 200 years there has been no crisis great enough to warrant the calling of another constitutional convention. And no one thinks there is such a crisis now.

Certainly none of the states that have called for a single-purpose constitutional convention seem to believe any general crisis exists. But such a crisis may well be created, if we go forward with a constitutional convention without first establishing satisfactory rules.

We cannot and should not play dice with the American political system, and with a constitution that has served us well for 200 years. The unintended consequences of holding any Constitutional convention now are too unknown and may well be too severe to risk.

"An ideal series of amendments to the American Constitution would include these, roughly in order of importance."

The Constitution Needs Amending

James L. Sundquist

James L. Sundquist is a senior fellow emeritus in the Brookings Government Studies program at the Brookings Institution. The Institution, founded in 1927, describes itself as "an independent organization, devoted to nonpartisan research, education, and publication in economics, government, foreign policy, and the social sciences." Mr. Sundquist has authored several books for the Institution, including *Dynamics of the Party System* and *The Decline and Resurgence of Congress.* The following viewpoint is excerpted from his most recent book, *Constitutional Reform and Effective Government.* In the book he reviews the debate about whether reform of the US Constitution is needed and raises practical questions about what changes might work best. Although he is skeptical that the Constitution can be changed without the prodding of a political crisis, he suggests several Constitutional amendments should a consensus for change develop.

As you read, consider the following questions:

1. What two dangers to the American political system does the author describe?
2. Why does he place his suggestion for "the team ticket" at the top of his list of recommended amendments?

James L. Sundquist, *Constitutional Reform and Effective Government.* Washington, DC: The Brookings Institution, 1986. Reprinted with permission.

That there has been no powerful popular, or even elitist, movement on behalf of fundamental alteration in the governmental structure at any time in two hundred years testifies that the government has, most of the time, lived up to the expectations of the people. When failures have occurred, they have proven to be temporary and correctable. Yet some of the experienced leaders who are advocating constitutional revision today are profoundly convinced that the United States has been lucky in the past and that, in the future, the deadlock and indecision built into the governmental structure will place the nation in continued peril. Perhaps the country's luck, if that is what it has been, will continue. But there have been enough periods of governmental failure in the nation's past to suggest the imprudence of continuing to rely on providence if the weaknesses in the governmental system can be identified and timely remedies adopted.

In today's world, two dangers seem paramount. One is that the division of power among the president, the Senate, and the House—coupled with a split in partisan control—will render it impossible to achieve what [former] Budget Director David Stockman called "fiscal sanity," and budgetary deficits will grow until they produce a sudden, or a gradual, economic calamity. The other is that division of power will produce a paralysis in foreign policy, with no president of either party able to conduct foreign relations in a coherent and effective manner with the harmonious assured participation and support of congressional majorities. And the consequences of foreign policy failure are magnified with every new generation of more deadly, destructive weapons.

If one accepts the proposition that indecisive, stalemated government can place the nation in peril—and that those risks outweigh the danger that decisive government will make unwise decisions—the preceding chapters suggest a range of remedies. Without regard to the question of what may or may not be politically feasible, an ideal series of amendments to the American Constitution would include these, roughly in order of importance.

1. *The team ticket.* The separation of powers is far more likely to lead to debilitating governmental deadlock when the organs of government are divided between the parties. Several measures give promise of discouraging the ticket-splitting that produces divided government, but only one would prevent it altogether. That is the team ticket, which would combine each party's candidates for president, vice president, Senate, and House into a slate that would be voted for as a unit.

2. *Four-year House terms and eight-year Senate terms.* Even a united government is constantly distracted by the imminence of the next election, which normally limits an incoming president to barely a year as his "window of opportunity" to lead his party in enacting the program for which it sought its victory. The

199

"Our No. 1 priority is to get re-elected.
Can't we shove last year's unfinished business under the rug?"

midterm election now gives the electorate an opportunity to express its objections if an administration performs poorly but it gives them no chance to remedy the situation, for the president remains in office. To eliminate that election and thereby lengthen the period of relative freedom from election pressure would require four-year House terms and either four-year or eight-year Senate terms, with the latter more in accord with the staggered-term tradition of the Senate. Presidents and Congresses alike would be better able to undertake short-term measures that might be unpopular, in order to achieve a greater long-run good, and the legislative process would profit from a more deliberate tempo.

3. *A method for special elections to reconstitute a failed government.*
If the mechanism is to be suitable for use in all of the kinds of

emergency circumstances that can produce governmental failure, the special election should be callable at any time, by the president or a majority of either house of Congress. All seats in both houses, as well as the presidency and vice presidency, should be filled at the election. Those elected should serve full terms (except half the senators would serve for only four years), and the terms could be adjusted by a few months so that the next regular election would fall on the customary November date.

4. *Removal of the prohibition against dual officeholding.* Permitting members of Congress to serve in the executive branch might turn out not to be practical, but removing the prohibition would permit constructive experimentation with that means of linking the executive and legislative branches.

5. *A limited item veto.* An item veto that could be overridden by absolute majorities of the two houses would give the president an important new power with which to combat the rising deficit, yet not upset the executive-legislative balance of power.

6. *Restoration of the legislative veto.* This, too, might be limited, permitting only two-house vetoes.

7. *A war powers amendment.* Writing the essential terms of the War Powers Resolution of 1973 into the Constitution would clear up the unsettled question as to whether that resolution is valid and presidents are required to conform to its provisions.

8. *Approval of treaties by a majority of the membership of both houses.* This would remove the power to dominate critical foreign policy decisions from a minority of the Senate and restore it, like other governmental powers, to the majority.

9. *A national referendum to break deadlocks.* Measures that are in deadlock could be submitted to referendum by both houses of Congress, or by the president and one house. The number to be submitted in any year could be limited to one or two.

These constitutional amendments could be supplemented by statutes and changes in party rules that would serve the same objectives, such as increasing the proportion of members of Congress, candidates for Congress, and other party leaders in presidential nominating conventions and providing for partial financing of congressional campaigns with public funds administered by party committees.

a critical thinking activity

Distinguishing Bias from Reason

A debate or discussion on the Constitution can be a passionate experience. Many citizens regard patriotism, and things American, with a religious-like fervor. Suggesting changes in the Constitution to them would be akin to altering the laws of nature. Other Americans, although taking pride in their national heritage, are more open to revising both their thinking about America and the possibility of amending the Constitution. All Americans have opinions on the functioning of American government. Some of these opinions are based on emotion, and others are based on fact. One of the most important critical thinking skills is the ability to distinguish between opinions based on emotion or bias, and conclusions based on a rational consideration of facts.

The statements that follow are taken from the viewpoints in this chapter. Consider each statement carefully. *Mark R for any statement you believe is based on reason or a rational consideration of the facts. Mark B for any statement you believe is based on bias, prejudice, or emotion. Mark I for any statement you think is impossible to judge.*

If you are doing this activity as a member of a group or class, compare your answers with those of other group or class members. Be able to defend your answers. You may discover that others come to different conclusions than you do. Listening to the reasons others present for their answers may give you valuable insights in distinguishing between bias and reason.

If you are reading this book alone, ask others if they agree with your answers. You will find this interaction very valuable.

> R = *a statement based upon reason*
> B = *a statement based upon bias*
> I = *a statement impossible to judge*

202

1. The Constitution, in fact, was fashioned to save the aristocrats (the govern-ors) from any populace (the govern-ees) intervention into the governing process.

2. A radical reform of basic schooling in the United States would have to precede any attempt by whatever means to improve our system of government through improving its Constitution.

3. The endeavor the framers began in Philadelphia, for a stronger central government to serve the commercial and industrial class, has continued and accelerated.

4. Of the six objectives stated in the Preamble, the first—to form a more perfect union—was the one most completely realized by the adoption of the federal Constitution.

5. The chance of a runaway convention would fall to one in one hundred million.

6. The unintended consequences of holding any constitutional convention now are too unknown and may well be too severe to risk.

7. The intent of the framers of the Constitution was to contain democracy, rather than give it free rein, and dilute the democratic will, rather than mobilize it.

8. Our fundamental law [the Constitution] was not the product of an abstraction known as "the whole people," but of a group of economic interests which must have expected beneficial results from its adoption.

Periodical Bibliography

The following periodical articles deal with the subject matter of this chapter.

Gary Benoit
"Bicentennial Plot: A Scheme Exists to 'Turn the Founders Upside Down'," *The New American*, February 10, 1986.

Charles Colson
"Is the Constitution Out of Date?" *Christianity Today*, August 8, 1986.

Archibald Cox
"The Constitutional Adventure," *Common Cause Magazine*, March/April 1987.

Lloyd N. Cutler
"To Form a Government," *Foreign Affairs*, Fall 1980.

Walter Dellinger
"Con Con Con," *The New Republic*, April 7, 1986.

Ed Doerr
"Our Secular Constitution," *The Humanist*, March/April 1987.

Robert A. Goldwin
"Why Blacks, Women & Jews Are Not Mentioned in the Constitution," *Commentary*, May 1987.

Lino A. Graglia
"Was the Constitution a Good Idea?" *National Review*, July 13, 1984.

A.E. Dick Howard
"The Constitution: Mirror of National Life," *U.S. News & World Report*, December 29, 1986.

Cleo Kocol
"Our Flawed and Glorious Constitution," *The Humanist*, May/June 1987.

Edwin Meese III
"The Battle for the Constitution," *Policy Review*, Winter 1986.

John G. Murray
"Editing the Constitution," *American Atheist*, March 1987.

John T. Noonan Jr.
"Calling for a Constitutional Convention," *National Review*, July 26, 1985.

The Public Interest
Winter 1987. Special Issue on the Constitution.

R.C. Sproul
"The Constitution's Last Chance," *Eternity*, February 1987.

Marvin Stone
"Amend the Constitution?" *U.S. News & World Report*, May 14, 1984.

5 CHAPTER

How Can American Democracy Be Improved?

American GOVERNMENT

Chapter Preface

Since 1982 a small nonpartisan group of influential Americans has been meeting to find solutions for the defects it perceives in American government. The group calls itself the Committee on the Constitutional System, and the first viewpoint of this chapter presents the structural changes it recommends. Also in 1982, the Joint Economic Committee of Congress held three days of hearings, bringing together academics, journalists, and former government officials to discuss how the American political system could be improved. It is clear that problems exist. Voter participation has eroded in recent years and public opinion polls show increasing public dissatisfaction with the functioning of government. Whether it is massive deficits, national borders out of control, or volatile economic cycles, something seems wrong. The Joint Economic Committee indicates a leading reason is a deteriorating political structure.

This chapter brings together the viewpoints of a number of experts. They all suggest different remedies. During the bicentennial celebrations of the next few years more solutions will undoubtedly surface. At least one academic, John Lukacs, in his book *Outgrowing Democracy*, suggests that American democracy reached its peak in the 1950s and has since been in decline. Is he correct? Has the United States, like previous great civilizations, passed its zenith? Or, does the future hold an even greater promise for America's democratic institutions?

"The difficulty lies mainly in the diffuse structure of the executive-legislative process and in the decline of party loyalty and cohesion at all levels of the political system."

The Structure of Government Must Be Changed

Committee on the Constitutional System

The Committee on the Constitutional System is a group of 200 prominent citizens, including present and former members of the Congress, Cabinet and White House staff, governors and party officials, members of academia, journalists, lawyers, and labor, business and financial leaders. It is non-partisan and nongovernmental. It is chaired by Senator Nancy Landon Kassenbaum, Republican of Kansas; C. Douglas Dillon, member of the Eisenhower and Kennedy cabinets; and Lloyd Cutler, former White House Counsel to President Carter. Its purpose is to study the problems of modern American governance and to assess proposed reforms. The following viewpoint proposes constitutional changes recommended by a majority of the Committee's members.

As you read, consider the following questions:

1. What examples does the Committee present to support its claim that the structure of American government is ineffective?
2. How does it suggest the situation be remedied?

Committee on the Constitutional System, *A Bicentennial Analysis of the American Political Structure.* Washington, DC: Committee on the Constitutional System, 1987.

In the last Federalist Paper, Alexander Hamilton urged that the Constitution be ratified despite the objections that were being raised, because there would be opportunity later to make amendments as experience revealed the need. James Madison and Governeur Morris likewise acknowledged imperfections in the framers' brilliant work.

For example, the same document that established the Bill of Rights also countenanced the continued practice of slavery. When that contradiction became apparent over the next century, the resulting constitutional crisis produced a terrible civil war. Abraham Lincoln called a distracted nation to attention with the words, "We must disenthrall ourselves." "The dogmas of the quiet past," he added, "are inadequate to the stormy present. . . . As our case is new, so we must think anew, and act anew." And the Constitution was amended to outlaw slavery, root and branch.

Thomas Jefferson considered the amendment process one of the Constitution's most important features. "I am certainly not an advocate for frequent and untried changes in laws and constitutions," he wrote. "But I know also that laws and institutions must go hand in hand with the progress of the human mind. As that becomes more developed, more enlightened, as new discoveries are made, new truths disclosed, and manners and opinions change with the change of circumstances, institutions must advance also and keep pace with the times."

As Jefferson foresaw, we too face unprecedented challenges. If aspects of the system framed in 1787 prevent the national government from meeting its present responsibilities, we must identify the outmoded features, separate them from the good and durable parts of the system and make the necessary modifications.

To do so is not to reject the great work of our forebears. It honors their spirit in the most sincere way: by seeking to emulate it.

Signs of Strain

As the bicentennial draws near, the signs of strain in our governing processes are unmistakable.

Perhaps the most alarming evidence is the mounting national debt, fueled anew each year by outsized and unsustainable deficits that defy the good intentions of legislators and Presidents.

Consistency in our foreign and national security policies is also frustrated by an institutional contest of wills between Presidents and shifting, cross-party coalitions within the Congress. Over forty treaties submitted to the Senate for ratification since World War II have either been rejected or have never come to a vote. Among those that have never come to a vote are SALT II, the 1974 and 1976 treaties on underground nuclear tests and explosions, maritime boundary treaties with Mexico and Canada, several UN and OAS human rights conventions, and a wide variety of bilateral trade, tax and environmental tactics. Meanwhile presidential concern over "leaks" and frustration with congressionally imposed restrictions have led Presidents and their staffs to launch important diplomatic, military and covert activities in secret and without consulting Congress.

Our System of Government Is Awkward

America confronts subtle, complex and terrifying problems, and our form of government is awkward for dealing with them. Under our present governmental structure, it is difficult to find out who is really in charge in Washington.

Richard L. Strout, *U.S. News & World Report*, July 20, 1981.

Further problems—particularly damaging in a nation dedicated to the principle of self-government—stem from malfunctions of the modern electoral system: the high cost of running for office, the corroding influence of campaign contributions from single-interest groups, the stupefying length of campaigns (for the presidency, usually several years from initiation to inauguration), and persistently low turnout rates (among the lowest in the world for nations with competitive elections).

Causes

Sensing the failures and weaknesses in governmental performance, people tend to blame particular politicians or the complexity of the modern world. But our public officials are no less competent, either individually or as a group, than they used to be. Nor do our problems, as complex as they are, defy rational solutions consistent with our basic constitutional liberties. The difficulty lies mainly in the diffuse structure of the executive-legislative process and in the decline of party loyalty and cohesion at all levels of the political system. . . . .

Effects

Because the separation of powers encourages conflict between the branches and because the parties are weak, the capacity of the federal government to fashion, enact and administer coherent public policy has diminished and the ability of elected officials to avoid accountability for government failures has grown. More specifically, the problems include:

Brief honeymoons. Only the first few months of each four-year presidential term provide an opportunity for decisive action on domestic problems. By the second year, congressional incumbents

209

are engrossed in the mid-term election and defer difficult decisions that will offend any important interest groups.

The mid-term election usually results in a setback for the President's party that weakens his leadership and increases the stalemate and deadlock in the Congress. After the mid-term election, the government comes close to immobility as the President and Congress focus their energies on the imminent presidential election.

Divided government. We have had divided government (one party winning the White House and the other a majority in one or both houses of Congress) 60 percent of the time since 1956 and 80 percent of the time since 1968, compared to less than 25 percent of the time from the adoption of the Constitution until World War II.

This has led to inconsistency, incoherence and even stagnation in national policy. Affirmative policy decisions, as well as the *non*decisions resulting from frequent deadlocks that block any action at all, are reached by shifting majorities built out of cross-party coalitions that change from one issue to the next.

Divided government in turn reflects the decline in party loyalty and the growing practice of ticket-splitting among the electorate. In 1900 only four percent of all congressional districts were carried by one party's presidential candidate and the other party's candidate for Member of the House. By 1984, because of the growth of ticket-splitting, this happened in 44 percent of all congressional districts.

One of Woodrow Wilson's themes during the campaign of 1912 —a time of divided government—was that only party government (with one party successfully bridging the separated powers by winning control of the Presidency and both houses of Congress) could carry a coherent program into effect. The voters in 1912 responded by choosing party government, and Wilson's New Freedom program was successfully legislated.

Lack of party cohesion in Congress. Even in times of united government, disunity persists between the branches—and between and within the two houses of Congress—because many members of both the President's party and the opposition party reject the positions taken by their leaders. Legislators today have less reason to stick with their party's position and more reason to follow the urgings of non-party political action committees, which provide more of their campaign funds than the party does. The summary rejection of President Reagan's budget in 1986, even by members of his own party in the Republican-controlled Senate, dramatically illustrates the lack of party cohesion in the current political environment. This lack of cohesion induces Presidents and their staffs to conceal important foreign policy initiatives even from the leaders of their own party in Congress.

Loss of accountability. Divided government and party disunity also lead to diffused accountability. No elected official defends the sum of all the inconsistent policy decisions made by so many shifting cross-party coalitions, and each successfully shifts the blame to others. Polls show the public is dissatisfied with the governmental institutions—especially Congress and the bureaucracy—that legislate and administer this hodge-podge of policies. But the public seldom holds a party accountable for these failures, and it hardly ever holds individual legislators responsible.

Since World War II, 90 percent of each party's incumbent legislators who sought another term have been reelected, even in years when their party lost the White House. In 1986 the figure was 97 percent. Benjamin Franklin's famous maxim, "We must all hang together, or assuredly we shall all hang separately," no longer applies to the Members of Congress of either party.

A Flawed Power

In other democracies the executive is formed by men and women drawn from the parliament and responsible to it. The American system was created to be different. The branches of government deliberately were set against one another in order to check abusive power. It is an extremely wasteful and inefficient system, but there is a reason for it. . . .

The United States is and will remain, in this respect, a flawed great power. The flaw does not lie in the national character, but in the nation's Constitution, 200 years old this year, and likely to be around for a long time to come.

William Pfaff, *Los Angeles Times*, May 14, 1987.

Lack of a mechanism for replacing failed or deadlocked government. Presently there is no way between our fixed election dates to resolve basic disagreements between our President and Congress by referring them to the electorate. The only way to remove a failed President is by a House impeachment and Senate trial for "treason, bribery, or other high crimes and misdemeanors." And between the fixed election dates there is no way to reorient a Congress in which one or both houses obstruct an important and popular presidential program.

Remedies

In seeking to adjust the constitutional system to modern conditions, we must be careful to preserve its enduring virtues. We must continue to respect the Bill of Rights, protected by an independent judiciary, and we must continue to insist that elected officials be able to monitor one another's performance and call one another to account.

Consistent with these principles, it should be possible to design improvements that would encourage party cohesion and lessen the deadlock between the executive and legislative branches without sacrificing essential checks and balances. The Committee on the Constitutional System offers the following proposals as sufficiently meritorious to warrant national consideration and debate. Some of these proposals call only for adopting new party rules or statutes, while others would require amendments to the Constitution.

Proposals Which Command Majority Support Among Our Membership

Strengthening Parties as Agents of Cohesion and Accountability

1. The Party Presidential Nominating Convention

The parties should amend their rules for the presidential nominating conventions so as to entitle all winners of the party conventions nominations for the House and Senate, plus the holdover Senators, to seats as uncommitted voting delegates in the presidential nominating convention. This would give the congressional candidates of the party a significant voice in selecting the presidential candidate, increase the loyalties between them in the election campaign, improve cohesion between the President and the legislative incumbents of his party and tend to make them jointly accountable to the voters in the next election.

2. Optional Straight-Ticket Balloting

Congress should enact a statute requiring all states to include a line or lever on federal election ballots enabling voters, if they so desire, to cast a straight-line party ballot for a party's candidates for all open federal offices.

A recent survey shows that nineteen states, including Illinois, New York and Pennsylvania, already have such statutes and that ticket-splitting is less common in those states. This would encourage party loyalty at the voter level and among a party's federal candidates. To the extent that it reduced ticket-splitting, it would lessen the likelihood of divided federal government, while still leaving voters free to split their tickets if they chose.

3. Public Financing of Congressional Campaigns

Congress should amend the campaign financing laws to create a Congressional Broadcast Fund similar to the existing Presidential Campaign Fund. This fund would be available to each party under a formula similar to that used for the Presidential Campaign Fund, on condition that the party and its candidates expend no other funds on campaign broadcasts. Half of each party's share would go to the nominees themselves. The other half would go to the party's Senate and House campaign committees, which could apportion the funds among candidates so as to maximize the party's chances of winning a legislative majority.

By requiring candidates to look to the party for a substantial part of their broadcast funds, this proposal would help to build party loyalty and cohesion. It would also provide a constitutional way of limiting expenditures on the largest single component of campaign financing costs.

Improving Collaboration Between the Executive and Legislative Branches

1. Four-year terms for House members and eight-year terms for Senators, with Federal elections every fourth year

The present system of staggered elections has the effect of pulling the branches apart. Members of the House, who run every two years, feel a political need to demonstrate their independence from the White House, particularly in off-year elections. So do the one-third of the Senators who face an election within two years. Every other time an incumbent in either house runs for reelection, there is no presidential campaign.

The effect is to encourage legislators to distance themselves from the President and from presidential programs that may involve a difficult, short-term adjustment on the way to a worthwhile, longer-term result.

Defective Constitution

I do not believe that the meaning of the Constitution was forever "fixed" at the Philadelphia Convention. Nor do I find the wisdom, foresight, and sense of justice exhibited by the Framers particularly profound. To the contrary, the government they devised was defective from the start, requiring several amendments, a civil war, and momentous social transformation to attain the system of constitutional government, and its respect for the individual freedoms and human rights, we hold as fundamental today. When contemporary Americans cite "The Constitution," they invoke a concept that is vastly different from what the Framers barely began to construct two centuries ago.

Thurgood Marshall, speech before the San Francisco Patent and Trademark Law Association, May 6, 1987.

The Constitution could be amended so that the President and Members of the House would serve concurrent, four-year terms, and one Senator from each state would be elected for an eight-year term at each presidential election. This would eliminate the present House and Senate elections in the middle of the presidential term. It would lengthen and coordinate the political horizons of all incumbents. Presidents and legislators could join to enact necessary measures with the promise of longer-run benefits,

213

without having to worry about an imminent election before the benefits were realized.

With fewer elections, the aggregate cost of campaign financing should go down, and legislators would be less frequently or immediately in thrall to the interest groups on whom they depend for funds. The honeymoon for enacting a President's program would be longer. With a four-year life for each Congress, the legislative process for the budget and other measures could be made more orderly and deliberate.

Alternatives: If the eight-year term for Senators were deemed too long, the Senate term could be shortened to four years, concurrent with the terms of the President and the House, which would also eliminate the mid-term election. Or, if the Senate would not accept a shortened term, we could keep the present six-year term. This would retain a limited mid-term election (for one-third of the Senate), permitting a partial referendum on government policy, at the cost of shortening the political horizon of one-third of the Senate.

2. Permitting Members of Congress to Serve in the Cabinet

The Constitution now bars members of Congress from serving as heads of administrative departments or agencies or holding any other executive-branch position. This provision was intended to prevent the President from dominating Congress by offering executive positions to key legislators. But its principal effect has been to deprive the nation of administrators who would have the confidence of both the executive and legislative branches.

If the barrier were moved from the Constitution, Presidents would have the option of appointing leading legislators to cabinet positions, and legislators would have the option of accepting such offers, without being required to give up their seats in Congress. Such ties between the branches might encourage closer collaboration and help to prevent stalemates. They would broaden both the range of talent available to a President in forming his administration and the base of political leadership in the executive branch.

Under such an amendment, of course, a President would not be obliged to appoint any members of Congress to his cabinet, nor would they be obliged to accept.

Woodrow Wilson strongly favored this amendment, as a means to encourage closer collaboration between the branches. While modern legislators may have less time and incentive to join the cabinet than earlier generations, there is no longer any reason for a constitutional barrier to an experiment that has considerable promise and little risk.

3. Relaxing the Requirements for Treaty Ratification

The ability to enter into formal agreements with other nations is vital to effective national government in an increasingly interdependent world. The present constitutional requirement that treaties require the approval of two-thirds of the Senate has been a major barrier to the use of treaties and has led to evasion of the treaty process by way of executive agreements.

To restore an appropriate congressional role in the making of agreements with foreign powers, this provision should be amended to require that treaties can take effect with the approving vote of a constitutional majority of both houses. If the Senate does not join in proposing such an amendment, it should at least approve an amendment reducing the present requirement of approval by two-thirds of the Senate to 60 percent.

Reducing the Costs of Campaigning for Election

The lack of any legal limit on total campaign expenditures has led to a spiraling, competitive escalation in campaign costs. In the 1986 mid-term election, the legislative candidates raised and spent $342 million, up 30 percent over 1984. The cost of campaigning has put a contested seat in Congress beyond the means of everyone who is not either personally wealthy or willing to become dependent on well-heeled special interest groups. The Supreme Court's interpretation of the First Amendment seems to prohibit Congress from limiting private campaign expenditures by legislation, although the Court has authorized public financing on the condition that candidates who accept it limit their expenditures to these federal funds.

A constitutional amendment allowing Congress to set reasonable limits on campaign expenditures would not endanger the freedom of expression guaranteed by the First Amendment. If such an amendment were adopted, many able citizens who now reject the idea of standing for election might be attracted to political office, and the divisive influence of interest group contributions might be reduced to the point where more cohesive government would again become feasible.

Conclusion

In presenting this analysis and list of proposals, the Committee wishes to stress its central conviction. The best way to honor the framers of the Constitution during this bicentennial era is to follow their example.

When the parlous state of affairs under the Continental Congress raised doubts about the fitness of the new nation's frame of government, George Washington and his associates took steps to meet the challenge. They adopted the changes necessary (in the words of the resolution that called the Convention of 1787 into being) to "render the federal Constitution adequate to the exigencies of government and the preservation of the union."

Two hundred years later, we stand in awe of their achievement. We disserve their memory, however, if we ignore signs that our political system today faces challenges that it is not equipped to meet.

We need to face up to these shortcomings in the capacity of our two-hundred-year-old political structure to cope with a global economy and prevent a nuclear war. We may ultimately conclude that these shortcomings can be remedied without major structural changes, or that any major changes needed to correct them would create even greater problems. But we cannot be confident of having reached the right conclusions until we confront the problems, trace them to their roots and examine the alternatives.

It is in this spirit that we offer these proposals.

"Agitation about constitutional reform is a form of escapism, a flight from the hard problem, which is the search for remedy."

The Structure of Government Need Not Be Changed

Arthur Schlesinger Jr.

Arthur M. Schlesinger Jr. won the Pulitzer Prize for History in 1946 for *The Age of Jackson* and the Pulitzer Prize for Biography in 1966 for *A Thousand Days: JFK in the White House.* He is the Albert Schweitzer Professor in the Humanities at City University of New York. In the following viewpoint, taken from testimony presented to a congressional committee investigating constitutional reform, Schlesinger argues that America's political problems are caused by a lack of leadership and not by some kind of structural logjam in our constitutional system. Although he does support some structural adjustments, the main remedies, he claims, are to be found in more effective leadership.

As you read, consider the following questions:

1. What evidence does the author present to support his claim that America's current problems are caused by a lack of leadership and not an inadequate structure?
2. Why does he think a parliamentary system would not work as well as America's current system?
3. What minor structural changes does Schlesinger suggest?

Taken from testimony by Arthur Schlesinger Jr. before the Joint Economic Committee of the Congress of the United States on November 17, 1982.

The question, I take it, that we are examining is this: Is the difficulty we encounter in devising effective remedy for the problems that assail us the consequence of defects in our leadership or of defects in the structure of our Government?

Given the separation of powers, the erosion of party responsibility, the influence of single interest groups and lobbies, is our political system capable any longer of making the decisions necessary to bring our problems under control?

Has not the time come to demand basic constitutional change that by checking or abolishing the separation of powers will restore the capacity of Government to act with decision and dispatch?

Such questions imply that we have only fallen latterly from a golden age in which the process of governmental decision was relatively efficient, political parties were disciplined and responsible, and single interest groups and lobbies were trivial or nonexistent.

But was there ever such a golden age? The historian is bound to observe there is nothing especially new about the conditions that are supposed to have brought our system into its alleged present state of paralysis and crisis.

After all, we have had the separation of powers from the beginning of the Republic. If parties arose in part as a means of overcoming the separation of powers and providing the link between executive and legislative, they have always done so in a haphazard way.

We have never had the disciplined party operation required by the parliamentary system. The reasons for this were clear from the start. Tocqueville pointed them out a century and a half ago. Our legislators, as Tocqueville wrote in 1840, must always "think more of their constituents than of their party—but what ought to be said to gratify constituents is not always what ought to be said in order to serve the party to which representatives profess to belong—hence it is that in democratic countries parties are so impatient of control and are never manageable except in moments of great public danger."

Separation of Powers Need Not Disable Government

Party indiscipline is hardly a latter-day novelty. A loose party system has been necessary to accommodate diverse interests and regions in a far-flung Federal Republic. Nor can anyone who has read the 10th federalist or recalls the Anti-Masons, the abolitionists, the know-nothings, the prohibitionists, the greenbackers, and so on suppose that "factions" as Madison called them—single-issue groups—are an invention of the late 20th century.

Nor can anyone who has read Mark Twain's "The Gilded Age" or meditated on the gaudy 19th-century career of Sam Ward, the "King of the Lobby," take powerful lobbyists as an appalling innovation of our own times.

The constitutional reformers, in short, are protesting what have been in fact the routine conditions of American politics. Yet these conditions—the separation of powers and all the rest—have not prevented competent Presidents from acting with decision and dispatch throughout American history.

The separation of powers did not notably disable Jefferson, Jackson, Lincoln, Wilson, or the Roosevelts. Why are things presumed to be so much worse today?

It cannot be that we face tougher problems than our forefathers: tougher problems than slavery; the Civil War; the Great Depression; the Second World War. Let us avoid the fallacy of self-pity that leads every generation to suppose that it is peculiarly persecuted by history.

Political Problems Should Not Be Mistaken for Structural Defects

Members of the self-appointed Committee on the Constitutional System maintain that they desire only "modest" alterations. But surprisingly radical proposals for change have emanated from the committee. . . .

The committee contends that further amending of the Constitution is required to rectify chronic governmental "confrontation, indecision and deadlock" that have diffused "accountability." Perhaps. But what the committee has proposed would do more harm than good. It would leave Americans with an overly powerful central government that could all too easily disregard public opinion in pursuit of its own agenda.

Members of the Committee on the Constitutional System may mean well enough but they have committed a fundamental error in confusing political problems with structural problems.

The bicentennial of the Constitution would be observed more wisely by considering how to faithfully follow its time-tested provisions than to rush into writing dubious new ones.

Steven Green, *Manchester Union Leader,* February 19, 1987.

The real difference, I submit, is that Presidents who operated the system successfully knew what they thought should be done and were able to persuade Congress and the Nation to give their remedies a try. That possibility remains as open today as it ever was.

In his first year as President, Mr. Reagan, who knew what he thought should be done, pushed a comprehensive economic program through Congress—and did so with triumphant success in spite of the fact that the program is manifestly incapable of achieving its contradictory objectives.

He is in trouble now, not because of the failure of governmental structure, but because of the failure of remedy. If his program had worked, he would be irresistible.

Our Problem Is That We Do Not Know What To Do

Our problem today is not at all that we know what to do and are impeded from doing it by some kind of structural logjam in our political system. Our problem today is that we do not know what to do. We are as analytically impotent before the problem of inflation, for example, as we were half a century ago before the problem of depression.

Our leadership has failed to persuade a durable majority that one or another course will do the job. If we don't know what ought to be done, efficient enactment of a poor program is a dubious accomplishment—as the experience of 1981 surely demonstrates. What is the great advantage of acting with decision and dispatch when you do not know what you are doing?

The issues involved are not new. A century ago foreign visitors levied the same criticism against our governmental structure. Bryce, next to Tocqueville the most illuminating foreign analyst of American institutions, reported in "The American Commonwealth" the British view that the separation of powers, party indiscipline, and the absence of party accountability made it almost impossible for the American political system to settle major national questions.

He also reported the response to this criticism by American political leaders. It was not, in their judgment, because of defects in structure that Congress had not settled these questions, but I quote Bryce:

> Because the division of opinion in the country regarding them has been faithfully reflected in Congress. The majority has not been strong enough to get its way; and this has happened not only because opportunities for resistance arise from the methods of doing business, but still more because no distinct impulse or mandate toward any particular settlement of these questions has been received from the country. It is not for Congress to go faster than the people. When the country knows and speaks its mind, Congress will not fail to act.

When the country is not sure what ought to be done, it may be that delay, debate, and further consideration are not a bad idea. And, when our leadership is sure in its own mind what to do, it must in our democracy educate the rest—and that is not a bad idea either. An effective leader with a sensible policy, or even— as in the recent Reagan case—with a less-than-sensible policy has resources under the present Constitution to get his way.

I believe that in the main our Constitution has worked pretty well. It has insured discussion when we have lacked consensus, and has permitted action when a majority can be persuaded that the action is right. It allowed Franklin Roosevelt, for example, to enact the New Deal but blocked him when he tried to pack the Supreme Court. The Court bill could not have failed if we had had a parliamentary system in 1937.

Do Not Need Constitutional Change

In short, when the Executive has a persuasive remedy, you do not need a basic constitutional change. When the Executive remedy is not persuasive, you do not want basic constitutional change.

Politics in the end is the art of solving substantive problems. There is no greater delusion than the idea that you can solve substantive problems by changing structure.

My frank opinion is that this agitation about constitutional reform is a form of escapism, a flight from the hard problem, which is the search for remedy. Structure may become an alibi for analytical failure. Much as I enjoy this hearing as an intellectual exercise, I cannot refrain from the conviction that your committee would be spending its time more usefully in trying to work out serious answers to the substantive questions of unemployment, inflation, growth, and equity.

I must add that constitution-tinkering could become more than an agreeable intellectual diversion. If there were any reality to the prospect of basic structural change, it would be an enterprise overflowing with hazard.

Burke was right when he warned of the danger of digging into the foundations of the State. As Bryce put it, "It's hard to say, when one begins to make alterations in an old house, how far one will be led on in rebuilding."

Experiment through statute is comparatively harmless. If the law does not work, there is no great difficulty about repealing it. Experiment through constitutional amendment is a very different matter. Once something is in the Constitution, it's hard to get it out—unless it flagrantly offends the good sense and taste of the people, like the 18th amendment [prohibition]. And, once imbedded in the Constitution, "reform" may have unpredictable and far-flung consequences.

I speak with diffidence because of the weight of responsibility and authority my cherished friends, Secretary Dillon, Senator Fulbright, and Dick Strout bring to their advocacy of the parliamentary model; but I must disagree.

Weaknesses of Parliamentary Systems

The argument for the parliamentary system is that the fusion of powers will assure cooperation and partnership between the executive and the legislative branches. In fact, fusion of powers

221

Dramatic Constitutional Change Is Unnecessary

Our political system is in need of repair. Yet I do not think we have reached a condition where, in the words of Livy, "We can endure neither our vices nor their remedies." There are remedies for our ills, we can identify them, and we can bear the costs of them. . . .

I don't happen to be one of those who believes that the problem is one that demands dramatic constitutional changes. It could be said perhaps that we have more anchor than sail in our system, but anchor is sometimes needed, as Watergate certainly showed, and sail is usually forthcoming in times of crisis.

I think that constitutional change can too easily create false expectation of dramatic improvement and, when that improvement is not forthcoming, a willingness to engage in even more Constitution making in the future.

So I would, Mr. Chairman, suggest that, rather than embarking on basic constitutional change, let us rather focus on areas of reform which can be effectuated within the constitutional rules of the game as they now exist.

And I would briefly mention three of the areas where reform is needed, where I think the results could be positive and significant. I have already, I think, said with respect to electoral reform that there are three present problems.

One of them is the power of special interest groups.

Second, I think there is growing evidence of irrationalities in the Presidential nominating process.

And, third, there is the existing structure and the immobility of our present party system.

John B. Anderson, in testimony before the Joint Economic Committee's hearings on Political Economy and Constitutional Reform, November 9, 1982.

---

assures the almost unassailable dominance of the executive over the legislative.

It is noted that the parliamentary system has marked superiority in the promptness and efficiency with which it enacts the executive program. This is true, but it is, of course, a function of Parliament's weakness, not of its strength.

Churchill made the point to Roosevelt in a wartime conversation:

You, Mr. President—

Churchill said—

> are concerned to what extent you can act without the approval of Congress. You don't worry about your Cabinet. On the other hand, I never worry about Parliament, but I continuously have to consult and have the support of my Cabinet.

The Prime Minister appoints people to office without worrying about parliamentary confirmation, concludes treaties without worrying about parliamentary ratification, declares war without worrying about parliamentary authorization, withholds information without worrying about parliamentary subpoenas, is relatively safe from parliamentary investigation, and in many respects has inherited the authority that once belonged to absolute monarchy.

As Lloyd George told the Select Committee on Procedure in Public Business in 1931, "Parliament has really no control over the executive, it is a pure fiction."

While American constitutional reformers muse about the virtue of fusion of power, British reformers yearn for the separation of powers. They want to set Parliament free. They want a formal written bill of rights.

They want standing parliamentary committees with increased professional staff and enlarged powers of investigation and oversight. They want the right to examine witnesses in committee during pending legislation. They want to reduce the power of the whip. They want to end designation of parliamentary candidates by the party organization in favor of open primaries.

They want fixed elections at regular intervals. A former Prime Minister spoke to me a few months ago with envy about our system of midterm elections.

> The only means we have between general elections of bringing national opinion to bear on national policies is through by-elections, and this depends on a sufficiency of MP's resigning or dying. Luck has been with Mrs. Thatcher, and she has had far less than average number of by-elections. How much better to give the whole country a chance to express itself every two years!

Fortunately, I think, given the nature of the American political tradition, the parliamentary system is an unreal alternative. The thought that in this era of conspicuous and probably irreversible party decay we can make our parties more commanding and cohesive than they have ever been is surely an exercise in political fantasy.

Centralized and rigidly disciplined parties, the abolition of primaries, the intolerance of mavericks, the absence of free voting—all such things are against the looser genius of American politics.

I Am Not Opposed to All Structural Adjustments

I would not want to conclude by leaving the impression that I'm opposed to all structural adjustments of our political system. I think there is much to be said, for example, for the proposal of Senator Pell to eliminate lameduck Congresses and lameduck Presidencies by providing that the new Congress after an election should begin on November 15 and the President and Vice

President be inaugurated on November 20.

The length of our transition is a puzzle and bafflement to the rest of the democratic world, and we could do that with much greater efficiency.

I would solve the dilemma of the Electoral College by the "national bonus" plan recommended by the 20th Century Fund task force—which, by awarding a national pool of electoral votes to the winner of the popular vote, would assure the popular winner a majority in the Electoral College while still preserving the Federal system and avoiding a proliferation of Presidential candidates.

I favor reforms of the nomination process which would restrict primaries to a 3-month period in the spring of the Presidential year. I believe that television networks and stations, growing rich off the people's airwaves, should be required to provide free prime time to major political parties during Presidential elections.

I think we must consider a constitutional amendment overriding the *Buckley* v. *Valeo* decision enabling Congress to place effective limits on what candidates for President and Congress can spend on their campaigns.

I'm opposed to the direct election of the President, to the abolition of midterm elections, to the limitation of congressional terms, to the single, 6-year Presidential term.

I would conclude with a reiteration of my plea earlier in these remarks: fascinating as constitution-tinkering may be, like the Rubik cube, let it not divert us from the real task of statecraft. Let us never forget that politics is the high and serious art of solving substantive problems.

"Political parties can serve as the mainspring of democracy, as the vital link between voters and rulers."

America Needs Strong Party Leadership

James MacGregor Burns

James MacGregor Burns is Woodrow Wilson Professor of Government at Williams College in Missouri and a past president of the American Political Science Association. In addition to authoring a number of influential books on American government, he is the the recipient of numerous awards, including the Pulitzer Prize, the National Book Award, and the Woodrow Wilson Foundation Award. In the following viewpoint, excerpted from his book *The Power To Lead*, he argues for a revitalization of political parties to provide elected leaders a stable basis for governing. The great weakness in the American system, according to Burns, is the inability of elected officials to make difficult decisions and take decisive action. A stronger party system would provide both an ideological and a practical base to enable leaders to make the hard and unpopular decisions that are necessary in the daily management of government and to make vital changes in the American constitutional system.

As you read, consider the following questions:

1. What three major steps does the author propose to strengthen the political party system?
2. What important contribution does he attribute to President Ronald Reagan?

James MacGregor Burns, *The Power To Lead*. Copyright © 1984 by James MacGregor Burns. Reprinted by permission of SIMON & SCHUSTER, INC.

Political parties can serve as the mainspring of democracy, as the vital link between voters and rulers. They organize and focus public opinion. They aggregate "special" interests. They provide meaningful cues to voters, present them with alternatives at election time, propose programs, develop among party followers and party leaders in office support for such programs. They unify legislators and executives among themselves and with one another. They help hold government officials accountable to voters. They mobilize popular support for candidates and officeholders and hence are indispensable to democratic leadership. . . .

Party Renewal Is Essential

One fact towers over all others in the relation of party renewal to presidents and other political incumbents: The average officeholder hates a strong party, unless she or he happens to control it. That hate is somewhat logical. Most politicians in America gain high office not through party organizations, as we have seen, but through their personal organizations. They win nominations not by working through the party structure but by winning a primary election. Of course vote seekers are greedy and will accept all the party support they can get. But their heart belongs to the men and women who have worked for them, over the years, through thick and thin, sometimes across party lines. . . .

To a large extent, the weakness of the party system itself permits and encourages casual disregard of the party on the part of other officeholders as well as the President. The gap between candidates and parties will not be bridged until the party regains control of its own nominating process. . . .

Formalizing Party Membership

To restore the national convention to its commanding role in the presidential nomination process, to restore state and local conventions and caucuses to a central role in nominations of candidates for all major offices, we must rethink many aspects of our present selection process. We must ask first, whom have we allowed into the nominating process by opening it up to anyone who wants to come to the polls on presidential-primary day? Largely, to any persons who care to call themselves Democrats or Republicans on one specific day every two or four years. But parties cannot function well if they lack an identifiable membership base, composed of persons who have a demonstrable and long-term commitment to the party. Allowing voters to declare their party affiliation at the primary-election polls (and deaffiliating shortly thereafter if they wish) undermines the foundation on which responsible parties must be built. The first step, then, is the introduction of a mandatory party registration or enrollment requirement necessitating that those persons participating in party processes must be members of that party.

Already, I can hear cries of "elitism!" but I challenge any critic to name a major organization that permits nonmembers to vote for the officers that represent that organization in public life. Why should our political parties operate under different standards when the stakes—for all of us—are so much higher? Such a requirement need not be elitist, exclusionary, nor burdensome—which is why participation reforms are so necessary. It would be the responsibility of the party and election officials overseeing the system to provide notice of enrollment and registration deadlines, actively recruit new members, and develop simple, well-publicized procedures for registration and enrollment.

Parties Are Vehicles for Ideas

In a democracy politics is about something more than the struggle for power or the manipulation of image. It is about the search for remedy. . . .

Ideas are produced by individuals working in solitude. They are refined and extended by informal discussions with other individuals. They are disseminated when political leaders, conscious both of the world's problems and their own ignorance, reach out for counsel. The incubation of remedy depends, not on techniques of party organization, but on the intelligence and resourcefulness of people outside the organization and on the receptivity and seriousness of individual politicians, who will then use the parties as vehicles for ideas.

Arthur M. Schlesinger Jr., *The Cycles of American History*, 1986.

Secondly, the presidential-primary tide must be reversed, even while we try to salvage the better features of the present nomination method. Presidential primaries do expose candidates to public scrutiny, allow them to demonstrate their popularity and electability in November, and provide a forum for discussing issues, however superficially. The problem is that primary outcomes turn on media appeal rather than party support. Let's recognize primaries for what they really are: popularity contests, political "beauty contests." A few states in diverse areas of the country should be permitted to hold advisory presidential primaries so that candidates could demonstrate their political and popular support, *but no national convention delegates would be awarded to candidates on the basis of primary results.* Delegates would be chosen through a party caucus and convention process and allocated proportionately on the basis of the presidential preferences expressed by those participating in this process, not by the voters in the primary. The "beauty contest" results would be merely one of many factors that a party member might take into account in deciding which presidential candidate to support.

My reasons for opposing primaries are not limited to the drawbacks I see in the primary system itself, but also reflect a more positive belief that a caucus-convention system is a superior method for choosing our nominees and has important fringe benefits for our political system. Caucuses offer the party an opportunity for its members who are primarily enthusiastic about a particular candidate to widen their participation by supporting candidates for other offices and taking part in a variety of party activities. Ideally, participants in a caucus not only would come to register their presidential preferences, but would be enlisted as party committee members, assigned to a working subcommittee with a specific function, such as fund raising, membership recruitment, publicity, issue development, or the like, thus reinforcing and expanding the active organizational base of the party. . . .

Enlarging the Role of All Party Members

Finally, the presidential nominating process must try to foster a better relationship among the party's candidates, officeholders, party officials, and party cadres at all levels. The thorniest issue here is the extent to which officeholders should claim favored, even automatic, membership in party nominating conventions—especially, of course, the presidential. . . .

Women and ethnic minorities have engaged in a long but victorious struggle to win their battle for inclusion in party affairs. The automatic granting of voting-delegate status to categories of officeholders—the vast majority of whom are white males—will undercut the party's actual and philosophical commitment toward equal rights and equal opportunity for participation, regardless of race or sex. Even if the "numbers" remained the same—an outcome that is problematic at best—a special class of delegates would be created: an uncommited bloc numerically significant enough to have disproportionate influence at the convention. Once again, and more significantly so, one group of Democrats would be "more equal" than all others. . . .

Such party changes may seem technical and humdrum, but they go to the heart of the problem of linking party to government. They could also help solve other pressing problems in presidential and lesser nominations. They could shorten the present interminable nomination process by requiring delegates to be chosen in the final weeks before the convention. They could diminish excessive media influence by enhancing the parties' deliberative processes. They could elevate the role of the individual delegates in a Burkean sense by making them true representatives of the party electorate. These are the kinds of party *reform* that immensely strengthen party *renewal*. Hence my emphasis on the three major steps I have proposed: formalizing party membership, drastically reducing the number of binding presidential primaries, and enlarging the role of all *party* cadres and leaders in presidential conventions. Other rules may influence the nature of the game and may influence candidate strategies for participating in it, but none will have as significant an impact as any of those three in terms of the long-range growth and true renewal of our parties. . . .

Effective Party Renewal and Constitutional Change

What is the prospect, then, of achieving a constitutional system that fosters majority rule, firm governmental authority, consistent policy, collective leadership, vigorous and principled opposition, open and responsible government? Our only chance, I believe, lies in beginning with modest efforts to strengthen both the constitutional and party structures in the hope that gradual renewals and reforms simultaneously in both the party and constitutional spheres would set up a symbiotic relationship out of which might come major changes. This is a strategy for gradual structuralists.

I would start with the force that serves as the indispensable cutting edge in social or structural change—ideas. In this case the ideas would be policy proposals embodied in party platforms, candidates' promises, and official utterances by leaders in office and in opposition. No basic change is possible, and no change if adopted would work, unless each set of party leaders stands united behind a coherent and balanced set of foreign and domestic policies. . . .

Once renewal was well on its way in both parties, modest efforts to amend the Constitution could be initiated. If the parties had managed sharply to reduce the number of state presidential primaries in which delegates were chosen, it would be safe to amend the Electoral College to make it more equitable, dependable, and more clearly representative of popular majorities. The presidential impeachment process might be strengthened to allow Congress to encourage or effect a resignation or removal of a President who had as clearly lost the confidence of the country for personal or political reasons as Richard Nixon had for moral dereliction. We might adopt the Reuss plan allowing the President to choose for high executive posts members of Congress who would retain their seats, from which they could seek to unify the executive and legislative efforts at collective governing. The "team ticket" might be established, at least covering presidential and House candidates.

Effective party renewal combined with a set of moderate constitutional "process" changes would bring about some modest improvement, at least, in our governance; and each would fortify the other. The question is whether it would be necessary, or even

The Reagan Lesson

Ronald Reagan, defeated in 1976 in his bid to lead the Republican Party, had gathered his followers together again, captured the Republican nomination, revitalized the Grand Old Party, and—in a feat the country had not seen in fifty years—ousted an elected White House incumbent. Now, in office, he was building a presidential team, establishing close ties with Senate and House Republican leaders, pushing big budget and tax programs through Congress, and—most remarkable of all—sharing campaign money and other political resources with the party that had put him into the White House.

Ronald Reagan, in short, was giving us a textbook demonstration of how a leader both mobilizes and engages with his followers, wins office, and works closely with party leadership in governing the nation. . . . Reagan was demonstrating something even more important—that political polarization was not necessarily bad for the American people and might even be good for it. This was bracing news for a people too long lulled by bland and comforting paeans to compromises, centrism, consensus, bipartisanship, "national unity." Leaders of opinion had forgotten that the great forward movements of American democracy had emerged not out of consensus but fiery conflict—out of the struggles between Federalists and Jeffersonians, Whigs and Jacksonians, Free Soil Republicans and slaveholding Democrats, Bryanites and McKinleyites, Roosevelt Progressives and Old Guard Republicans, FDR Democrats and Hoover and Taft Republicans. These conflicts produced a reinvigoration of American democracy and new and more positive directions for the American people. . . .

Ronald Reagan in effect was conducting an experiment for us all—an experiment in party government. He was depending less on the reorganization of *machinery* to enact and implement his policies than on the organization of *power* rising out of militant conservative Republicanism and flowing into the federal government. He might not conduct this experiment well; he might even fail; but he was forcing the American people to re-examine a century-and-a-half-old formula—party government—as a foundation for successful presidential leadership and a strategy for effective government.

James MacGregor Burns, *The Power To Lead*, 1984.

---

possible, to proceed to *structural* change. This is hard to predict. If the initial moves toward party renewal and moderate constitutional change worked well, the pressure for major constitutional restructuring, such as adoption of a parliamentary system, might be lessened. Indeed, these party and constitutional changes might be enough to make the system work tolerably well. If they did not, some leaders would want to return to the old system of divided powers and individualistic leadership.

Others might press for major constitutional restructuring. I doubt that Americans under normal conditions could agree on the package of radical and "alien" constitutional changes that would be required. They would do so, I think, only during and following a stupendous national crisis and political failure. By then any reform might be too late, but if not, at least we should have done our homework. And we can watch the unfolding constitutional experiments abroad. If we should ever make fundamental changes, the remarkable French combination of presidential and parliamentary government may be especially relevant to the American situation. I doubt that we would ever import the pure, classic form of parliamentarianism, as in Britain.

One thing is clear in all this murk. Major changes in process and structure will not be brought about by spontaneous action on the part of the mass public. People as a whole are not interested in the complexities of party organization and constitutional structure; they are interested in practical results. Changes will be brought about by leadership, as in the drafting and adoption of the Constitution of 1787. But today such changes will not be allowed to remain in the hands of a small set of elites, like the fifty-five men who drew up the Constitution. The second and third cadres of American leadership must be fully involved. The most heartening precedent for constitutional change today goes back to the thousands of grass-roots activists who took part in the state constitutional ratifying conventions of 1787-1788.

Do we have a third-cadre leadership of similar intellectual power and creativity today? The answer can be found in the civic and religious groups, in the local Leagues of Women Voters and local bar associations, in the unions and Chambers of Commerce, in the professional organizations, in the schools and colleges and universities of America. . . .

My Proposals

I would propose:

1. Strengthening party and collective leadership in House and Senate and between Congress and the President through reorganizing and integrating committees, agencies, and liaison offices.

2. Converting impeachment into a means of removing Presidents not only when they have committed high crimes and misdemeanors but when they have dramatically and irremediably lost the confidence of the nation.

3. Make the major parties more organized, disciplined, programmatic, and principled so that they might offer meaningful alternatives to the voters, sustain their leadership in office, and pull the government together behind the winning platform.

4. Through constitutional amendment create the "team ticket" by which the voter could cast a single party ballot for President,

senator, and congressman (as voters do now for President and Vice-President), thus creating electoral support for congressional-presidential linkage.

5. Through constitutional amendment adopt the Reuss proposal, enabling the President to choose senators or representatives for Cabinet membership without requiring these legislators to give up their seats in Congress.

Crucial to this whole effort is the development of a leadership and a followship in the Democratic Party that will move the party to the liberal-left, draw to the polls a huge army of the presently non-voting, strengthen the grass-roots foundation of the party, and make clear to the American people not only *what* it proposes to do but *how* it proposes to do it. Inevitably, this would compel the Democratic Party leadership to confront the structural weaknesses discussed [here].

There is a grand precedent for such a grand strategy—the leadership that Jefferson and Madison and their fellow Republicans demonstrated in the 1790s in organizing a new "party of the people," leading it to victory, converting the opposition party into the governing party, creating party instruments in the executive and legislative branches, and generating new sets of leaders in nation, state, and community. Where are the Jeffersons and Madisons today?

"At this point in American history we need a political revitalization as badly as—and in large measure because—we need an economic one."

America Needs a Restructured Political Economy

Robert B. Reich

Robert B. Reich teaches business and public policy at the John F. Kennedy School of Government at Harvard University. Formerly the director of policy planning for the Federal Trade Commission, he is a contributing editor of *The New Republic* and his articles have appeared in numerous publications, including *The New York Times, The Washington Post,* and *Business Week.* In the following viewpoint, exerpted from his book, *The Next American Frontier,* Mr. Reich argues that America's political system must be restructured if it is to reverse its current political and economic decline. He claims adaptation is America's challenge. It is America's next frontier.

As you read, consider the following questions:

1. What point does the author make when using the term America's "ideology of escape"?
2. Why does he claim America's economic decline since the 1960s has political roots?

Since the late 1960's America's economy has been slowly unraveling. The economic decline has been marked by growing unemployment, mounting business failures, and falling productivity. Since about the same time America's politics have been in chronic disarray. The political decline has been marked by the triumph of narrow interest groups, the demise of broad-based political parties, a succession of one-term presidents, and a series of tax revolts.

These phenomena are related. Economics and politics are threads in the same social fabric. The way people work together to produce goods and services is intimately tied to the way they set and pursue public goals. This link is perhaps stronger today than at any time in America's past because we are moving into an era in which economic progress depends to an unprecedented degree upon collaboration in our workplaces and consensus in our politics. . . .

America's Two Cultures

Americans tend to divide the dimensions of our national life into two broad realms. The first is the realm of government and politics. The second is the realm of business and economics. Our concerns about social justice are restricted to the first realm; our concerns about prosperity, to the second. Issues of participation, equality of opportunity and civil rights, public education and mass transit, social security and welfare, housing, pollution, and crime are seen as aspects of government and politics—the substance of our civic culture. Issues of productivity and economic growth, inflation and unemployment, savings, investment, and trade are seen as aspects of business and economics—the substance of our business culture. Democrats and liberals traditionally lay claim to the first realm; Republicans and conservatives, to the second.

Americans whose principal frame of reference is the civic culture charge business with undermining civic values by compromising politicians with campaign contributions, polluting air and water, and endangering workers and consumers. Americans whose principal frame of reference is the business culture feel that government and politics intrude mischievously on the free market, at best distracting businessmen from the vigorous pursuit of national prosperity, at worst subverting the system of individual enterprise. . . .

In countless ways Americans are called upon to choose between these two sets of central values—social justice or prosperity; government or free market; community or freedom. A debate over environmental pollution becomes a contest between the vision of a restored community flourishing within a scenic and healthy environment and the opposite vision of unfettered enterpreneurs whose ambition and daring would create new products and pro-

234

cesses to benefit all. A debate over taxes and government spending becomes a divisive dispute over the relative value of business investment versus such intangibles as education, public health, and income security.

America's Choice

America confronts a choice. We can continue to endure a painful and slow economic transition in which industrial assets and managers are endlessly rearranged through paper entrepreneurialism, political coalitions seek and obtain shelter from foreign competitors, and a growing share of American labor becomes locked into dead-end employment. This kind of transition can lead only to a lower standard of living for many Americans. It will be coupled with political rancor and divisiveness as the steadily shrinking economic pie is divided into ever smaller slices.

The alternative is a dynamic economy in which capital and labor adapt to engage the new realities of international competition. Rapid adjustment offers Americans a rising standard of living. But the politics that must underpin a dynamic economy are far more difficult to achieve. Ultimately America's capacity to respond to economic change will depend on the vitality of its political institutions. Only by acknowledging the powerful links between the social and economic dimensions of our national well-being can we forge a consensus for progress. And only through such a consensus can we craft vigorous institutions and forward-looking strategies to accelerate economic evolution. America's choice is fundamentally a political one.

Robert B. Reich, *The Next American Frontier*, 1983.

This choice is falsely posed. In advanced industrial nations like the United States, drawing such sharp distinctions between government and market has long ceased to be useful. Government creates the market by defining the terms and boundaries for business activity, guided by public perceptions of governmental responsibility for the overall health of the economy. Business, meanwhile, is taking on tasks that once were the exclusive province of government, involving responsibility for the work communities that are coming to be many Americans' most important social environment. The interwoven organizations of government, business, and labor together determine how America's resources are allocated and employed. Public and private spheres are becoming indistinguishable. . . .

The cleavage between the business and civil cultures in America is a legacy of the nation's singular history. That history shaped both America's economic and social organizations and ideology that developed alongside them.

Many of the first settlers came to this continent precisely to escape oppressive governments. The young country's formative political experience involved defying a strong central state in England. The original colonies, many populated by wary social minorities, were anxious to ensure that no one of them would come to dominate the others by gaining control of a powerful government.

During the years when the foundations of America's culture were being fixed, avoiding social conflict was far easier than settling it. The vastness of America's territories enabled generations of Americans to solve social problems by escaping from them, instead of working to change them. So long as the frontier beckoned, the sensible way to settle disputes was not painful negotiation, but simply putting some distance between the disputants. American notion of civic virtue came to center less on cooperating with the neighbors than on leaving them alone.

The ideology of escape from social problems lived on in America long after the nation's physical boundaries set limits to flight. It found expression in nineteenth-century utopian cooperatives and in twentieth-century suburban sprawl. It is still represented in America's vast network of highways and its "love affair" with the automobile. And it continues in our reluctance to acknowledge the end of the era of cheap fossil fuels and to devise strong measures for energy conservation; in our inability to halt the dumping of toxic wastes into aquifers; and within America's wealthy, suburban enclaves, whose residents are almost oblivious to the presence of real poverty in nearby central cities. . . .

Today's Situation

This sparring between the business and civic cultures did little damage while the United States was largely isolated and economically unrivaled. The two cultures could set and pursue their agendas independently—even antagonistically—without disastrous consequences so long as the strength of the economy depended on producing large amounts of standardized products primarily for the nation's huge domestic market. In this era of substantial economic autarky, it did not matter that social and economic policies were at odds with each other and that America lacked any mechanism to accelerate economic change or to forge a social consensus that would allow adaptation. The American economy grew not by evolving, but by taking its basic style of production to its limits—ever larger volumes of standardized goods at ever lower unit costs. This required no real alliance but, at most, a truce, between America's business and civic cultures.

This has changed. The reasons are well known, even if their implications are still not widely recognized. First, Western Europe and Japan have fully recovered from World War II and its disruptive aftermath, and America is now one among several mature industrial countries. The second change will prove to be even more important in the sweep of world economic history: Many developing countries—members of the third world—are emerging as industrial powers. Already much of the world's steel, textiles, rubber, ships, and petrochemicals come from countries not long ago dismissed as backward. Economic development in Asia and Latin America is at least as uneven and traumatic as it was in Europe; but the long-term trend is unmistakable, and it is irrevocably altering the dynamics of international competititon. Finally, postwar technical and institutional innovations have made finance, physical resources, and finished goods more mobile, so that the world is fast becoming a single, highly competitive marketplace. . . .

Adaptation Will be Difficult

Adaptation will be difficult. America's current patterns of organization were once so successful that they have endured long after they have outlived their usefulness. To change the way we conduct our businesses and our government implies a more general change of customs, attitudes, and values which are parts of our cultural heritage. This more fundamental change is emotionally difficult. It becomes even more difficult as economic decline sets in because then change threatens the economic security of people who are desperately trying to hold onto what they have. A new consensus is difficult to achieve when each person seeks to preserve his standard of living but finds that he can only do so at the expense of someone else. But failure to adapt will rend the social fabric irreparably. Adaptation is America's challenge. It is America's next frontier.

Robert B. Reich, *The Next American Frontier*, 1983.

These developments—Europe's and Japan's reconstruction, third world industrialization, and more efficient world trade—should surely be welcome. But together they pose an unprecedented challenge for America. How will the United States adjust to the changing world economy? . . .

The recent progress achieved by Japan and several European countries, and America's relative decline, require no convoluted explanations. For largely historical reasons these countries are organized for economic adaptation. And for largely historical reasons America is not. . . .

America's Choice

America confronts a choice. We can continue to endure a painful and slow economic transition in which industrial assets and managers are endlessly rearranged through paper entrepreneurialism, political coalitions seek and obtain shelter from foreign competitors, and a growing share of American labor becomes locked into dead-end employment. This kind of transition can lead only to a lower standard of living for many Americans. It will be coupled with political rancor and divisiveness as the steadily shrinking economic pie is divided into ever smaller slices.

The alternative is a dynamic economy in which capital and labor adapt to engage the new realities of international competition. Rapid adjustment offers Americans a rising standard of living, but the politics that must underpin a dynamic economy are far more difficult to achieve. Ultimately America's capacity to respond to economic change will depend on the vitality of its political institutions. Only by acknowledging the powerful links between the social and economic dimensions of our national well-being can we forge a consensus for progress. And only through such a consensus can we craft vigorous institutions and forward-looking strategies to accelerate economic evolution. America's choice is fundamentally a political one.

The burdens and benefits of rapid economic change inevitably fall unevenly in the first instance: Older jobs are threatened; older investments, jeopardized; sacrifices are demanded of some for gains that others reap, at least in the first round. But unless citizens trust that these gains and losses will be shared equitably, the groups that stand to lose disproportionately will resist change with every resource at their command. They will prevail. Economic minorities in America hold the power to veto proposals that jeopardize their well-being. This is an invaluable virtue of our political system—giving force to the guarantee against tyranny by the majority—but under the imperative of economic change it is also a substantial challenge. The wide diffusion of effective veto power requires complex negotiations and creative solutions to the problems of economic "losers" before change can occur. American democracy often makes economic change enormously difficult while ensuring that once brought about, the change will by and large be fair. . . .

The Issue Is Political

The issue is political, not economic. The underlying economic relationships are the same in the typical American company as they are in the typical Japanese and continental European company—employees are the major beneficiaries of industrial success and the major victims of industrial failure. But the political relationships are vastly different. The fates of American workers are not directly linked to the success of the particular companies they work for, and they have no formal means of participating in company decisions. In West Germany employees are directly represented on workers' councils and on supervisory boards. In

Japan employees participate through elaborate systems of consultation at all levels of the firm. (Sixteen percent of the board members of Japanese companies have previously been trade union leaders.) In Sweden formal, influential union boards represent workers.*

Present System Not Working

The fact remains that our present federal system is simply not working well—not well enough, in any case, to meet obvious national needs—in a number of areas of decision where the entire future of the country may be at stake. These concern, in the main, matters that require the long view: environmental protection, immigration, drug control, public finance, and, above all, nuclear arms control. In all of these matters the failures are evident; in some of them the Congress even confesses its helplessness. It is idle to shrug these failures off with the comforting reflection that our institutions have worked well enough in the past. So great have been the changes in the physical and technological environment of our lives in this present century that there can be no assurance that what was adequate to the past will continue to be adequate to the future.

George F. Kennan, *The New York Review of Books,* November 6, 1986.

Because the institution of professional management has never taken firm root in continental Europe or Japan, there is not the sharp division of labor between the planning and execution of work that has characterized Anglo-Saxon enterprises. This radical bifurcation of the work force is now having disastrous results in America and Britain. It has defined two distinct corporate cultures that communicate primarily through formal channels of management directives and union complaints. It is keeping the vast repository of information embodied in the work force locked out of the processes of decision. It is sapping workers' sense of common cause with their firms and forcing unions to rely on cumbersome and inefficient shop-floor rules to protect their members' interests. In short, it is destroying the foundation of economic community that now underpins industrial vitality. . . .

Symptoms of America's Political Failure

Economic managers in America and Britain have come to measure the health of their national economies in terms of abstract rates of inflation, interest, unemployment, trade balances, investment, and productivity. They view the world through the eyes of bankers and traders—wedded to abstraction and thus prone to sacrifice the real to the symbolic and the future to the present. They ignore the importance of structural change and adaptability to the nation's economic health and the central role of political choice and compromise in making such change possible.

In their obsession with economic aggregates, these economic managers confuse means with ends. Proximate goals become disconnected from ultimate goals and take precedence over them. The only sensible end of a nation's economic policy should be improving its citizens' standard of living. The concept of "standard of living" is, of course, vague and subjective. But most people probably would agree that it is comprised of at least three elements: the goods and services bought by the nation's citizens; the availability of goods that are not purchased directly but that weigh heavily in most people's sense of well-being, such as clean air and water, protection from crime and accident, and security against medical or financial disaster; and finally, the sense that these goods and services, both private and public, are justly shared among citizens. Such economic goals as growth, higher productivity, lower inflation, and a strong currency are means of achieving a higher standard of living, but they are not ends in themselves. Policies of these aggregate, proximate goals are justifiable, therefore, only as means to achieve an even higher standard of living in the future. The debate over economic abstractions in America and Britain has obscured this most fundamental premise.

A Reliance on the Courts

A further symptom of America's political failure is the nation's increasing reliance on courts and judges to allocate the burdens and benefits of economic change. In recent years political dialogue has been supplanted to an extraordinary degree by adversarial litigation. Courts are now called upon to decide such things as where power plants should be located, how the burdens of a certain bankruptcy should be shared among shareholders and workers, how many trees can be cut from watersheds, how many salmon can be caught by American Indians, which workers should be laid off when a certain factory is automated, who should pay compensation to victims of asbestosis, which large mergers and acquisitions should be barred because they lessen competition, and who should bear the costs of Love Canal and Three Mile Island.

Suffering that at one time would have been a personal misfortune—the random consequence of fate—is now perceived as injustice open to redress through the legal process. The reason is simple. The dynamic behind economic change in America is now understood to be neither the benign neutrality of the free market nor efficient management. The forces propelling economic change in modern America, even if unacknowledged, are the same as in every other advanced industrial nation: the highly discretionary decision of executives in giant companies and administrators in giant government agencies. By virtue of these decisions, some people lose and others gain. But lacking political forums in which these benefits and burdens can be acknowledged and negotiated directly, the losers in America have taken to the courts. Litigation is the only way most citizens can bring officials of large corporations and government agencies to account for their decisions clearly, directly, and truthfully.

But the courts are ill-equipped to settle such issues. These controversies are not so much disputes among individuals as they are political contests among whole segments of the population. Their resolution depends less on findings of fact or interpretations of law than it does on widespread public discussion, negotiation, and consensus. . . .

Reordering the Economy

True democracy must come to the workplace and to the ordering of our economy as a whole. Despite the myth of a free market, all capitalist economies are planned—and have been, to a greater or lesser degree, since at least World War I. When President Reagan rigged the tax system so people would "choose" savings over consumption, that was planning, even if accompanied by hymns to the Invisible Hand. . . .

But it is more dangerous now than ever before. We face a choice between democratic planning on behalf of humane values and the kind of authoritarian, top-down, corporate-governmental planning we have had a taste of in the last few years. If the latter approach prevails, America will come to have the appearance of a Disney World Main Street, programmed by computer-assisted design to yield maximum private profits, while hunger, poverty, and despair are hidden from public view.

Michael Harrington, *Harper's,* March 1984.

These manifestations of America's political failure have a common message. Managerial government, the presumptive neutrality of macro-economic policy, and even the logic of judicial law cannot substitute for political dialogue and choice. There is no "best" solution to how the gains and losses from economic change should be allocated and rearranged. There is an almost infinite range of solutions. And the fairest among them—the one that will generate the broadest commitment to active adjustment—is discoverable only through the messy process of political debate and choice. . . .

The notion that the economic and political spheres of our lives can be separated is relatively new. The very word "economics" was not firmly established until Alfred Marshall wrote his *Principles of Economics* in 1890. Before then the term was "political economy"—with the adjective serving as a constant reminder of the "economy's" origins and effects. The entire field branched off in the late eighteenth century from moral philosophy, the study of citizens' rights, duties, and social obligations. In earlier eras it seemed nonsensical to consider economic relationships in isolation from their specific political and social contexts. Which functions society would entrust to markets and how trade was to be structured were explicitly political issues. . . .

Conclusion

At this point in American history we need a political revitalization as badly as—and in large measure because—we need an economic one. But there is no simple route to such a civic renaissance. Much will depend on the quality of America's future political leadership—not only in our federal, state, and local governments but also in our labor unions, political parties, corporations and business associations, and civic groups. We will need leaders who are not afraid to recognize frankly the political choices that are entailed in major economic change and who are willing to choreograph openly the bargaining about them. American statesmanship must rise above both the myth of the unmanaged market and the myth of neutral management. It must devote itself instead to helping our citizens perceive the consequence of public choices about economic change and to hold accountable those who make these choices in the first instance.

As citizens we must transcend the old categories of civic culture and business culture and recognize the relationship between the nation's social and economic development. Americans concerned with social justice must become familiar with the subtleties of American business and recognize the importance of profit seeking and investment in economic growth. American businessmen must accept that claims for participation and fairness are not obstacles to their mission, but ultimately its very substance.

Finally, we will need political institutions capable of generating large-scale compromise and adaptation. Some of these institutions will be at local and regional levels. But we will also need a national bargaining arena for allocating the burdens and benefits of major adjustment strategies. Such an arena would enable the nation to achieve a broad-based consensus about adjustment. It would enable government, business, and labor to fashion explicit agreements to restructure American industry. Protectionist measures and bailouts to preserve the status quo would be difficult to elicit from government if they were demanded and debated in full view of industrial purchasers, emerging industries, and other groups on whom their costs would fall. Companies seeking financial support or import protection would enter restructuring agreements to ensure that the measures would be temporary and would serve to benefit the overall economy. By the same token, labor and management facing industrial decline would be in a position to negotiate a package of public adjustment assistance designed explicitly to buttress their most competitive operations, retrain their work force, and shift other resources to more profitable uses. Perhaps most important, the single arena could povide a focus for an ongoing national debate about human capital investment and the appropriate allocation of the gains and losses from such change. . . .

The answer is not "national planning," if we take that term to mean the centralized drafting of detailed blueprints for future economic management. We already have that sort of planning. We have had managerial planning for decades—within our giant corporations and government agencies. Managerial planning depends on stability, predictability, and control. It seeks to be apolitical—a legacy of the management era in America. It is becoming dangerously obsolete as America is caught up in the unpredictable dynamic of international competition. Instead, we need political institutions that are as versatile as flexible-system enterprises—less concerned with making "correct" decisions than with making correctable ones; less obsessed with avoiding error than with detecting and correcting for error; more devoted to responding to changing conditions and encouraging new enterprises than to stabilizing the environment for old enterprises. The instruments for implementing active adjustment will not be the blunt tools of historic preservation—broad gauge tariffs, desperate corporate bailouts, and prayerful macroeconomics—but more supple tools like restructuring agreements, training and employment vouchers, regional development funds, and tax and financial codes that guide and accelerate market forces while discouraging paper entrepreneurialism. If we are to become a truly adaptable society, our political choices need to be flexible and experimental. They must be compatible with evolving approaches to emerging problems and opportunities. Change and adaptability must be built into our public and private institutions; rigid planning must be avoided. . . .

We will be able to conquer unemployment and inflation and enjoy enduring economic growth only to the extent that we harness the energy and ideals of all our citizens to the process— spreading the burdens and benefits equitably, making good the losses attendant upon economic change, and striving for justice and decency. A social organization based on greed and fear will fail because it cannot enlist the commitment of all Americans. The notion that social justice must be sacrificed for the sake of economic growth is simply wrong. Social justice is not a luxury bought at the expense of national economic health. It is the means for achieving and maintaining prosperity.

To put it simply, we need an economics that reaffirms our

political life together and a politics that promotes our mutal prosperity. In an advanced industrial economy like ours this is the only
economics, and the only politics, that make lasting sense. Either
we will adapt to this new reality, or following our historical
predecessors, the American ascendancy will needlessly come to
a close.

*For more detailed discussions of these systems of participation, see Japan Federation of
Employees Association (Nikkeiren), *Report of the Committee for the Study of Labor Questions*
(Tokyo, March 1981); Benjamin C. Roberts, Hideaki Okamonto, and George Lodge, *Collective
Bargaining and Employee Participation in Western Europe, North America, and Japan* (New York:
Trilateral Commission, 1979); Beat Hotz, "Productivity Differences and Industrial Relations
Structures," unpublished (1982).

> *"American political life . . . requires a polity in which morally reflective persons debate and decide public questions on the basis of what they and their neighbors believe is just and right."*

America Needs Religious Guidance

Harvey Cox

Harvey Cox, a theologian, has been Victor Thomas Professor of Divinity at Harvard Divinity School since 1970. He has written numerous books on religion and American culture and is a member of the editorial board of *Christianity & Crisis* magazine. In this viewpoint he claims it is essential that religion and religiously motivated people participate in the policy decisions of government. He warns that American democracy is endangered by a process that has become too technical and elitist. He advocates a political process where decisions are based on considerations of what is just and are imbued with moral purpose.

As you read, consider the following questions:

1. The author claims Americans have been distracted from considering religious and moral values in their political deliberations. What two factors does he identify as being partially responsible?
2. What does he think of the presence of religiously motivated people, and the Christian "biblical tradition" in particular, in the political arena?

Harvey Cox, "Our Politics Needs Religion," *The Washington Post National Weekly Edition*, September 17, 1984. © The Washington Post. Reprinted by permission.

The root question raised by the current debate about the role of religion in American political life is surely not whether religious convictions should influence political choices. The answer to that is they always have; they do now; and they probably always will. The question rather is how the larger universe of religious and moral discourse can help to invigorate an enfeebled American political process, which has become so technical and so elite it has nearly ceased being democratic.

America's Political Discourse Needs Religious Input

I believe the vigorous presence in the public arena of religiously motivated people (whether a Jesse Jackson or a Mario Cuomo or the Roman Catholic bishops or the evangelical preachers) should not be viewed as a nuisance but as an opportunity. These people and the millions of others they represent should be welcomed as sources of renewal in a critical conversation that had become jaded and effete, the privileged domain of experts and "policy makers."

Naturally, because we are a religiously pluralistic people, and because our governing institutions are so vast and intricate, the problem of how the religious, moral and political arenas can be brought back in touch will not be an easy one. Still, finding such connections is essential for three reasons:

1. Our politics needs it.
2. Our faith requires it.
3. Our people want it.

In Western political theory moral reasoning and political choice belong together. From Aristotle to Reinhold Niebuhr, from Thomas Aquinas to Abraham Lincoln, our sages have taught that when the two are separated both are diminished. Politics without a vision of the common good becomes something less than politics. It is reduced to the art of brokerage between power interests. It becomes war carried on by other means. In light of this tradition, the present high visibility of religious and moral terms in our political life must be understood as arising not just from some new assertiveness by religious institutions, but as an understandable response to the continuing impoverishment of American political discourse itself.

Cultural Changes Have Subverted Political Discourse

The thinning out of the discourse is not, however, just the result of bad theory. It stems from massive cultural changes that have subverted the Founders' idea of an "active and informed citizenry." One such change comes from the impact of a huge, bureaucratic state, which reduces citizens to clients. The other is the growth of an economy fueled by greed and acquisitiveness, which inevitably twists citizens first into customers and then into consumers. This transformation of sturdy citizens into suppliant clients and bemused consumers of campaign hype has been abetted by the detachment of political judgment from the religious and moral frames of reference within which it was once lodged, for most of our people, throughout most of our history.

Almost all American religious traditions stand in direct opposition to these citizenship-subverting forces. Our religious traditions emphasize restraint. They teach that there are moral limits on acquisitiveness, which are not in keeping with the calculated stimulation of the need for ever more commodities. They deny that one can single-mindedly pursue private gain and yet somehow automatically contribute to the public good. Most important, American religious traditions emphasize the bringing together of citizens to discuss their policy choices in terms of their moral values. Remember the New England town meetings, which often took place in the church. This tradition rejects the notion of citizens as audiences to be researched, persuaded and cajoled.

Religion Strengthens Political Life

At its best, religion deepens politics. It is a wellspring of the civic virtues that democracy requires to flourish. It promotes hard work and individual responsibility. It lifts each citizen outside himself and inspires concern for community and country. At the same time, it offers a sense of purpose and a frame of reference for the claims that transcend everyday politics—claims like our collective responsibility to foster liberty around the globe, and to be kind and good and decent and forgiving in our homes, our schools, and our communities.

US Secretary of Education, William J. Bennett, 1986.

These changes have produced the so-called "market model" of politics, and the result has been the trivialization of ethics. The "ethics commission" of a legislative body today is reduced to dealing with who is stealing the pencils. Meanwhile, the vital link between politics, morality and ultimate beliefs is lost sight of.

Religious Traditions Seek Justice

The most prominent religious traditions in the United States, the Jewish and the Christian, are not accidentally or peripherally concerned about politics. They are essentially and intentionally concerned. They are religious world views in which the political arena is enormously important because they are religions of justice. Think of Moses confronting the Pharaoh; the prophets denouncing the wayward kings; Jesus before Pilate; the popes and the emperors; Martin Luther King at the March on Washington.

In the Jewish and Christian beliefs, God not only created the world but also built into it the foundations of public and private morality: not the specifics, but the foundations. Further, the God of the Jewish and Christian traditions does not dwell beyond history but is active within it as the One who vindicates the poor, comforts the sorrowing and brings peace to the nations. All this necessarily impels the people who believe in such a God to participate in politics.

The purpose of public policy, according to this religious tradition, is not merely to maintain rules of fair play. Its purpose is to seek a justice that is measured in concrete terms by how the most vulnerable and the weakest members of a society fare.

I am not arguing, as some of the "Christian America" advocates sometimes do, that the biblical tradition is the only one we have in American history. There were and are others: the Enlightenment one, and the even older one of republican virtue among them. Still, the biblical traditions are surely ones that deserve to be heard and, with the others, to have a share in the shaping of our common public life. '

Decisions Should Be Based on What Is Just

In the United States, a genuinely public political ethic will have to make room for discussions based on a religious vision of the good because—quite simply—that is the way the majority of our people envision it. Making room for this tradition does not mean allowing it to dominate all others. The critics of those who make political choices on religious grounds often talk about the danger that some people will "impose" their beliefs on others. There is of course always such a danger. But the irony is that a public political discourse that debars religious values would also have to be an imposed one, since the majority of our people think about moral values on the basis of religious beliefs nurtured in liturgy and doctrine, in sacred song and story.

Understandably, some people are afraid that the din of conflicting religious claims will inevitably shred the fragile tissue of civility. I disagree. The word "civility," before it acquired its current sense of politeness and decorum, once meant "that which has to do with the *civitas*," with the obligations and rights of citizens. Those who wish to protect civility in American political life should realize that genuine civility rests on an authentic *civitas*. It requires a polity in which morally reflective persons debate and decide public questions on the basis of what they and their neighbors believe is just and right. This is something neither clients nor consumers can do. But it is something citizens must do.

Still, those of us who draw on religious traditions in the strengthening of the *civitas* should bear in mind that religious people have not always treated their adversaries with restraint and respect (if nonreligious people have been equally guilty, that is another question). The fact is that when religion touches politics it enlivens us but also taxes our capacity for patience and fairness. Consequently, we have a special responsibility. We must demonstrate the kind of civility that reassures others that they are not being accused of bad faith. I doubt that President Reagan helped much when, speaking at the ecumenical prayer breakfast in Dallas, he described those who disagreed with his position as "intolerant of religion."

Moral Purpose Must Inform Political Life

Reinhold Niebuhr used to say that the core insight of all religious faith is the belief that "there is a purpose beyond my purpose." I believe Niebuhr was correct. Against any merely technical view of politics, faith insists that there is a moral purpose that must inform political life. But against any kind of fanaticism it also insists that this purpose cannot be equated with my purpose or the purpose of my group.

Indispensable Supports

Of all the dispositions and habits which lead to political prosperity, religion and morality are indispensable supports.

President George Washington, Farewell Address, 1796.

Perhaps the most important thing faith does for politics is to dignify it: to invest it with a certain weight and seriousness, but not permit it to claim its own ultimacy.

In this, as in so many other things, Abraham Lincoln is still a trustworthy guide. Often attacked and harassed by religious groups, he remains the most profound theologian who has ever served as president. In 1862, during the worst hours of the national agony, when there was every political reason to demonize the South and to sanctify the cause of the Union, Lincoln wrote that "in the present civil war it is quite possible that God's purpose is something different from the purpose of either party." Lincoln went far beyond a politics of brokerage. He saw the larger moral and religious purpose within which politics must proceed. But he refused to claim God for his side even in the midst of a bloody war. He was right on all counts then, and he is still right today.

"I am concerned not so much as to whether you agree with my prescriptions as I am that these prescriptions stimulate you to think about the issues."

Ten Ways To Improve American Politics

John J. Harrigan

A former foreign service officer with the US Information Office, John J. Harrigan is currently a professor of political science at Hamline University in St. Paul, Minnesota. He is the author of several books on political science, including *Political Change in the Metropolis*, and most recently, *Politics and the American Future*, from which the following viewpoint is taken. He suggests ten ways to improve American politics that are primarily prescriptions to strengthen habits of mind rather than to make institutional changes. He claims the challenges facing America are so important that all responsible citizens must become involved, not just politicians.

As you read, consider the following questions:

1. The author suggests that American government show greater concern for those, as he phrases it, "who are left behind." Do you agree?
2. After reading this viewpoint, or better yet, after reading all of the book's viewpoints, how would you prioritize these ten suggestions, from most to least important?

There are no sure-fire ways to reinforce the strengths of the American political system and rectify the weaknesses. I am not inclined to promote a revolution that would radically change the system. And I am also impressed by the limits of what can be accomplished by reform and the tendency to reform to produce unintended consequences. Nevertheless, the challenges our nation faces are so important that I think all responsible citizens have an obligation to begin discussing ways to alleviate some of the political system's weaknesses and to strengthen its virtues. As students of American government, you and I especially have a responsibility to do so. Accordingly, I want to propose for your consideration and discussion ten very modest steps that in my mind would improve the quality of American politics and help our nation cope with its challenges of the future. I am concerned not so much as to whether you agree with my prescriptions as I am that these prescriptions stimulate you to think about the issues involved and develop positions of your own.

1. *Foster an ethic of restraint rather than a philosophy of aggrandizement.*

We should put our support, our votes, and our contributions behind those politicians who have some practical sense of what they can accomplish, who are willing to make sensible compromises to achieve their goals, and who have enough restraint not to seek the destruction of people and groups with viewpoints different from their own. We should not support demagogues who promote unrealistic either-or visions of a world divided into "good guys" and "bad guys" and who lack any sense of restraint in promoting witch hunts that destroy the reputations and careers of their opponents. Former Senator Joseph McCarthy is a typical example of an aggrandizement approach. Fortunately, there are many examples of restraint. Among Democrats there are former Vice President Hubert H. Humphrey, former Senator William Fulbright, and President Franklin D. Roosevelt. Among Republicans there are Senate majority leader Howard Baker and President Dwight D. Eisenhower.

Achieving a philosophy of restraint rather than one of aggrandizement is, of course, much more difficult than advocating it. Most political people are ambitious by inclination. It is hard to imagine many of them going through the rigors of a campaign for office and accepting the personal costs of public life unless they had a considerable amount of ambition to start with. It is certainly very difficult to reach the top of American politics, and for most politicians it takes a heavy dose of ambition to succeed. But I still would prefer to support politicians whose ambition is tempered by a sense of restraint. In my view, candidates who are so single-minded in their pursuit of high office that they are willing to destroy anybody or anything that stands in their way are very

Jim Morin. Copyright © 1987. The Miami Herald. Reprinted with permission.

dangerous.

2. *Strengthen the political parties.*

This is the paramount institutional reform that needs to be made. . . . Unless we reverse the decline of the political parties, we are very likely to see a continuation of several unfortunate trends in American politics. The decline of parties has contributed to making members of Congress increasingly dependent on PACs and increasingly vulnerable to the pressures of single-issue interest groups. It has weakened the ties between presidents (especially Democratic presidents) and Congress. Moreover, the decline of parties has made it more difficult for average citizens to sort out the meaningfulness of elections. To the extent that votes are influenced by televised imagery rather than by partisan affiliation, it is difficult for people to sort out which candidates support their best interests. Because the decline of parties contributes to making elections less meaningful, it also seems to have a logical connection with the decline in voter turnout rates in the last two decades. Party decline is not the sole cause, or even the primary cause, of all these developments. But it has contributed to these trends, and it is hard for me to see how they will be arrested unless we strengthen the party system in this country.

3. *Simplify government, wherever possible.*

There are simply too many governments in America. The number of governments and levels of government involved in administering any particular domestic program often create staggering problems of coordination. The research literature on urban and metropolitan politics is replete with studies showing that poor accountability and limited effectiveness are the common results of the contemporary intergovernmental system. The Reagan Administration made strenuous efforts in its first two years to sort out some of the overlapping responsibilities between federal, state, and local levels of government and to determine which levels of government could best perform particular duties. The administration eventually seemed to lose interest in intergovernmental reform, however, as more pressing political problems drove the issue into the background.

4. *Show greater compassion for the people left behind.*

In St. Paul, Minnesota, where I live and work, the Dorothy Day Center provides free meals and shelter in the winter for the city's street people. For these people, the often subzero winter temperatures are dangerous. The Dorothy Day Center is located downtown in a grubby old building sandwiched between an elegant redevelopment project and a gentrifying neighborhood, where many upper-middle-income people are refurbishing old houses and turning rundown apartments into chic condominiums. Both the downtown redevelopment project and the gentrifying neighborhood have received substantial federal and local government subsidies. However, the Dorothy Day Center receives no federal funds and is staffed by volunteers from local church groups, who often comment that the patrons of the center are truly helpless people. These are the people who have been left behind. They often are mentally retarded, severely emotionally disturbed, or physically handicapped people, who for whatever reason do not qualify for much, if any, government assistance. In my opinion, it is a sad commentary on a society as rich as ours that our government has so little compassion for the patrons of the Dorothy Day Center and its counterparts in other cities around the country.

In addition to truly helpless people such as these, there is a new class of marginally poor people being created by the economic dislocations. These are people who previously held steady, well-paying jobs in factories, steel mills, mines, and other economic sectors that are severely depressed today and that are not likely ever again to employ the numbers they employed in the 1970s. Unless we make significant changes in our social welfare system, restimulate economic growth, and invest substantial sums of money in retraining and resettlement programs, millions of these people are going to be marginally poor for the rest of their lives.

People may honestly differ on the best ways to deal with social problems such as these. Conservatives may propose different solutions than liberals will propose; Democrats different solutions than Republicans. But whether one is a Democrat or Republican, liberal or conservative, I think that as a society we need to show considerably more compassion for the people left behind by economic progress than we have shown for the past several years. Without some sense of compassion, I do not see how we will be able to address the question of an equitable distribution of the benefits of our economy, no matter how much economic growth we stimulate.

The American Tradition

To me, the American Revolution did not end with the battles of Bunker Hill, or in Saratoga or even Yorktown. Our whole American history has been a two hundred year struggle to strengthen and enlarge the benefits of democratic freedom; to include women and minorities and young people in our democratic system; to protect the individual rights and welfare of *all* our citizens; to build social and economic opportunity for *everyone*.

Today there are those who argue that the way to achieve this dream is to go it alone, to forget about those less fortunate. The new morality says that the young should forget about the old, the healthy ignore the sick, the wealthy should forget the poor.

That is an alien philosophy. We Americans believe in looking out for the other guy. That is our tradition, from the early days when settlers joined together for barn-raisings to the recent generosity of little school children to raise money for the starving in Africa.

This is a country that has insisted from its earliest beginnings that the individual human being is of fundamental value, that the humblest, meekest person has the right to be treated with dignity and with respect.

US House Speaker Thomas P. ("Tip") O'Neill in a speech before the Hubert H. Humphrey Institute, November 12, 1986.

5. *Remain vigilant about protecting our constitutional freedoms.*
   I firmly believe that the next thirty years will pose grave threats to the constitutional freedoms and the civil liberties that we enjoy today. There is no reform mechanism capable of preserving these freedoms. Nor is it reasonable to rely on the Supreme Court or any other specific institution to protect them. In the last analysis, we will have the level of freedom and civil liberties that we demand. And the best defense of our freedoms and liberties lies in a population that understands the sources of its liberties, perceives the nature of the threats against them, and vigilantly demands that these liberties not be infringed.
   6. *Remember the limits to reform.*

Although I am arguing that many reforms are still needed in our political system, it is important for any political reformer to have some humility about the proposals he or she makes. Reforms, as we have noted repeatedly, tend to have unforeseen and unintended consequences. Because of this distinct possibility, there are limits to the inroads that reform can accomplish.

7. *On foreign issues, a little common sense would be helpful.*

In our conduct of foreign relations, we Americans have a history of meddling in the affairs of other nations while being woefully unknowledgeable about the internal politics of those nations. This trait often leads us to be greatly surprised when those internal politics upset our foreign policy plans. We also have a tendency to distort the motives of other nations. Depending on whom one talks to, for example, the Soviet Union may be pictured as a devious force lying in wait for an opportunity to attack the United States or as a benign, well-meaning nation in the forefront of the struggle for human liberation. A little common sense would tell us that the Russians have self-interest to guide their foreign policy, just as the Americans do. Another area where common sense appears to be lacking is in the procurement policies of the Pentagon. A corporation that purchased its supplies as inefficiently as the Pentagon purchases military hardware would have trouble avoiding bankruptcy. A final example where common sense is lacking, it seems to me, is in much of the theorizing about nuclear strategy. It may well be an inescapable fact of life that nuclear weapons are necessary as a deterrent. However, nuclear strategists who plot out nuclear exchanges and talk of victory lack common sense. A nuclear war involving the Soviet Union, the United States, and Europe would destroy so much of Western culture and Western society that it would make the concept of victory meaningless. Even if the United States were to "win" such a war by having missiles left after the Soviets' missiles had either been exhausted or destroyed, the way of life we know in this country would cease to exist.

8. *Reinforce groups that aggregate interest; work against groups that are single-issue.*

Single-issue groups do contribute positively to the political system. In the 1980s, however, there has been a proliferation of single-issue and ideological groups, and members of Congress are in danger of being whipsawed between them at election time. The National Rifle Association, for example, is a single-issue group, as are the various right-to-life groups and the National Wildlife Federation. The AFL-CIO, by contrast, and the Business Roundtable tend to take a broader perspective on political issues. Political parties, by definition, are not single-issue groups. If we truly value moderation and continuity in national politics (as I do), those groups that aggregate interests and promote compromise among them will help achieve those goals much better than will groups inclined to fight uncompromisingly for a single issue.

9. *Foster effective participation.*

A democratic political system that is at all responsive to people's and groups' demands is necessarily unresponsive to people who do not place demands on it. In the United States, those who do not place demands on the system tend to be unorganized people and people of low socioeconomic status. If we want a political system that responds to the real needs of all the people, we need to create ways of broadening effective political participation. For example, labor unions have become effective institutions at representing the interests of their members and work hard at increasing the political participation of their members. There are, however, no comparably effective institutions for the poorest third of the population.

Increasing participation is important in order to make the political system more responsive to the needs of the unorganized and poor members of our society. It is important for other reasons as well—for increasing the legitimacy of government, for example. . . . Stronger political parties would probably contribute to more participation. Tax credits could be made available to the poor to encourage the formation of interest groups among them. Removing a number of registration barriers could conceivably increase voter turnout by as much as 9 percent.

10. *Protect the integrity of our national institutions.*

Finally, to enhance the effectiveness of our government in coping with our challenges of the future, it is important to protect the integrity of our national political institutions—the political parties, the presidency, Congress, the Supreme Court, and the bureaucracy. As individuals, there is one very important thing we can do in this regard. We can refuse to use the popular language that derides our national institutions. We can stop using the word "politician" as though it were a dirty word and an insult. We can stop referring to "bureaucrats" as though there were something inherently disreputable about being a government employee. We can also refuse to vote for, support, or contribute to candidates whose campaigns constitute an attack on the integrity of our political institutions.

I think the best remedy is exactly that provided by all our constitutions, to leave to the citizens the free election and separation of the aristoi from the pseudo-aristoi, of the wheat from the chaff. In general they will elect the real good and wise.

Thomas Jefferson

Choosing the Best Political Candidates

In 1813, Thomas Jefferson, the author of the Declaration of Independence and a former president, wrote to John Adams, another former president. In his letter he discusses his belief in "a natural aristocracy among men." He also presents his reasons for believing that American citizens will choose wisely, and vote for the candidates from this aristocracy with the most virtue and talents to fill the offices of government.

Read carefully the following excerpt from the letter. Familiarize yourself with Jefferson's arguments. Compare his observations with your knowledge of the current state of American government. Do you think Jefferson was right or wrong in his analysis of American voters? Has his prediction of the prudence of voters, choosing those with the most virtue and talents, been proven true? Why or why not? Present three arguments either supporting or attacking Jefferson's thesis.

257

I agree with you that there is a natural aristocracy among men. The grounds of this are virtue and talents. Formerly bodily powers gave place among the aristoi. But since the invention of gunpowder has armed the weak as well as the strong with missile death, bodily strength, like beauty, good humor, politeness and other accomplishments, has become but an auxiliary ground of distinction. There is also an artificial aristocracy founded on wealth and birth, without either virtue or talents; for with these it would belong to the first class. The natural aristocracy I consider as the most precious gift of nature for the instruction, the trusts, and government of society. And indeed it would have been inconsistent in creation to have formed man for the social state, and not to have provided virtue and wisdom enough to manage the concerns of the society. May we not even say that that form of government is the best which provides the most effectually for a pure selection of these natural aristoi into the offices of governments? The artificial aristocracy is a mischievous ingredient in government, and provision should be made to prevent it's ascendancy. On the question, What is the best provision, you and I differ; but we differ as rational friends, using the free exercise of our own reason, and mutually indulging its errors. You think it best to put the Pseudo-aristoi into a separate chamber of legislation where they may be hindered from doing mischief by their coordinate branches, and where also they may be a protection to wealth against the Agrarian and plundering enterprises of the Majority of the people. I think that to give them power in order to prevent them from doing mischief, is arming them for it, and increasing instead of remedying the evil. For if the coordinate branches can arrest their action, so may they that of the coordinates. Mischief may be done negatively as well as positively. Of this a cabal in the Senate of the U.S. has furnished many proofs. Nor do I believe them necessary to protect the wealthy; because enough of these will find their way into every branch of the legislation to protect themselves. From 15 to 20 legislatures of our own, in action for 30 years past, have proved that no fears of an equalisation of property are to be apprehended from them.

I think the best remedy is exactly that provided by all our constitutions, to leave to the citizens the free election and separation of the aristoi from the pseudo-aristoi, of the wheat from the chaff. In general they will elect the real good and wise. In some instances, wealth may corrupt, and birth blind them; but not in sufficient degree to endanger the society.

Periodical Bibliography

The following periodical articles deal with the subject matter of this chapter.

James MacGregor Burns	"Coming to the Aid of the Party," *Psychology Today*, July 1984.
Greg Easterbrook	"What's Wrong with Congress?" *The Atlantic Monthly*, December 1984.
William E. Johnson Jr.	"Lincoln and Watergate: The American Past Speaks to the American Future," *The Christian Century*, June 25, 1973.
Peter McGrath	"In Order To Form a More Perfect Union," *Newsweek*, May 25, 1987.
Warren P. Mass	"Constitutional Vandalism," *The New American*, May 25, 1987.
Norman Ornstein	"The System of Checks and Balances Is Alive and Well," *U.S. News & World Report*, January 18, 1985.
M. Scott Peck	"A New American Revolution," *New Age*, May/June 1987.
Lawrence W. Reed	"The Fall of Rome and Modern Parallels," *Vital Speeches of the Day*, August 1, 1979.
Kirkpatrick Sale	"Why Voters Don't Care," *The Nation*, May 31, 1980.
James L. Sundquist	"Improving the Capacity To Govern," *The Brookings Bulletin*, Fall 1980.
Time	"To Reform the System," February 23, 1981.
U.S. News & World Report	"Too Many Presidential Primaries?" November 19, 1979.

Annotated Book Bibliography

Mortimer Adler

We Hold These Truths: Understanding the Ideas and Ideals of the Constitution. New York: MacMillan Publishing Company, 1987. A popular philosopher illuminates the ideas and ideals that form the core of the Declaration of Independence and the Constitution.

American Bar Association

Amendment of the Constitution by the Convention Method under Article V, 1974. The results of a Bar Association study committee calling for Congress to clarify the procedures for calling a constitutional convention and concluding that such a convention would not harm the country. Available for $3.50 from the Taxpayers' Foundation, 325 Pennsylvania Ave., SE, Washington, DC 20003.

Charles A. Beard

An Economic Interpretation of the Constitution of the United States. New York: The Free Press, 1986. An American classic, claiming the Constitution was fashioned by men of property and wealth, working to protect their interests from a growing population and the demands for greater democracy.

Robert N. Bellah

Habits of the Heart. Berkeley: University of California Press, 1985. The results of a five-year study of American communities and individuals conclude that Americans' emphasis on self-interest harms the common good.

Sidney Blumenthal

The Rise of the Counter-Establishment: From Conservative Ideology to Political Power. New York: Times Books, 1986. An analysis of the conservative elite in America, which the author labels the "counter-establishment." He identifies a rise of ideological politics replacing the old party system, and describes the conservative elite behind the Reagan presidency.

Daniel Boorstin

The Genius of American Politics. Chicago: University of Chicago Press, 1953. A Pulitzer Prize-winning historian argues that America's acceptance of common values is so pervasive that an explicit political philosophy is superfluous.

Robert E. Brown

Charles Beard and the Constitution: A Critical Analysis of "An Economic Interpretation of the Constitution." Princeton, NJ: Princeton University Press, 1956. A detailed refutation of Charles Beard's thesis.

James MacGregor Burns

The Power to Lead: The Crisis of the American Presidency. New York: Simon & Schuster, 1984. A Pulitzer Prize-winning political scientist argues for the revitalization of political parties to provide a base for restoring missing leadership to American government.

Joseph Church

America the Possible: How and Why the Constitution Should be Rewritten. New York: MacMillan Publishing Company, 1982. A psychology professor analyzes the American scene and presents a thought-provoking case for reorganizing American government and rewriting the Constitution.

Committee on the Constitutional System — *A Bicentennial Analysis of the American Political Structure,* 1987. A 20-page booklet, presenting the recommendations of a non-partisan group of scholars, politicians, and others to improve the structure of American government. Available free from CCS, Suite 410, 1755 Massachusetts Ave. NW, Washington, DC 20036.

Robert A. Dahl — *Pluralistic Democracy in the United States.* Chicago: Rand & McNally & Company, 1967. An expert in power structures at both the local and national levels claims pluralism, not elite control, describes American democracy.

Alexis de Tocqueville — *Democracy in America.* New York: New American Library, 1956. An American classic. Written in the 1830s by a French political scientist after visiting America, it remains the best study ever written by a foreign observer of American culture and political institutions.

Donald J. Devine — *The Political Culture of the United States.* Boston: Little, Brown & Company, 1972. Claims that the political culture of the US reflects a broad consensus involving all groups in the population, anchored in the basic principles of Lockean liberalism.

Robert E. DiClerico & Allan S. Hammock, eds. — *Points of View: Readings in American Government & Politics.* New York: Random House, 1986. A collection of readings, debating many of the issues currently challenging American democracy.

G. William Domhoff — *Who Rules America Now? A View for the '80s.* New York: Simon & Schuster, 1983. A professor of sociology and psychology claims that a ruling class of privileged people dominates the American economy and government.

Wilber Edel — *A Constitutional Convention: Threat or Challenge?* New York: Praeger Publishers, 1981. An investigation of calls for a constitutional convention over the course of American history, exploring many of the problems and questions that would arise if a convention were called.

Robert A. Goldwin & William A. Schambra, eds. — *How Democratic Is the Constitution?* Washington, DC: American Enterprise for Public Policy Research, 1980. Seven essays debate whether the Constitution is an aristocratic document garbed in democratic rhetoric or the truly democratic instrument the American populace believes it to be.

Edward S. Greenberg & Richard P. Young, eds. — *American Politics Reconsidered: Power and Inequity in American Society.* Belmont, CA: Duxbury Press, 1973. A valuable anthology, debating many of the issues raised in this book.

Alexander Hamilton, John Jay & James Madison — *The Federalist.* New York: Modern Library, 1964. A compilation of newspaper articles, written in 1787 and 1788 by supporters of the new Constitution, that has been referred to as America's closest approximation of a written political philosophy.

John J. Harrigan — *Politics and the American Future.* New York: Random House, 1984. A textbook that examines the American political system and the problems currently challenging it.

Louis Hartz — *The Liberal Tradition in America.* New York: Harcourt, Brace & World, 1955. Claims America's political philosophy is liberalism, based on the theories of John Locke.

The Hearst Corporation — *The American Public's Knowledge of the US Constitution: A National Survey of Public Awareness and Personal Opinion.* New York: The Hearst Corporation, 1987. A forty-page survey reveals that the American public has "neither adequate factual nor conceptual knowledge of the U.S. Constitution." Available free from the Hearst Corporation, 959 Eighth Ave., New York, NY 10019.

Samuel P. Huntington — *American Politics: The Promise of Disharmony.* Cambridge, MA: Belknap Press, 1981. Examines the conflict between America's creed of liberty and hostility to authority and its increasing reliance on a more bureaucratic government.

Steven Kelman — *Making Public Policy: A Hopeful View of American Government.* New York: Basic Books, 1987. Argues that a concern for the common good is a better explanation for the national public policy-making process than is the more commonly accepted theory of Madisonian factions or self-interest.

Joint Economic Committee of the Congress of the US — *Political Economy and Constitutional Reform.* Washington, DC: US Government Printing Office, 1983. Two-volume compilation of testimony taken from a variety of experts, debating the strengths and weaknesses of America's government. Numerous remedies are suggested and resisted.

John Lukacs — *Outgrowing Democracy.* Garden City, NY: Doubleday & Co., 1984. A gloomy view of American government and society that argues it has passed its zenith and reached a state of bureaucratic inefficiency.

Forrest McDonald — *We the People: The Economic Origins of the Constitution.* Chicago: University of Chicago Press, 1958. Another detailed refutation of the Beard thesis.

Richard B. McKenzie — *Bound to be Free.* Stanford, CA: Hoover Institution Press, 1982. A cataloging of the ways large government in America has eroded personal freedoms and democracy. It suggests ways governmental taxation and the impact of special interest groups can be limited.

C. Wright Mills — *The Power Elite.* New York: Oxford University Press, 1956. An argument that a power elite of politicians, corporate executives, and military men determine public policy in the US, relegating the official governmental structure to a secondary role.

Peter Navarro	*The Policy Game: How Special Interests and Ideologues Are Stealing America.* New York: John Wiley & Sons, 1984. An economic researcher makes a detailed argument, focusing on specific issues, claiming that special interests and ideologues have mastered the techniques needed to manipulate public policy to the detriment of the public interest.
Michael Parenti	*Democracy for the Few.* New York: St. Martin's Press, 1983. A critical examination of the mechanics of America's political system, claiming the idealized textbook versions of American democracy are far different from what is actually practiced.
M. Scott Peck	*The Different Drum.* New York: Simon & Schuster, 1987. A recommendation to revitalize American government without structural changes, by replacing the current "obsolete presidency" with a communal model.
George S. Reedy	*The US Senate: Paralysis or a Search for Consensus.* New York: Crown Books, 1986. An insider compares the productive Senate of the 1950s with today's Senate, illustrating why the current Senate does not work.
Robert Reich	*The Next American Frontier.* New York: Times Books, 1983. A political economist claims that America's challenge, and next frontier, is the adaptation of its economic system to compete successfully in the new worldwide economy. He argues that necessary economic change can only occur after political restructing.
Robert J. Ringer	*Restoring the American Dream.* New York: Harper & Row, 1979. An attack on big government by a libertarian, listing the sins of America's bureaucracy and suggesting solutions to restore the American dream.
Donald Robinson, ed.	*Reforming America.* Boulder, CO: Westview Press, 1985. A valuable anthology, sponsored by the Committee on the Constitutional System, presenting alternative views on the problems confronting American Government along with proposed solutions.
Arnold M. Rose	*The Power Structure: Political Process in American Society.* New York: Oxford University Press, 1967. Claims the power structure identified by Mills is not united and effective, largely because of the plurality of competing interests in America.
Arthur M. Schlesinger Jr.	*The Cycles of American History.* Boston: Houghton Mifflin Company, 1986. A lucid and eloquent book by a Pulitzer Prize-winning historian, examining and taking a stand on many of the issues debated in this book.
William E. Simon	*A Time for Truth.* New York: Berkeley Publishing Corporation, 1978. A former US Secretary of the Treasury describes how a growing American bureaucracy has eroded freedom.

263

David G. Smith   *The Convention and the Constitution*. New York: St. Martin's Press, 1965. Investigates the intentions of the Constitution's framers and concludes that they placed republican principles and the common interest before their personal interests.

Theodore C. Sorensen   *A Different Kind of Presidency: A Proposal for Breaking the Political Deadlock*. New York: Harper & Row, 1984. A Special Counsel to President Kennedy proposes a one-term depoliticized presidency to halt the decline of the office.

James L. Sundquist   *Constitutional Reform and Effective Government*. Washington, DC: The Brookings Institute, 1986. The best available review of the debate about whether reform of the US Constitution is needed, raising practical questions about what changes might work best, and suggesting remedies to improve the governmental system.

Rexford Tugwell   *The Emerging Constitution*. New York: Harper's Magazine Press, 1974. The result of several years of deliberations by the Center for the Study of Democratic Institutions, presenting the draft of a new constitution and the rationale for its adoption.

Gordon Wood   *The Creation of the American Republic, 1776-1787*. Chapel Hill, NC: University of North Carolina, 1969. A detailed analysis of the development of political thought from the Declaration of Independence to the ratification of the Constitution.

Index

theory of balanced government in, 37-38
tradition of, 30-31, 254
was feared by founding fathers, 173, 175-176
works well, 145
see also political theory, American
Devine, Donald J., 55
Domhoff, G. William, 129
Druker, Peter, 128

economy, US
and democracy, 238, 241
and politics
division between, 234-236
and world economics, 236-237
division of labor in, 238-239
dynamic behind change in, 240-241
failures of, 239-240
must be restructured, 233-244
solutions for, 241-244
Eisenhower, Dwight D., 75, 251

factions
definition of, 40
effects of, 42-45
varieties of, 41-42
Ferrara, Peter, 81, 82
Friedman, Milton, 80, 84

Giordano, Joseph, 75
Goodwin, Richard N., 131, 135
government, American
cultural changes have subverted, 245-247
dangers to, 199
flaws in
are moral, 245-249
are political, 217-224, 233-244
founding fathers' intentions for, 66
institutions must be protected, 256
largeness of
destroys
private property, 84-85
the balance of power, 69-70
democracy, 65-72
the economy, 67-68, 84-85
is natural, 78-79
promotes
dependence, 68-69
dishonesty, 70-72
the general welfare, 76, 146
myth of, 81-85
liberty, 75-76
myth of, 77-85
social equality, 86-94
tyranny of the status quo, 80
waste, 79-84

must be simplified, 252-253
must help the disadvantaged, 253-254
proposed reforms for, 222, 231-232, 250-256
should be activist, 75
should be guided by
common sense, 255
restraint, 251-252
social role of, 87-88
future of, 92-93, 94
history of, 89-92
reduces poverty, 88, 90
strengths of, 90-91
successes of, 93
structure of
is awkward, 209
is flawed, 211, 213
must be changed, 207-216, 239
problems with, 208-211, 218-219
solutions for, 211-215, 223-224, 229
see also Constitution, US; political parties, US; welfare state
Green, Steven, 219

Hamilton, Alexander, 195
and mistrust of big business, 123-124, 127
and ratification of the Constitution, 208
and strong central government, 89
fear of democracy of, 173
Handlin, Oscar, 29
Harrigan, John J., 250
Harrington, Michael, 241
Hartz, Louis, 48
Hobbes, Thomas, 18-20
Hofstadter, Richard, 34, 36
Hoover, Herbert, 125, 127
Humphrey, Hubert H., 21, 251

Jacobson, Norman, 50, 51
Jefferson, Thomas
and big business, 124, 127
and constitutional amendments, 208
and the general welfare, 76
and government versus liberty, 78
and property, 182-183
and strong central government, 89
leadership of, 232

Kelman, Steven, 143, 145, 148
Kennan, George F., 239

liberalism
American